Presen

Other Titles by the Author

The Dastgah Concept in Persian Music (2004)

PRESENT PAST

NOTES FROM THE LIFE OF
A PERSIAN AMERICAN COMPOSER
IN IRELAND

HORMOZ FARHAT

Ibex Publishers,
Bethesda, Maryland

Present Past
Notes from the Life of a Persian-American Composer
by Hormoz Farhat

Copyright © 2019 Hormoz Farhat

Manufactured in the United States of America

The paper used in this book meets the minimum requirements of the American
National Standard for Information Services—Permanence of Paper for Printed
Library Materials, ANSI Z39.48–1984

Ibex Publishers strives to create books which are as complete and free of errors as
possible. Please help us with future editions by reporting any errors or suggestions
for improvement to the address below, or corrections@ibexpub.com

Ibex Publishers, Inc.
Post Office Box 30087
Bethesda, Maryland 20824
Telephone: 301–718–8188
Facsimile: 301–907–8707
www.ibexpublishers.com

LIBRARY OF CONGRESS CATALOGING-IN-PUBLICATION DATA

Farhat, Hormoz.
Present past : Notes from the life of a Persian American composer in Ireland / by
Hormoz Farhat.
Bethesda, Maryland : Ibex Publishers, [2017] | Includes
bibliographical references.
LCCN 2017000173| ISBN 9781588141415 (hardcover : alk. paper) |
ISBN 9781588141521 (pbk. : alk. paper)
LCSH: Farhat, Hormoz. | Composers--Biography. | Iranian
Americans--Biography. | LCGFT: Autobiographies.
LCC ML410.F2195 A3 2017 | DDC 780.92 [B] --dc23

To my wife
Beloved Maria,
whose ceaseless prompting is responsible
for the pages that follow

Contents

Introduction

The long span of my life has been divided into four distinct segments. The first of these was the period of my childhood and teen years in my native Persia, when that country was still a very isolated and underdeveloped place, with no more than 15 million population, 80% of whom lived in rural areas. At the same time, under the forceful and visionary rule of Rezā Shah, the country was in the throws of modernization and westernization. In my teen years, I witnessed the Allies' invasion and occupation of Persia followed by a period of internal political upheaval, menacing threats by the Soviets, and the growth of American influence.

The second phase of my life can be identified with my move to America in 1949, university years, struggle to sustain myself while studying to become a composer, taking American citizenship, and finally establishing an academic career. The third period, lasting from 1968 to 79, brought me back to Persia, when a great deal of reform and progress were underway. During that period, I was active as Professor and Head of the Music Department at University of Tehran, and Head of the Music Council at the Radio and Television organization.

In the final fourth segment of my life, which has lasted longer than any of the previous three, I have been in Ireland since 1979. Initially, I came to Belfast in Northern Ireland as a Visiting Professor at the Queen's University. This was followed, three years later, by a move south to the Republic of Ireland, when I was appointed to the Chair of Music at Dublin University, Trinity College Dublin. After my retirement in 1995, I have continued to live in Ireland, with my wife Maria Baghramian, a philosophy professor, and our son Robert Kambiz, in a country that we love and admire, a green and gentle land with warm and charming people.

It has been, I believe, a singularly eventful life rich in diversity and challenge. About half of my life, consisting of the two middle periods and ten years into the fourth, has been exceptionally turbulent. They have been eventful, in many ways arduous, but also rewarding. Much of the upheaval I have experienced has been of private nature, while some was related to circumstances in my professional life.

Over the past many years, a few people close to me have pressed me to write an account of my life believing that it would be of interest to some readers. My wife, Maria, has been particularly encouraging in urging me to write. This, I have resisted until now for one overriding reason. I have not been so satisfied with myself to feel comfortable enough to write about myself. I believe an autobiography, no matter how modestly tackled, tends to be an exercise in self-promotion, which I do not like to do. Also, I am obviously not a Jean-Jacque Rousseau and I do shy away from divulging personal accounts of domestic life. My private world has been colorful, often fraught and painful, but I like to keep that to myself. However, within the limitations that I have set, I am now convinced that some form of expression in written words, pertaining to some of my experiences and observations, may merit publication.

This book, therefore, is not an autobiography; it is not a narrative and is not sequential throughout. As it is not a book based on research, and it is not intended to create or establish positions of discourse, no footnotes are given. Intimate accounts of private life, domestic issues, both in my paternal home and in my adult life, do not come into the picture. Most of the book's content (Chapters 1 through 12) is admittedly in the nature of a selective memoire. The final three chapters are specific to musical discussions; they are didactic or even polemic in character. I imagine that these chapters may be of greater interest to the musically informed reader.

Chapters 1 and 2 are related to memories of childhood and youth in Persia during the transformative years of 1930s and 1940s. My childhood corresponded with the heady years of Rezā Shah's forceful reforms and secularization. In my teen years, I saw the Shah's abdication, witnessed the upheaval of the war years and the chaos that followed the end of the Second World War. During the same period I became enchanted with western classical music to the point of total commitment. The next three, Chapters 3, 4 and 5, also pertain to my childhood and youth, but deal with specific issues that stand out in my memory. These Chapters convey social conditions that were present some seventy years ago in Persia but survive no longer. I hope that they prove to be of interest to the reader.

In Chapters 6 and 7, I have written about my arrival in America and my confrontation with a country that I knew only through movies: the America of Mickey Rooney in the Andy Hardy series, America of the Philadelphia Story, the Maltese Falcon and Abbott and Costello comedies. I was a stranger in a strange land, totally at odds with the American ways. I could barely manage a few words in English, was so out of step with my surroundings as to wear a suit and necktie to my Freshman classes, and yet had to support myself by part-time employment, often menial jobs, in order to survive.

Chapters 8 and 9 are related to my return to Persia in 1968 and the musical life of the country in the last two decades before the Revolution of 1978/9, including an account of the Shiraz/Persepolis Festival - a major event in the musical and artistic life of the country prior to the Revolution - and my own part in the planning and provisions for some of the Festival's programs.

Chapter 10 contains a summary overview of the events in the1970s that led to the Revolution. Much has been written, and will continue to be written, through authoritative research, on this so-called 'Islamic' Revolution. It has been one of the most consequential events of recent history. I do not claim to have any original contributions to the polemics of the issue; but I do have an individual non-political point of view, and, as such, my observations may be of interest.

Chapter 11 stands on its own, yet maintains relevance to both my life and some of the preceding material. Here, I have written about five exceptional individuals I have known in my life. An octogenarian who has lived in three continents and has travelled a great deal is bound to have known many people including some who were 'interesting'. Nevertheless, one is not likely to come across truly exceptional individuals often. The five men I have written about were quite extraordinary, not necessarily always in positive or admirable ways, but definitely exceptional. Two of the five were family relations, the other three were not. They are all deceased but are very much on my mind; I trust that the reader will come to appreciate why I remember them fondly and why I wish to write about them in this book.

The next four Chapters, in one way or another, pertain to music. In Chapter 12, I have written briefly on my experiences with each of my composition teachers, since at least three of them were among important composers of the 20th century. Chapter 13 brings together my teaching experiences in universities in America, in Iran and in Ireland as a basis for comparison of third level music programs at different institutions. In particular, I have made comparisons between approaches to the inclusion of music, and the content of respective curricula, at universities in the U.S. with those of Europe.

Chapters 14 and 15 are entirely concerned with my findings and views on two very different musical cultures, both of which I know well. In 14, I discuss the urban musical tradition of Persia. There is a great deal of confusion and misunderstanding about this music. It is quite astonishing that the theoretical foundations of Persian music are still subject to individual points of view. I have given a brief account of the history of this music and have presented the various theoretical theses on its structure. I have also argued the problems that music and musical activity face in an Islamic society.

The final Chapter presents a personal assessment of musical trends of the last one hundred years in contemporary western musical composition, or what is generally identified as 'modern' music. The views expressed are my own and are based on 70 years of involvement with western music, as a student of nearly every aspect of music history, theory and composition, and as a practicing composer. I am certain that my views will jar with those of some who will readily characterize them as 'conservative' or 'reactionary'. I believe others, both among professional musicians and the music loving public, will receive them with approbation.

༚ ༚

The reader will note that I have frequently used the name Persia for the country of my birth in preference to Iran. Every country with a long presence in world history, for various reasons, has a name used internally that differs from the name that identifies that country in the world at large. Egypt, Greece, China, Japan, Germany and even Finland, to name a few, are known by different names within their own borders. In the case of Persia, the name Iran, or a variant of it, has been the internal name for many centuries, at least since the Sassanid period (224 to 651 CE). To the outside world, however, for reasons that go back to the founding of the Persian Empire in 550 BCE by Cyrus the Great, Iran has been known as Persis, Parsa, Persia, La Perse, Persien, and the like. The Persian government's misguided decision, in 1935, to require the use of the internal name by the outside world has been nothing short of a disaster. By enforcing the name Iran in place of Persia the historic identity of the country has been effectively removed from her. To many people in the west, Iran is one more of the countries of western Asia that were created after the First World War such as Jordan, Iraq, Kuwait, UAR and Qatar, or more recently by colonial powers in Africa, such as Zambia, Zimbabwe, Ivory Coast, Burkina Faso and the rest. Even to the mind of the better-educated westerner, Persia may be one of those ancient entities that have long since ceased to exist, like Phoenicia, Babylon or Carthage.

In fact, only in the company of Greece and China, Persia is a country with a remarkable historic continuity for at least 26 centuries. Despite repeated invasions and catastrophic destruction it has maintained its language, traditions and distinct cultural character. It has made significant contributions to world civilization. The Islamic civilization that achieved brilliant heights between the 9th and the 14th centuries owes heavily to its Persian components; the great scientists, philosophers and sages of Islam were overwhelmingly of Persian nationality. All this, in the western world, is identified with the name Persia, not Iran.

Had I written this book in Persian, of course I would have used the name Iran. As I am writing in English I have chosen mostly to use

the name Persia hoping to evoke, in the mind of the reader, the right
associations with the country's history and culture. An additional consideration is the unfortunate but common association of the name Iran
with notions of religious fanaticism and the atrocious behavior of the
Islamic Republic - the obstreperous child of the Revolution of 1978/9
- all of which has made daily negative headlines in recent years. I have
tried, perhaps in vain, to circumvent such associations. A further problem with the name Iran is the similarity of its spelling with Iraq. This
confusing similarity comes about only in the transliteration of the two
names into Latin script and is resented by Iranians. Iraq is one of the
countries within the Arab world; Iran, of course, is not.

Some Iranians may believe that they have a compelling argument
against the use of the name Persia; they point to the fact that Persia,
or Fars (Pars), is only a province within the greater Iran. They do not
realize that this, although true, is only known to them and not to the
rest of the world, which has known the whole country as Persia. To the
world outside, Persia is synonymous with Iran, and all citizens of Iran
have been known as Persians and not only those who speak the Persian
language.

This reference to the language also invites me to include a few words
about the recent use of the adjective Farsi, instead of Persian, for the
language spoken by the majority of Iranians. In the English language
the word for the language spoken in Iran is Persian and not Farsi; the
word for the language of Germany is German and not Deutsch; the
language of Spain is Spanish and not Espagnol; the language spoken in
Sweden is Swedish and not Svensk, etc. There is no justification for the
use of the word Farsi in the context of spoken or written English, as
indeed in the context of spoken or written Persian one would not use
the word English for the language of Engelestan (Persian for England)
and would say Engelisi. It is also important to appreciate that the magnificent literary heritage of Persia is identified, in the west, as Persian
literature and not Farsi literature. The adjective Farsi, in the context
of written or spoken English, is new and unfamiliar; it has no identity
and no lineage. Its currency will be at the expense of all associations of
Persian culture with that country, whether we call her Persia or Iran.

Notes on Transliteration

Persian is an Indo-European language and its sounds are in common with most other languages of this large family. It is written, however, in the Arabic alphabet, which does not serve it well. No suitable and consistent system of transliteration into Latin script has been developed. In this book I have employed one of the more familiar methods but have refrained from doubling letters, to represent a single sound, wherever possible. My main objective has been to represent in Latin script the sounds of Persian language. In transliteration, in my view, it is not important how a word or a name is written in the original language, what is important is how it is read.

The following table shows the letters, as used in this book, for consonances of Persian language:

B	as in English
Ch	as in church
D	as in English
F	as in English
G	as in get, not in gem.
H	as in English
J	as in English
K	as in English
Kh	as in German pronunciation of ch in Bach, or Scottish ch in loch.
L	as in English usage
M	as in English
N	as in English
P	as in English
Q	as a guttural sound similar to the French pronunciation of r (gh is not used)
R	as in English
S	as in English

Sh	as in English
T	as in English
V	as in English
Y	as in yes, never as a vowel.
Z	as in English
Zh	as the sound of s in 'pleasure' or 'measure'.
	The vowels of Persian are expressed with the following letters:
A	short a as in hand
Ā	long a as in hard
E	as in desk (e at the end of a word is always sounded.)
I	as in pierce
O	short o as in omit
Ō	long o as in over
U	as in blue (ou and oo are not used)
	(' after a vowel represents a short glottal stop in the flow of sound, as in ta'zie.)

Names have been spelled according to the way they sound, not the way they are written in Persian. For example: Safieddin and not Safi al-Din; Nasereddin and not Naser al-Din. Some Persian words end with the vowel e. Since in the Arabic alphabet has no letter assigned to e, the letter h acts as the ending e. In the transliteration of such words, in this book, the h is omitted and the word is spelled with an ending e, for example: gushe and not gusheh, or sine-zani, not sineh-zani.

⚜ 1 ⚜

Childhood in the Age of Rezā Shah

Rezā Shah was proclaimed king in December of 1925; he ruled until September of 1941, when the British and the Russians who had invaded and occupied Persia forced his abdication. He was exiled by the British first to Mauritius Islands in the Indian Ocean and later to Johannesburg in South Africa, where he died in July of 1944, at 66 years of age. His 16 years on the Peacock Throne were among the most momentous in Persian history. His detractors, particularly the venomous propaganda machine of the Islamic Republic, would like to say that he was placed on the throne by the British, served them throughout his reign, and then was removed when he was no longer needed. This is sheer calumny. There is no doubt that the coup of February 21st, 1921, had the consent of the British forces stationed in Qazvin, and its commander, General Sir Edmund Ironside. In those days, nothing of any significance could have happened in Persia without the endorsement of the British. At the time, the northwestern provinces of Persia were under Soviet occupation; they had even created a Soviet Republic of Gilān in the south Caspian region. Under such circumstances, the British were naturally supportive of the only standing Persian army, the Cossack Brigade under Rezā Khān, to make a move to bring order and to confront the Russians, as the central government in Tehran was totally powerless to act. The Foreign Office in London had nothing to do with the decision and was only informed of it after the fact. Brigadier Rezā Khān was hardly known to the British. Once the coup succeeded and he emerged as the power broker and man of the hour, first as War Minister, then Prime Minister, and eventually as the elected King, the British realized that they could not count on him as any sort of an ally. He gradually, and often blatantly opposed their policies. The archives of the British Foreign Service contain many documents that demonstrate how Rezā Shah obstructed British interests throughout his reign.

(For documented accounts of Rezā Shah's rise to power and his relations with the British refer to Homā Kātouziān's State and Society in
Iran and to Cyrus Ghani's Iran and the Rise of Rezā Shah)

A proper understanding of what was accomplished during the Rezā
Shah era cannot be had without an understanding of where Persia
stood at the time of the 1921 coup. The country was in a state of
near total disintegration. The preceding 15 years had seen Persia in a
series of catastrophic convulsions. The revolution of 1906 had led to
the adoption of a constitution in which the powers of the monarch
had been reduced and defined. A parliamentary system was devised
and elected representatives of the people were vested with authority
to oversee the workings of the government and to pass laws to which
the king and the government were beholden. The constitution had received the endorsement of a sickly monarch, Mozaffereddin Shah, who
passed away only a few days after having given his reluctant consent.
However, only a year later, his successor, Mohammad Ali Shah, with
the outright military assistance of the Russians, attempted to destroy
the democratic government and to discard the constitution. In the civil
war that ensued the democratic forces won the day, but they were so
weakened in the process that the country was effectively run by the
British and the Russians who, in a covert pact, had divided Persia into
two 'spheres of influence'. Mohammad Ali Shah's attempts to abolish
the constitution and the parliament failed; he was dethroned, found
refuge in the Russian Embassy and eventually managed to escape to
Russia. His teenaged heir Ahmad was made king with a Regent who
worked in concert with the parliament.

A most revealing account of conditions, shortly after the reestablish-
ment of democratic government, appears in W. Morgan Shuster's outstanding book, *The Strangling of Persia*. Shuster was an American finan-
cier who, on the request of the Persian government, was dispatched, in
1911, by Washington to Tehran. His mission, as the Treasurer General
was to set in order the chaotic financial affairs of the country. Schuster's
policies, all to the benefit of the nation he was hired to serve, proved so
abhorrent to the 'interests' of the Russians that they forced the Persian
government, by virtual threat of armed intervention, to dismiss him

within eight months of his arrival in Tehran. His book, written and published shortly after his return to America, gives a vivid picture of the conditions in Persia just before the outbreak of First World War, conditions that got even worse during the war. Not only the country's declared neutrality was disregarded, opposing forces even fought within Persian territory. Russians and British who were initially allies, fought against the Ottomans in western parts of the country. After the demise of the Tsarist regime in 1917, the British fought the Bolshevik forces, who had practically annexed parts of Persia's northwest. The famine that was caused by both confiscation and destruction of crops and live stock in Persia during the period between 1917-19 resulted in some two million deaths, in a country whose population at the time was less than ten millions. The central government in Tehran was barely capable of controlling the capital; it had virtually no authority in the provinces, some of which were on the verge of being detached from the empire altogether. This was the general condition of Persia at the time of the coup of 21 February 1921 that eventually brought Rezā Shah to power.

It is not my object here to give an account of Rezā Shah's policies and reforms, nor is it befitting the purpose of this book to assess the pros and cons of his dictatorial rule. What is relevant to my story is the extent to which my childhood was affected by his towering presence. Had he not appeared on the scene, undoubtedly my formation as the person that I am would have been significantly different. As a child of a patrician family I would have had some education, mostly through private tutoring, in traditional subjects with emphasis on reading Persian literature and penmanship, some mathematics and maybe French language. It is possible that I might have been sent to the existing third level institution that was for training lawyers run by French teachers. The least conceivable outcome would have been that I might choose a career as a composer in the western classical tradition.

Before Rezā Shah's time few schools were run by the government. Most of the schools – and there were very few of them – were governed by the clergy as *maktabs* and their curricula were mainly focused on the Koran, the hadith and the sharia. There were only a handful of secondary schools, also dominated by the clergy, and only a couple of third level institutions in the capital city that were modeled on French *ecole normale.* There were no universities. Literacy, mainly among men, did not exceed ten per cent of the population. Among women only the ladies of the nobility had a smattering of education.

By 1935, when I was old enough to attend school, some ten years had passed since Rezā Shah had begun his fast-paced, some would say his ruthless, program of modernization. There were hundreds of primary schools throughout Tehran and in provincial large cities; also, a large number of secondary schools. All schools were governed by the Ministry of Education; the clergy had no authority over them or the subjects that were taught. A few of the primary schools, in the capital, were coeducational with boys and girls sitting in the same classrooms, a cause of immense resentment on the part of clerics. The University of Tehran had been founded and there was also a teacher training college. The primary school I attended had a curriculum that included, in addition to basics of reading and writing, such subjects as literature and poetry, grammar, creative writing, history, geography, drawing, mathematics, geometry, sports and, in the final two years (out of 6), music. In music classes, rudiments of western notation were taught and we learned to sing a number of hymns and patriotic songs. There was also a subject called '*āyāt-e montakhabe*', reading of selected brief chapters from the Koran. This was meant to pacify the clerics. The class met only once a week and the reading of the Koranic verses, which are in Arabic, made no meaningful impression on the children who could not understand what they were reading. We attended school for a total of six hours per day, from 8 to 12, and again from 2 to 4 in the afternoon. We only had one day of rest per week, Friday; however, on Thursdays there was no afternoon session.

Although only a child at the time, I have distinct memories of the way Rezā Shah had intimidated the clerics. One of our primary school teachers had been a *mollā* (low ranking Shiite cleric), but he could not wear his vocational garb to school; he had to appear before us in civilian clothes. In fact, only the clergy who had been licensed by the state as recognized preachers were allowed to wear their professional garment. Our third year teacher was a woman; this would have been unthinkable only a few years earlier.

Concurrent with the inauguration of the University of Tehran in 1935, an imperial edict was issued banning the use of the chador, the traditional tent-like sheet with which women covered their hair and body frame when appearing in public. The clothing worn in public had to be in line with European fashions. Men wore suits and western chapeau; women were required to discard the chador; their hair had to be exposed or covered by appropriate ladies hats; not even kerchiefs were allowed. I distinctly remember, on a number of occasions, seeing the police actually pulling down the coverage from women's heads. The clerics' outcry was ignored and demonstrations against the edict were crushed; disobedience simply was not tolerated.

In the late 30's, the organization of Boy Scouts was introduced. When I was in the 5th grade, with all my classmates, I had to join the Scouts, with its well-known uniform and other paraphernalia pertaining. On the 26th of October, the Crown Prince's birthday, we participated, wearing our uniforms, in parades and joined kids from other schools in putting on well-rehearsed shows in the city's stadium. Children from girls' schools also participated. There was an atmosphere of joviality in all this extracurricular activity, which the children greatly enjoyed.

The most striking aspect of the educational policy promoted in the Rezā Shah era was emphasis on nationhood and the glorification of the pre-Islamic history of the Persian Empire. This policy was nationally advanced by various means. In schools, the pre-Islamic history of Persia was taught in detail. Some of the buildings, erected during the reign of Rezā Shah, were designed in imitation of palaces from the Achaemenid and Sassanid periods. Attempts were made, by an academy established for this purpose, to rid the Persian language off Arabic words. A significant number of Persian words came into usage – and still remain – that had no currency before Rezā Shah. These words were either resurrected from old Persian texts or were constructed from the currently familiar nomenclature. It was during my primary school days that names of all state institutions of government were changed from Arabic to Persian: the Municipality (*Baladiye*) became *shahrdāri*; Police

Stations (*Nazmiye*) became *Kalāntari*; Ministry of Justice (*Adliye*) was changed to *Dādgostari*; Finance (*Māliye*) to *Dārāi*, etc. Also, hospital (*marizkhāne*) became *bimārestān*; school (*madrese*) was changed to *dabestān* (primary school), *dabirestān* (secondary school); teacher (*moallem*) became *āmuzgār* and *dabir*. This goes on and on; hundreds of words and names that had Arabic roots were replaced by Persian equivalents. It did not take long before the old Arabic words were completely forgotten.

Prior to Rezā Shah's reign, Iranian children were commonly named after the holies of shiism: Mohammad, Ali, Kāzem, Fāteme, Khadije, etc. Also common were names with religious connotation, i.e. Seyfollāh, Valiollāh, Rokneddin, Shamseddin, Ma'sume, etc. Although there was no compulsion, but from the beginning of Rezā Shah's reign, many among the middle and upper classes named their children after ancient Persian kings and worriers. My own parents and my grand parents all had Islamic names, which were of course Arabic. My three siblings and I were given Persian names. Such names as Kurosh, Ardeshir, Bahrām, Dāryush, Hormoz, Rostam, Sohrāb, Sudābe, Manizhe, Purān and many others became popular. The main source for most of these names was Ferdowsi's great epic the *Shāhname*. Some names were simply chosen from Persian language for their beautiful meaning, such as Afsāne (Legend), Omid (Hope), Giti (World), or Shādi (Happiness), etc. Practically none of these names had any currency before the age of Rezā Shah.

Another development was the introduction of a law that required everyone to have a surname as family name. In Persia, traditionally the nobility were given titles by the king. These tittles were not graded in importance as in the European titles of Duke, Marquis, Count, Viscount, Baron, etc. The Persian titles were chosen to project a dignified meaning, and usually ended with the words *saltane* (of the kingdom), *dowle* (of the government), *molk* (of the state), *mamalek* (of states). There were also tittles that referred to military positions, i.e. *sālār* (military lord), and *sardār* (commander). To a few highly esteemed personalities, the shahs would bestow honorific titles quite out the norm such as *Farmānfarmā* (giver of command), *Sāheb Ekhtiar* (possessor of authority), or *Sadrol-Ashrāf* (pinnacle of nobility). The common folk were only known by their names given at birth; sometimes they would acquire added sobriquets referring to their professions, or the place of their birth, or as the son of so and so. From late in 1920s, by the orders of the Shah, every citizen was required to choose a surname, which had to be registered with the Office of Census and Identity. My father, whose title, given by Mozaffareddin Shah, was *Amjadel-Molk*, chose as a surname, the word *Farhat*, from the old Persian word *Farr*, meaning splendor.

The emphasis on the importance of national holidays became particularly noticeable. We know that the *Nōruz* (new day) has been celebrated by the Iranians, both within Persia and beyond the present boundaries of the country, for thousands of years. *Nōruz* is the first day of spring, the spring Solstice. But the importance attached to it was another feature of the Pahlavi era, when seven days of holiday was observed and great attention was paid to decorating city streets and shops for the occasion. Towards the end of Rezā Shah's reign there were plans to revive the ancient autumn solstice festival of *Mehregān*. Also, around Christmas time many shops in the more fashionable parts of cities would decorate their windows with appropriate imageries of Santa Claus, Holy Child in the manger, and the like. The king's birthday (14 March), the heir to the throne's birthday (26 October), the Coup d'Etat Day (21 February), and the Constitution Day (5 August) were also important holidays. On the whole, the regime wanted to emphasize joyful occasions and chase away the mournful, which seems so dear to the Shiite clergy.

The Islamic lunar calendar was replaced by Persian solar calendar. Some religious holidays were eliminated and the fanatical demonstrations on commemorative occasions of martyrdom of saints were prohibited. All these measures had a profound impact on the public at large and more specifically on the youth of the country. The nationalism that is so pronounced among Iranians, a thorn in the side of the ruling clerics of today's Islamic Republic, was largely planted and nurtured in the Rezā Shah period. In all fairness, it must be added that the 37 years reign of the second Pahlavi monarch, also, greatly advanced the cause of national pride. Where Mohammad Rezā Shah deviated from the policies of his father was in his appeasement of the clerics who steadily regained their lost strength.

An event that made a great impact on me as a child was the advent of the telephone. While the invention of the telephone goes back to the 19th century its availability to the general public in Persia came decades later. By early in the 20th century the Royal Court and some government offices had obtained telephones of the type that a central operator had to be contacted in order to make the needed connection. In mid-30s the Siemens Company of Germany was contracted to construct a network of auto-dialing phones for private homes and offices. However, the system initially provided only 6000 numbers for Tehran, a city of some half a million population at the time. This included numbers allocated to all government offices and major businesses. Needless to say only people of some social standing and influence were the beneficiaries of receiving a telephone line with a four-digit number. I think it was around the year 1937 when we got our phone. This was a point of great pride and happiness; the very sound of the phone ringing, or the wonder of dialing the number of a relative or friend's phone and being able to talk to someone at a great distance were marvels that excited us children. It took a long time before the novelty wore off and the nuisance aspect of having a telephone also became known to us.

One of Rezā Shah's greatest achievements was the construction of the trans-Iranian railways. The dream of a railway system in Persia goes back to the second half of the 19th century. During the reign of Nāsereddin Shah (1848-96) the idea had surfaced from time to time but had never moved beyond preliminary talks with foreign governments who vied with one another for every conceivable concession or contract. Only a 6 kilometers long stretch of narrow gauge rail track was laid, in the 1890s, between Tehran and the shrine city of Rey to the south of the capital. The trans-Iranian railway was a pet-project of Rezā Shah, constructed within an eight years period in the 1930s, entirely financed by taxes levied on tea and sugar. It is a south/north line that connects the Persian Gulf to the Caspian Sea, traversing immense mountain ranges. This was in deliberate defiance of the British who had lobbied for an east/west line, to connect their India with Iraq, which was also under their control.

When I was eleven years old I had my first experience of riding on a train. My family took me on a train trip, during the *Nōruz* holidays, to the end of the southern stretch of the line, to the oil refinery city of Ābādān. This is a thousand kilometers long track that cuts through immense mountain ranges. I recall vividly the wonderment of travelling by train, going through innumerable tunnels, seeing the beauty and grandeur of the Zagros Mountains. Perhaps even more impressive is the line that connects Tehran to the southeast corner of the Caspian Sea, cutting through the high Alborz Mountains. A trip through that section of the line came later when I was in my teens.

The 16 years of Rezā Shah's reign, also, saw the construction of thousands of kilometers of roads. I remember how happy and proud I felt when we drove once to the shores of the Caspian Sea. The newly constructed road that took us there rose to some 7000 feet in order to cross the Alborz Mountains, taking us from the interior of the country to the Māzandarān province on the Caspian littoral. This road had also been one of the Shah's pet projects. Rezā Shah, who was a native of Māzandarān, was particularly interested in opening access to the northern provinces that are so different in their lush vegetation from the interior of the Iranian plateau. This road is also a marvel of engineering; it provided, with two other roads from the interior to the north, for a connection between parts of the country that were largely secluded from one another. Most people living on the plateau had never seen the Caspian Sea, nor had they seen the dense rain forests that cover the northern slope of the mountains. Holidaying by the shores of the Caspian, something that the Tehranis now relish, was unheard of before these roads were built.

As a child of 13, I remember well the feeling of emptiness and anxiety when the Russians and the British invaded Iran and forced the king to abdicate. Many rejoiced his departure. That included the clerics, the outlawed communists, some of the grandees of the Qājār era, and those who immediately jockeyed for position and power in the hope of receiving British support. But many, as was the case with my family, regretted the removal of a king who, although autocratic and ruthless, had done so much towards the creation of a proud, independent and unified Iran. I was deeply saddened and hated the allies for having entered my country and exiled my king. There is no denying that Rezā Shah's rule was deeply flawed. It was a severely dictatorial regime. The Shah's increasingly avaricious accumulation of land, his mistrust and ultimate destruction of a number of those who had served him well, some of whom were honest and effective instruments of his reforms, and his complete intolerance of any criticism were among the weaknesses of his regime. But, given the shambolic and effete conditions of the country at the time of his rise to power, Rezā Shah remains a towering figure, a veritable savior, in the long history of Persia.

❧ 2 ❧

Teen Years in Troubled Times

The years that began with the reign of the second Pahlavi monarch, Mohammad Rezā Shah, in September of 1941, until the fall of the government of Prime Minister Mosaddeq in August of 1953, were highly charged and chaotic. In some respects, Persia underwent a kind of semi-democratic experience that had only been known in the early years after the constitutional revolution of 1906. Political parties and newspapers proliferated overnight. As the legislative branch of the government became assertive, the executive branch of the government became unstable and ineffectual. Prime ministers came and went within a matter of months. With the entry of the United States into the war in December of 1941, American soldiers also arrived in Persia, adding to the large numbers of British and Soviet forces that had the country under occupation since their invasion in September. The order and security that was a hallmark of the Rezā Shah era were gone. Much of the country's produce were consumed by the occupying forces; food items became scarce; coupons were distributed by the government for the purchase of such items as bread, cooking oil, rice, sugar and meat.

As I grew into manhood, I became increasingly aware of the unfolding political events and the dangers that my country faced. The communist party of Iran, known as the *Tudeh* (Masses) Party, directly linked with and subservient to Moscow, had become a vocal and troublesome social force. This was aided by the presence of Russian forces in the country. In the treaty that was drawn at the time of the invasion in September of 1941, the Allies had given assurance that Persia's independence and territorial integrity shall be respected. The agreement had also specified that all occupying forces are to depart from Persian territory within 6 months after the cessation of all hostilities. This meant that by February of 1946, half a year after the Japanese surrender, all foreign forces had to be out of Iran. The Americans and the British forces did leave by that date, but the Soviets remained in the northwestern provinces of Āzarbāijān and Kordestān. Two entities under the guise of 'Republic' were created in those two regions that proclaimed independence from the central government in Tehran. They were structured on Soviet models and were directly under Russian control.

I should make clear that, historically and geographically, Āzarbāijān is only the region south of the river Aras (Araxes), which is now and has always been within the Iranian domain. The area to the northwest of the river, bordered by the Caspian Sea, was always known as the provinces of Shirvān and Ārān. Azerbaijan (their spelling), as a republic of the Soviet Union, now an independent political unit, is a misnomer. At no time in history before the late 19th century has that region been called by that name. Any map predating the mid 19th century, will not designate the name Āzarbāijān to that area. The application of that name to the provinces of Shirvān and Ārān, lost to Russia in early 19th century, has been in line with the Tsarist, and later Soviet, designs on Persian territory south of the river, which is the historic Azārbāijān.

It took ten months of hard negotiation, referral to the UN's Security Council, and eventually the threat of intervention by the U.S., before the Soviets withdrew their support, and their military presence, from those regions. On the 12th of December 1946, Āzarbāijān and Kordestān were once again reunited with the rest of Iran, a date that was celebrated throughout the country. I remember the joy I felt to see my country in one piece again, free of the presence of all foreign forces.

In late summer of 1941, shortly after the invasion of Persia by the British and the Russian forces, I began my first year of high school, which was called the 7th class. During the six years of primary school I had been consistently among the top students; however, in the first three years of high school I steadily slid downwards and did poorly in most subjects. Our secondary school curriculum was quite extensive. It included mathematics, geometry, algebra, physics, chemistry, history, geography, botany, drawing, Persian literature, foreign language, and sports. The subjects that I particularly disliked were the sciences, specially algebra, trigonometry, chemistry and physics. By the time I was in the 9th grade my love for American movies had blossomed to near obsession. On occasions, in the company of one or two likeminded classmates, I would sneak out of the school compound in the afternoon and head for the nearby cinemas. My teenage rebelliousness did not really amount to waywardness, but my interest in school, and attention to my studies did suffer. The worst punishment I received was failing a few of my courses in the May/June final examinations, which meant having to re-sit exams in those subjects at the end of summer. This, in turn, meant a partially ruined summer break to which all youngsters looked with such anticipation. The 9th grade proved hard going; in the finals, I failed in two subjects and had to study during the summer and re-sit exams in September.

In the Persian schooling system at the time, the six years of secondary school were divided into two three year periods. In the first three years, called the First Cycle, all students had a uniform curriculum except for the foreign language for which they could choose either English or French. I had chosen the latter because my family had more of a French orientation. In the next three years, the Second Cycle, students had the choice of either 'Scientific' or 'Literary' strands of courses. This, I believe, was modeled on the French system of secondary schools, as indeed much else in the education system was also based on the French models including marking of assignments and exam papers from 0 to 20. In my case, it was clear that if I made it through the end of summer exams and finished with the 9th Grade, I had to take the 'Literary' Second Cycle, for the last three years of high school. Not only had it been proven that I had no gift for sciences, but I had shown some artistic sensibilities. I had serious romantic tendencies; I loved reading poetry and was very fond of French Romantic literature. I devoured works of poets such as Chateaubriand, Lamartine, Victor Hugo, and Alfred de Musset; they were available both in French and in Persian translation. Privately, I saw myself in the guise of such romantic figures as Paul (in *Paul et Virginie* of Bernardin de Saint Pierre), or Goethe's *Werther*, or as the young Lamartine in his youthful Italian romance as told in *Graziella*. I also wrote occasional poems and fantasy essays.

During the summer of 1944, when I was preparing to retake exams in September in the failed subjects, I happened to learn about a three-year secondary school, which only offered courses in the Second Cycle, entirely devoted to literary subjects plus courses in foreign languages, economics and law. This was *Dabirestān-e Dārāi* (High School of Finance), administered, not by the Ministry of Education as all other schools were, but by the Ministry of Finance. The graduates of this school could compete for admission to the University of Tehran in the fields of humanities, literature, law or economics. They could also apply for employment at the Ministry of Finance where, as a graduate of *Dabirestān-e Dārāi*, their employment was guaranteed.

Fortunately, in September, having passed the two subjects I had failed in the June exams, I applied for admission to *Dabirestān-e Dārāi* and was accepted. At that point a serious transformation seemed to have taken place within me; from the outset, at *Dārāi*, in some respects, I became an exemplary student. My teenage rebelliousness had proved short lived. While I was not among the top students in achieving high marks, I managed to conduct myself well; most of my classmates seemed to look up to me as a sort of a gentleman to be treated with some deference. As was the pattern in my previous schooling I did not attract many friends, but the few with whom I became friendly were devoted and always accommodating. The Principal, Mr. Vasiqi, was very fond of me and treated me with marked consideration. He was not an educator but was a cultured man with a distinguished background in the Ministry of Finance. I maintained occasional contact with him after my graduation before my departure for America.

The three years at *Dabirestān-e Dārāi* proved to be on the whole a happy period in my young life. At the end of the three years I graduated with a high school diploma. Meantime, I had begun my musical studies with violin lessons; my teacher was Vahe Djingheuzian, an Iranian/Armenian who had studied in France and was an excellent violinist. He also gave me lessons in music theory and solfeggio. Vahe was a strikingly handsome young man in his late 20s. He was tall and lean with sleek black hair parted in the middle. He bore a striking resemblance to Rudolf Valentino, the silent star of the 20's. He always wore a while shirt, a black bow tie and a black suit. I idolized him and found him in every way fascinating. My music lessons with Djingheuzian had the added benefit of improving my French. He had been born in Tabriz, where his family had found refuge after escaping the Turkish and Kurdish massacres during the First World War. He had been sent to France for his education at an early age. Accordingly, Vahe was most fluent in French and he also spoke Armenian, but his Persian was deeply flawed. I had to communicate with him in French, which was at first difficult but gradually became comfortable.

By the time I received my high school diploma, I still had no clear idea as to what I wanted to do with my life. I had begun to toy with the dream of a career in music; but the dream was full of uncertainties. I was a late starter in music and felt very insecure. I went to the Music Conservatory (*Honarestān-e Āli-ye Musiqi*) to see if I could be accepted as a music student, but was told that the Conservatory takes students at the beginning of their secondary school level. I was already 18 years old and could not contemplate recommencing the secondary school years. I competed for admission to the University of Tehran to study law, but failed the entrance exams. (Ordinarily no more than a quarter of the applicants succeeded in these exams.) The failure strengthened my resolve to seek musical studies at university level. This was not possible in Iran; at that time there were no music courses offered at third level institutions. An account of my decision to seek musical training at university level in America has been given in Chapter 6.

During my late teens, I had become increasingly aware of the political turmoil in the country. This was a period that saw the resurgence of clerical power. One of the clandestine groups with supposed Islamic credentials was the *Fadāiyān-e Eslām*. This was a terrorist organization that set out to eliminate those who were seen as enemies of Islam. One of the most heinous acts committed by this group was the assassination of Ahmad Kasravi, the noted lawyer and courageous writer and historian. Kasravi had written and published a number of books and articles that challenged the validity of Shiite myths, including the concept of the hidden Imam, the awaited messiah. There were a number of other assassinations and attempted assassinations by the *Fadāiyān*, some of which occurred during the years after I was no longer living in Persia.

The thugs, who perpetrated these murders, are now celebrated by the Islamic Republic of Iran, even streets have been named after them.

In the post Rezā Shah era, some of the old religious practices were revived and the government did not find it expedient to oppose them. Women from the less privileged and more devout sectors of the population reverted back to the habit of wearing a *chādor* in public. During the month of *Moharram*, processions by bands of chanting men, beating their chests (*sinezani*), or whipping their backs with chains, in commemoration of the martyrdom of Hoseyn, the third Shiite Imam, were once more allowed. New mosques were built and *mollās* regained greater presence in society and in politics. Nevertheless, the secularism fostered by Rezā Shah remained largely intact. Above all, civil laws that had been adopted based on Belgian models remained in force; sharia laws had no place in the legal system. Women were free to choose how they wished to appear in public, and were free to take on any job outside home they were qualified to perform. There were no restrictions on the sale of alcoholic beverages or any meat and fish products that might have been considered *harām* (forbidden) by Islamic laws.

The musical life of the country was significantly livelier. By 1945, there was a Symphony Orchestra in Tehran associated with the Tehran Conservatory of Music. The Conservatory (*Honarestān-e Āli-ye Musiqi*) was established in the 1930s; it was in fact a transmutation of the old music school that had been established in the 19th century for the training of military band musicians. The new Conservatory was modeled on European musical institutions where courses on the theory and techniques of western music, together with instruction on various instruments and voice, were taught. Most of the teachers were engaged from abroad, they included Czechs, Russians and Italians. A number of Iranian Armenians were also on the teaching staff, including the excellent violinist Rouben Gregorian. He was from a very musical family and was active, not only as a violinist, but also was a composer of considerable accomplishments. One of his major contributions was a published collection of Persian folk songs arranged for a-cappella choir. The collection includes some 20 pieces that were tastefully written in four-part harmony. This was a very important pioneering effort as it demonstrated that native folk songs are not incompatible with poly-phonic treatment based on the harmonic system of western music.

The head of the conservatory, in post WWII, was Parviz Mahmoud, the Belgian trained Persian composer and conductor. Mahmoud and Gregorian had jointly created the Tehran Symphony of which the for-mer was the conductor and the latter the leader. This was a small or-chestra of about 40 to 45 players. The small size did not necessarily make for a poor ensemble. The Esterhasy Orchestra of Hayden was smaller than that; the orchestra that gave the premier of the Eroica Symphony, that greatest of all symphonies, in 1804 was also certainly smaller. The problem was that most members of the Tehran Symphony were amateurs or students; many did not attend rehearsals regularly. Nevertheless, the concerts of this orchestra were, for me, the apogee of musical fulfillment. To be able to sit and listen to a Mozart or a Tchaikovsky symphony coming to life, for this impassioned novice, was the greatest thrill, an unforgettable experience, even if the orches-tra was of poor quality.

The periodic concerts of the Tehran Symphony were the absolute high points of my life. On occasions, these concerts included some of Mahmoud's own compositions. They affected me deeply. His com-positions were all based on Persian folk melodies. I remember an or-chestral piece called *Nōruz*, and a beautiful Violin Concerto, the solo part of which was played, at a concert, by my own violin teacher, Vahe Djingeuzian. Mahmoud's works reinforced my dream of becoming a composer. I don't know how I would judge his music now, but, at the time, they sounded quite magical. Sadly, after leaving Persia, I never heard any of his compositions again. I do know, however, that Mahmoud also left Iran and emigrated to America, as did Djingheuzian and Gregorian.

The years after the war also saw the beginnings of occasional visits to Persia by foreign musicians. At that time very few would venture to travel to such an out-of-the-way place, but I do recall a piano recital by a Virom Bellas, a Greek pianist. And, I did attend a recital by the French violinist, Ginette Neveu. She played, among other things, the

Cesar Franck Violin Sonata which remains to this day one of my beloved works of chamber music literature.

The main venue for concerts was the hall of *Nurbakhsh* (later called Rezā Shah Kabir) High School. The stage of this hall was large enough to seat the small Tehran Symphony Orchestra. It was a rather long and narrow hall with the capacity to seat about 500 people. The small hall at the Armenian Club was also used on occasions for recitals. The Armenian community in Tehran, in those days, was in the forefront of musical and theatrical activity. As a Christian minority the Armenians had the advantage of freedom from some of the restrictions that Shiism imposed on the Moslem community.

⟡   ⟡

As I have stated in the Introduction, this book is not concerned with my private life. However, I like to conclude this chapter, which is about my teen years, with a brief reminiscence of my youthful infatuation with a girl of my own age who dominated my thoughts during the last four years before leaving for America. This love story, in its purity and innocence, stands apart from all other romantic involvements I have known. Its inclusion may serve a purpose in availing, to the reader, a glimmer into a life style of a bygone age and an environment that is forever lost.

The high school I attended during the first three years was *Dabirestān-e Irānshahr*. It was located very close to our home; it took me no more than seven minutes walk to reach it. The high school I attended for the final three years, as related above, was *Dabirestān-e Dārāi*, which was considerably farther, at a distance of about 20 minutes walk. In the post Rezā Shah period, all schools, primary or secondary, were of one gender. There was a girl's high school very close to our home on Shahabad Avenue. As of the start of the school year on the 22nd of September 1944, every morning, as I walked to *Dārāi*, I would pass by the girls who were walking to this school, called *Dabirestān-e Shāhdokht*, in the opposite direction, usually in groups of two, three or more.

In Iran of my youthful years, any contact, friendship and romantic relationship between boys and girls were extremely hard to come by.

One would meet girls of similar age if they were among family relations and friends, but it was very difficult to cultivate any contact with
strangers. Romantic feelings were largely forged in the realm of fantasy
and were devoid of intimacy. In my case, such feelings were of dreami-
est purity. For me, love was an exalted emotion unsoiled by physicality.
This wholly innocent and redolent conception of love found its object
in one of the girls that I observed every day, as she passed me by on her
way to her school near our house. She always walked in the company
of one or two of her friends, followed by her black servant who carried
her books.

The 'black servant' needs some explanation. It is not known at what
stage in Persian history slavery had been introduced; I suspect some
slave holding had existed since very ancient times, as was common in
all conquering empires. Even after the Islamic conquests the practice
had continued. Slavery did, in fact, exist among the Arabs, even at the
time of the Prophet Mohammad and thereafter. However, there is no
evidence that, at least in the past two centuries, there had been any
'slave markets' in Persia. Nevertheless, there were a few cases of de-
scendants of African slaves who remained in some old families among
the nobility. They were not 'owned' by the family but were more of
auxiliary family members. I had seen a number of such servant/family
members in my own greater family. They were treated above the hired
hands and their position was permanent. There was no question as to
their freedom to leave if they so desired, but that was simply not con-
templated. The family of the girl whom I saw on my way to school, and
fell in love with, apparently had this old African as an adjunct family
member. He was very small, thin and quite old; he always walked a few
paces behind her carrying her books.

The subject of my admiration and eventual adoration was a young
lady of extraordinary beauty. She was of slightly above average height,
with a luminously clear complexion, blue/green eyes and long black
hair, always braided in two strands that were turned upwards into a
loop on her back. She had an uncanny resemblance to Vivien Leigh, as
I remembered, in *Gone with the Wind*. I was particularly taken by her
bearing, always stately and dignified, unlike many girls I saw on the

way to school who were a bit rowdy, giggling as they walked in groups of four or five.

In those days, the seed of love was planted by mere glances, which gradually would become ardent and longing. Ultimately, a furtive smile on the part of the lady in question may give a hint of encouragement. At that point, detective work had to be mounted to find out who she is and to see if there can be any way of making contact without appearing brash. My closest friend at that stage in my life was Hassan whom I knew form the previous high school; we remained very close until my departure for America. When I opened my heart to him, he told me that he had a cousin who was also a student at the same girls' school. A short time later, having made queries, Hassan reported that the girl who has stolen my heart was named Giti; she is the only daughter of an aristocratic family, and that her home is located at a short distance beyond Dabirestān-e Dārāi. This investigation had, at the same time, revealed to Hassan's cousin, and in turn to Giti, both my identity and my sentiment.

After several weeks of seeing Giti and her friend, every morning, on their way to their school, one day I noted a faint smile and a lingering glace as she passed me by. More surprisingly, the black servant who followed a few paces behind stopped and greeted me, followed with the customary query as to my health. The encounter lasted only a few seconds but I took the few words exchanged with this old man to be immensely portentous. Clearly he would not have accosted me without having been so instructed by Giti. From that day on I felt encouraged enough to greet her and Hāji Khān (her African attendant) and we exchanged smiles, but we never stopped to talk to one another.

Throughout the remainder of my years in Iran before leaving for the United States, the relationship between Giti and I did not progress too far. She was one year older than me and finished the secondary school a year before I did. Near the end of her final high school year her graduating class organized a celebratory party at a sort of restaurant/night club on Istanbul Avenue called The Continental. Attendance was by invitation, which was distributed by the students to their friends; Hassan obtained an invitation ticket for me. I was thrilled, the idea of attending a party where Giti was among the hosts set my heart racing. On the night of the party I saw her, amid a large number of guests, more radiantly beautiful than ever. I managed to talk with her briefly and perfunctorily, but sadly the place was crowded and the occasion was such that could not have availed any opportunity for a more private conversation.

After Giti graduated from her high school, I saw her less regularly. Occasionally, I saw her in movie theatre lobbies, where she was usually with her parents. In summertime, I saw her more frequently in the course of evening strolls in Tajrish. Persian city dwellers are very fond of their leisurely walks, called *gardesh*, in certain localities, at certain times of day or evening. In the old days, during the cold season in Tehran, this *gardesh* took place in midday on sunny days in the vicinity of *Lālezār* and *Istanbul* Avenues. During the hot summers, this ritual promenade was moved to sunset and the favored area was *Sar-e Pol* in *Tajrish*. *Tajrish* was part of a group of villages (collectively called *Shemirān*) spread at a distance of about 10 to 15 kilometers to the north of Tehran, right in the foothills of the *Alborz* Mountains. In the 1940's, *Tajrish* had already become a sizable town that contained numerous summer homes of the wealthy Tehranis, who regularly moved to their villas in late June and retuned to their city dwellings in September. All of the *Shemirān* villages, at considerably higher elevation than the capital city, had cool and pleasant summers; on the average, temperature in the northern foothills was 5 to 8 degrees centigrade lower than in Tehran city center.

Giti's family owned a summer home in *Tajrish* to which they relocated for the duration of the hot season. Every evening throughout the summer, I went for the ritual stroll, usually in the company of my friend Hassan, to *Sar-e Pol* in *Tajrish*. *Sar-e Pol*, meaning Bridge Head, or over the bridge, was a vast plaza under which the *Darband* river flowed. The plaza was effectively a widened bridge over a river that was quite insignificant in summertime but sizable in winter and spring. There, with cool breeze from the mountains towering above us, I would see Giti, in the company of her parents and her young brother, also having their *gardesh*. We exchanged furtive smiles, but that was all.

This type of romantic connection with strangers, in those days, had to be concealed from parental knowledge. Parents disapproved of such relations no matter its utter purity.

Some four years had passed since I had first seen her on the way to her school. I had cultivated a deep feeing of admiration and love for this beautiful girl, a feeling that bordered on the sublime; but as to any relationship, I had hardly made any progress. There was something quite unreal about my feelings for Giti; it certainly remained a unique sensation that was never duplicated in any of the other experiences with women I had in the rest of my life.

In early June of 1949, as I was in the final stages of preparation for my flight to the United States, Giti was still very much on my mind. On the 8th of June, the day before my departure, the urge to see Giti for the last time took hold of me. I made what was for me a very bold move, as I was not only very timid but was also highly conscious of maintaining self-respect. I decided to go to her home to say goodbye. The summer move to *Tajrish* had not yet taken place and she was still at their big ancestral home not far from the old *Dabirestān-e Dārāi*. It was around 11 in the morning that I knocked on the big wooden door. I was nervous and apprehensive; I thought if any servant other than Hāji Khān should open the door I would simply ask for a made up name as if I had come to the wrong address by mistake. As the door opened, I was greatly relieved to see the friendly face of Hāji Khān. I told him that I was to leave for America the next day and would like to say good-by to Giti, if she can see me, (meaning that if she is available and that the coast is clear). He asked me to wait a few minutes and went back inside.

A few minutes that seemed like a few hours passed when the old man returned and asked me to come in. I had never been inside this house, which like all old Persian homes was built behind walls and therefore not visible from the street. There was a large courtyard with trees, flowers and a central pool. From the courtyard, he guided me up a flight of stairs into a large well-furnished room. All well-to-do Persian homes have an *Otāq-e Pazirāi*, or reception room that is used only when guests arrive. I sat on a comfortable chair; a few more tension-filled minutes passed before Giti entered the room. She appeared as if she just had a shower; her magnificent shinny black hair was not braded but was flowing behind her not yet quite dry; her face was radiant and her cheeks seemed as veritable rose petals. We shook hands and sat down. I related to her my love of classical music and my wish to pursue composition as my future occupation; she said that she had heard about the depth of my involvement with music. I told her of my trip to America the next day and the possibility that I may never come back. At that point she became quiet and remained silent for a few seconds, then she said that she was sorry to hear that I may never return but no doubt I have made the right decision.

Four years had passed since I had first seen Giti and had fallen in love with her. Now, at the time when I was to leave and perhaps never to see her again, I was at last with her, just the two of us, closer than we had ever been before. How I had dreamed of being near her with no one else around. Now the moment had arrived, just before I was to move away, to the other side of the world. Here was, next to me, the girl of my dreams, yet I didn't know what to do or what to say. I didn't even know what kind of a person she was. Was she good, gentle, kind, thoughtful, truthful and sensitive? I really had no clear idea. All I knew was that she was beautiful and I loved her. The irony and sadness of the moment was too painful. I had never told her of my feelings, but she surely knew how I felt about her. As for me, I had only some inkling that the feelings were not entirely one-sided.

Before leaving, I told her that I would like to send her a souvenir, a piece of music that I have composed for her. She seemed very pleased and gave me the address of their home in *Tajrish*, to which they were to move for the summer in a few days time. I cannot remember, now that well over six decades have passed, what else we talked about, but I did not stay more that 10 or 15 minutes. With tears in my eyes I kissed her hand, said goodbye and left.

In the course of the following summer, while I lived in Logan, Utah, I posted the violin piece I had composed for Giti to the address she had given me. The package contained no letter, just a piece of notated music. I cannot imagine what it meant to her to receive a piece of music called 'Amore'; what possible meaning could it have had for someone who did not read music!

I never heard from her.

❧ 3 ❧

Cinema in My Childhood and Beyond

My mother used to tell me that as a small child I loved movies and that I used to pester her to take me to cinemas. Later, when I was in elementary school, I fondly remember Friday afternoons when my father would give money to the male servant of the house to take my brother Manuchehr and me to the movies. In those days, the films we loved to see were the serials. In the 1930s and 40s, some of the Hollywood studios, mainly Republic, Universal and Columbia, made serials intended for very young viewers. Most serials were made of 12 or 15 chapters, about 20 minutes in length each, contained in one reel of film. Each chapter ended with a kind of cliffhanger scene when the hero is in perilous straights. The next chapter would pickup the story with further adventures ending with another cliffhanger. The final chapter would bring the tortuous, but highly repetitive, story to a close with the hero both triumphing and also winning the girl. By far the majority of serials were either cops and robbers stories or cowboys and Indians fights. They were simple-minded good guys and bad guys tales with the good eventually coming on top.

In the U.S., serials were shown on matinee programs and were followed by a main feature. Each week one chapter would be screened; the next chapter would be on the program the next week, and so on until the final episode. That way the audience, particularly the children, would be encouraged to come every week to see the story unfold to its end. In Persia, the serials were put to an altogether different use. There were cinemas that mainly catered to kids and the lower social classes. These cinemas, usually, showed three or four chapters of a 12 or more episodes serial in a row, amounting to a total of about an hour and twenty minutes, preceded by a cartoon; no feature (full length) movie was shown at these houses. There was a five to ten minutes pause between each of the three or four reels of film. During the pause lights would be turned back on and a couple of vendors would circulate in the isles selling refreshments on trays strapped to their necks, propped horizontally below their chests. They sold soft drinks, chocolates and nuts. Altogether, about two hours were taken, during which time the viewer would see, with interruptions, three or four chapters of the serial.

Children loved these adventure stories; they were simple to follow, there was much action, right and wrong were clearly drawn, villainy would be punished, and the ending would invariably be a happy one. Poor people, mostly young men of menial occupations, also came to see serials; the tickets were cheap and the feel good stories gave them needed relief from their humdrum existence. In those days the films were not dubbed. As the language spoken in the picture was not understood, the audience saw no reason to restrain from talking; the halls remained noisy throughout the show. Following the old pattern of the silent movies, periodic translation of some of the conversations would appear on the screen, interrupting the flow of the film. At that point loud reading of what appeared on the screen was customary as many of the adults who were illiterate relied on those who could read to do so aloud.

In 1930's, there were seven cinemas on Lālezār and Istanbul Avenues, within walking distance to our house. Five of these were first run houses where films from major Hollywood studios were imported and shown; these houses would never show serials. Two cinemas on Lālezār Avenue, Pārs and Melli, were devoted to the screening of serials and cartoons. As children, those were the places we wanted to go; we wanted to see serials. The experience was absolutely exhilarating. The Friday afternoon movie was the highlight of our week. The world depicted on the screen by these pictures was so removed from the experience of life in Persia of the 30s that it seemed like being transported to an alien world. This world of fantasy became all the more magical when, in the late 30s, science fiction serials were marketed. The most captivating was Flash Gordon with Buster Crabbe in the title role. This serial became the biggest hit among children. It had been, apparently, quite popular also in the U.S. for it spun a number of sequels.

When I was in my teens, corresponding to the secondary school years, I lost interest in the serials. Feature films of all kinds captured my imagination. The earliest favorites were films of Laurel and Hardy. The pair had formed the supreme comedy team of all time. They were unquestionably the most graceful and loveable of all comedians. I loved equally the swashbucklers of Errol Flynn, melodramas with the likes of Bette Davis and Joan Crawford, the situation comedies of James Stewart, Carol Lombard and Katherine Hepburn, the crime dramas with Humphrey Bogart or James Cagney. The musicals of Fred Astaire and Ginger Rogers became great favorites enthralling me with their grace and joyful exuberance. The famous stars of golden age of American cinema were idols whose movies I would see over and over again. The likes of Clark Gable, Gary Cooper and Greta Garbo were figures to be revered.

Usually, first run motion pictures were shown in Tehran cinemas a few years after they were released in America. The delay was particularly lengthy during the war years. I recollect distinctly that *Gone With The Wind*, which was released in the U.S. in December of 1939, was first shown in Tehran in 1944. This monumental production made a tremendous hit in Persia; it was shown in two segments and was on the screen for several months. I saw it 11 times.

The five cinemas that showed feature films were within ten minutes walk from our house. They were large well-upholstered theatres that even had box seats and balconies. The seats were comfortable and ticket prices were graded in three categories. First class seats were in the loggias in the back of the hall. Most of the rest of the hall was set for second class seating, and a few rows in the front were designated as third class. Ticket fares were very cheap for the front rows but quite expensive for the first class seats. Most people bought tickets to the second class seats at a moderate price. Curiously, all the good cinemas had a central box in the back, with velvet paneling, very comfortable seats and a heavy curtain that could be drawn if so desired, reserved for the Royal Family. This was clearly a gesture of courtesy for I never saw anyone seated in those boxes.

In the post war years, before my departure for America, I discovered that a number of movie magazines were imported and sold in Tehran. The one that I favored was *Photoplay*. This was a monthly periodical that contained articles, interviews, news items, film reviews and lots of pictures of stars, directors, producers, etc. Copies of *Photoplay* usually arrived a few months after it had been published in the U.S.; the shipment in those days was by sea and took weeks to arrive. There was a kiosk at the crossroad of Lālezār and Istanbul Avenues, close to my beloved cinemas, where I bought my *Photoplay*. At this same kiosk, whose owner had become friendly with me, I used to leave my violin after my violin lessons, before going to one of the nearby cinemas, to be retrieved on my way home. I would not even open the *Photoplay* before arriving home; the pleasure of relaxing in my own room and looking through its pages was not to be spoiled by browsing casually beforehand. Among the secondary school subjects, students had the choice of either French or English as the required foreign language course. My choice had been French. The fact that my English was nearly nonexistent did not stand in the way. I would read the shorter items such as the write-up under the pictures and the brief synopsis of movies stories and the like. Interest and eagerness was such that I would usually manage to arrive at some understanding of what I read.

It is not easy to grasp fully the impact that Hollywood movies had on a Persian teenager some seventy years ago. America was not just on the other side of the world, it seemed more like being altogether on a different planet. Nothing about what one saw on the screen was familiar. It made very little difference if the film was a western, a musical, a crime drama, a historic epic or a situation comedy; every genre appeared utterly removed from life as we knew it. In those days, there was some familiarity with the countries of western Europe; it was easy to meet people who had been to Europe. But hardly anyone from Persia ever travelled to America. America was, and still is, different. The buildings, the streets, the homes, the way people act and dress, the gaiety, abandon and freedom that typifies the life style, are all uniquely American. These manifestations of the American way of life were invariably mirrored in the films I saw and I found them sources of endless fascination.

My love of movies continued into adulthood. In the early years after coming to America, being very hard pressed for money, I had found a cinema in the West Lake district of Los Angeles, where second run double features were shown for 25 cents. Although this cinema was at a considerable distance from where I lived, on weekends, for diversion from the rigors of study and piano practice, I used to drive to this cinema and spend four hours watching two movies. There were also a number of theatres on Hollywood Boulevard that showed older movies inexpensively. Rarely could I afford to see a first run film at the more posh movie houses in Westwood village or on Wiltshire Boulevard in the nearby Beverly Hills, where a ticket sold for one dollar.

One time, when I did manage to pay the high price of the ticket to a first run motion picture, I had an interesting run-in with the Beverly Hills police. It was during my first year in America, a beautiful British film called Red Shoes, with ballerina Moira Shearer, was being shown at a cinema on Wilshire Boulevard in that city. Beverly Hills, a suburb of Los Angeles, was an even more posh and exclusive city in those days, and the police in that city are known for being very protective of their citizens. I arrived at the cinema about half an hour before the next showing of the film was to begin. I bought my ticket and decided to pass the time by having a walk on Wilshire. As I passed in front of one of the side streets, I noticed a police car that was parked there with two officers seated in it. As I walked by one of the two men stepped out of the car and approached me. I was wearing a suit, white shirt and necktie. With this outfit I must have appeared highly suspicious to him, particularly for the fact of I was walking in a city where no one walks. He stopped me and asked what am I doing there. I said I am walking. Why, he asked. I like to walk, I said. He wanted to know if I lived in Beverly Hills, and when I said no, he asked why are you walking here then. I told him that I am going to see the film at the cinema that was only a block away and informed him that I have already purchased the ticket and am waiting for the right time to go in. He asked to see the ticket, which I showed him. At that point he seemed satisfied but told me emphatically, 'ok, but don't go into any side streets!'

Some years later, my interest in movies took a new turn. When I was back in Iran in late 1960s and into the '70s, film director, Dāryush Mehrjui, approached me to see whether I might write music for some of the films he was making. I knew Mr Mehrjui from the time he was a student at UCLA in the early 60s. He had studied psychology and later had switched to film studies. He was also a good musician. He played the Persian dulcimer, *santur*, quite well. He participated in the Persian Music Study Group that I had organized within the Ethnomusicology Institute, an arm of the Music Department. He even occasionally played at concerts in the instrumental ensemble that I had created.

On his return to Persia, Mehrjui had quickly established a reputation as a serious movie director. The first of the films for which he asked my cooperation in composing background music was *Gāv* (The cow). This was a very simple yet profound study of the bleakness of rural life in Persia, based on a short story of the well-known writer, Qolām Hoseyn Sāedi. I was shown the film in its rough cut and liked it. It needed a simple and spare score, with the use of Persian instruments. The outcome was quite effective; the film won international acclaim and I was even given a trophy for the music by Empress Farah. I wrote music scores for two more films of Dāryush Mehrjui, Mr Simpleton (*Āqā-ye Hālu*), a charming comedy, and *Postchi* (The Mailman), a gripping drama.

Another filmmaker who sought my assistance in providing background music for two of his films was Nasser Taqvāi, also a talented and serious director. I wrote music for his *Ārāmesh dar Hozur-e Digarān* (Tranquility in the Presence of Others) and *Sādeq Korde* (Sadeq the Kurd). The three films of Mehrjui and the two of Taqvāi remained the extent of my venture into motion picture music writing. It would be fair to say that I never really felt comfortable with this type of creative activity. It was a short phase in my career as a composer; it was an experience that I enjoyed but did not wish to make it a major part of my professional life.

In my old age I still love cinema. Sadly movie making is now very different from what I knew in my youth, which corresponded to what is generally known as the 'golden age' of Hollywood cinema. Perhaps today's movies, in some respect, are more realistic. But, if filmmaking purports to be an art form then realism is not necessarily its purpose. I am particularly referring to the language, which is so predominantly foul and clothing that is so shabby. In the old films everyone, including the bad guys, spoke without the use of profanities, and they all dressed neatly. Films were made so that every scene could be clearly seen; the lighting was always bright so that the viewer could see everything clearly. In today's movies some of the scenes are so dark as if electricity has not yet been invented. Another axiom of old movies was that the spoken words must be audible; now the actors mumble and chew up their words; this is supposed to be more natural and 'cool'. I would rather hear and understand what is being said; if that is not very realistic, so be it. In my view, in the Golden Age of American Cinema (1920's, 30's and 40's) just about every motion picture was watchable and entertaining, even the B pictures. Present day Hollywood movies rarely satisfy me. In some ways the technical advancements in filmmaking, particularly in what is called 'special effects' is quite astonishing. Most films have very strong and commendable sound track and background music; the acting also is no less accomplished. On the other hand, movies have become far more limited in genres. Comedies are few and tend to be on the vulgar side with sexual innuendoes that are so clichéd to be boring; bedroom scenes and mandatory nudities in dramas are even more tedious. Romantic and tender stories, clean comedies and graceful musical seem no longer to be of interest. Every other film seems to be of the ludicrous 'out of this world' science fiction or action fantasy type; I find them immensely repetitive and tiresome. Maybe it is an old man talking, but I firmly believe that the best days of motion picture industry passed long ago.

❧ 4 ❧

The Unexpected Guests

In the course of my lifetime, Persian social customs have changed a great deal. I don't imagine any period, in the country's long history, has seen so great a transformation. My childhood and teen years roughly correspond to the 1930's and 40's. At that time, despite accelerated modernization, an age-old aristocracy still ran the country. They produced most of the well-educated class, the professionals and the technocrats. Some thirty years later, when I was back in Iran in the 1970's, this tight circle had widened considerably. Some of the high officials of the government were from the former 'lower' classes whose families had obtained better economic conditions and were among the ever enlarging middle class. It is significant to appreciate that no rigid caste system had ever existed in Persia; this is particularly true of the period after Islam came to be the dominant religion.

After the Revolution of 1978/79, however, the social order has become the exact reverse of what it was during my youth and before. The old aristocracy has been entirely decimated and has been purged from governance. They are either in self-exile abroad or have been neutralized, in some cases executed. Authority now mostly rests with the clerics who, before the Revolution, were generally considered as an under class affiliated with merchants and shopkeepers. The cities have grown immensely. Most of the growth has been due to movement from the rural areas to cities, and the greater rate of childbirth among the less privileged, which is true throughout the world.

Some of the traditions maintained by the old aristocratic families are gone forever. One of these customs was the open door policy in respect of visitors who had remote and tenuous relationship with the host family. I am not referring to invited guests, family relations or friends. For the invited, the traditional Persian hospitality remains intact. Persians are hospitable to an exaggerated extent. Every traveller and tourist to the country has experienced that. You only need to read the Lonely Planet Guide to Iran to see what the writer/travellers Andrew Burke and Mark Elliott have to say about this subject. In the following, I shall recount, from my childhood memories, the sort of reception given to those who can best be described not as just unexpected but unwanted guests. I imagine that in today's Iran, where the traditional 'upper class' has been eliminated, that kind of hospitality is no longer available.

One type of guest that appeared at our home, at least two or three times a week, was the lunch time arrival of any number of people who had rather remote connection with our family as former employees and their relatives. For example, there was my mother's infancy wet nurse, an elderly woman, lovable and jocular, who would show up, from time to time, unannounced, usually around eleven in the morning. She was rarely alone, one or more of her daughters, possibly some of her grand children, would accompany her. My own childhood wet nurse was another woman who occasionally appeared in the house. She was a peculiar woman, slightly unhinged and bad humored. There were any number of women who, at some period in the past, had been housemaids, not necessarily of ours, but, say, of my grand parents. There was a kind of enduring loyalty and bond that existed between these people and my immediate family. They would arrive have lunch, have long chats with my mother about their lives and family problems, receive some money and old clothes and depart by late afternoon. We would receive them warmly, not just in the spirit of charity, but more than that, as if they were almost part of the family.

This type of unexpected arrivals was common to all patrician homes. I know for a fact that all our relatives also received a stream of visitors from the ranks of former employees and their relations.

Another category of arrivals, that my family in particular had to put up with, was more rightly the unwanted and highly disruptive guests. These were guests that would arrive at times of their choosing and stay on for periods of weeks or months.

The Zeyni Family

My maternal grandmother had left my grandfather, Sālaār Moazzam, when her daughter, her only child at the time, was only two years old. Evidently, she disapproved of Sālaār's life style; she was very pious and he was, according to her, irreverent. Upon getting a divorce she had moved to the city of Karbala in Iraq. Karbala is a Shiite holy place where Imam Hoseyn, the martyred grandson of the Prophet Mohammad, is supposed to be buried. It is a place of pilgrimage favored by Iranians who form a large minority in Karbala. There, some years later, she had married a man who was among the keepers of the shrine of Hoseyn. This man, named Ahmad Zeyni was reputed to be half Persian and half Arab. This was probably true, as over centuries many devout Persians had settled in the Mesopotamian holy cities; moreover, Zeyni spoke Persian as well as Arabic.

From the time that I was about five years old, I can recall with horror the disagreeable sudden entrance of Mr. Zeyni into our house. We had a large old style Persian house in, what was then, slightly to the north of the center of Tehran, on an alley off Shahabad Avenue, very close to the Parliament Square. One entered the house by descending a few steps into a garden with a central pool. Around the pool were flowerbeds and a number of venerable trees. We had four very tall Pine trees, half a dozen spruces, two pear and two plumb trees, a pomegranate and a very big mulberry tree. On three sides of the garden there were rooms built some one and half meters above ground. Beneath the rooms was a lower level, partly below the surface of the garden. Some of the chambers of this basement level were used as cool summer retreats and some rooms were for storage. From the street, in order to enter the house, one had to pass through a roofed octagonal (*hashti*) entrance hall. Inside the *hashti* there were two doors, the one on the right led to our house; the left door led to my uncle's house. On passing through the door to our house one had to descend a broad stairway to arrive at the garden level. During the day, the heavy wooden doors, both the one from street to the *hashti*, and the one from there to our garden, were left unlocked. Accordingly, Mr. Zeyni had no need to knock, he simply entered our house, upon arrival from Iraq, at his chosen time in early summer. No prior notice had been given as to the date of his arrival, the length of his stay or those who may accompany him.

My grandmother and Ahmad Zeyni had four sons, my mother's half-brothers. The youngest was about my age; the other three were older with two or three years age difference between them. Usually one, some times two, of the boys came with their father. The grandmother seldom accompanied her husband, which was a relief, as she and my mother did not get along at all. The Arab invasion, as we used to call these visits, usually began in late June and lasted until late August. There were two reasons why Zeyni and family came to Tehran, one was to get away from the scorching Iraqi summer and the other was for Mr. Zeyni to collect *zakāt* from the devout Persian merchants he knew. *Zakāt* is a category of alms that the wealthy Moslems give to the needy. The concept of needy, in this case, was rather malleable. Zeyni was not poor, but as he was in the service of the shrine of Imam Hoseyn, he was considered to be in need of support.

For the Zeyni family this was a win/win situation. They had a summer vacation in a more pleasant climate, free room and board, plus *zakāt* money that was collected and taken back to Karbala. For us it was the imposition of one or more coarse and demanding near strangers for the duration of summer. My father was a very tolerant gentleman and would take the ungainly presence of Ahmad Zeyni in good humor. My mother was a tempestuous and impatient lady, who deeply resented these unwanted guests, but bound by tradition and hospitality, she remained restrained. For my brother Manuchehr and I – we were very close in age - these prolonged visits amounted to the partial ruin of our summer holiday. We disliked Zeyni who was brooding and imperious and who, on occasion, voiced disapproval of the fact that we were not attentive to our religious duties. For example, he questioned why we did not perform daily prayer, or why we had not learned Arabic so that we could read and understand the Quran. He was an imposing tall man with a stentorian voice, and was quick to show anger. We deeply resented this intruder coming into our lives and questioning why we do this or don't do that.

On rare occasions, my grandmother accompanied her husband on these visits. Curiously, she was even more religiously committed than her husband. She chided my mother about her total disregard of religious duties. My mother, however, was not the type to trifle with; she would not hesitate for a second to tell her to mind her own business. Actually, the two women had no real affection for one another; they had hardly ever lived together and the usual mother/daughter feelings simply did not exist. Whenever any of their sons came along on these summer holidays, a different kind of nuisance had to be tolerated. These were ill-mannered and rowdy boys with habits quite alien to us. We simply did not want them around, but there was not much we could do about it.

Once or twice, in the course of the two months that Zeyni stayed with us he would go on short trips within Iran. He knew wealthy businessmen in a few other cities such as Rasht and Mashhad. He would travel to those cities to collect zakat from these men and return within a few days. We certainly looked forward to his brief side trips. The yearly arrival of the Zeynis was an unpleasant summer routine; it continued, as I was told, for a few more years after my departure for America in 1949. Some time in the mid 50s, Ahmad Zeyni passed away; my grandmother died a few years later. Their sons, my mother's half brothers, according to letters I was receiving from my parents, occasionally did come for short stays but the routine of Arab summer invasions gradually ended.

The Shāpuri Family

In my childhood days there were very few hotels in Persia. None existed in smaller towns. In Tehran there were a few hotels that catered mostly to foreign visitors and businessmen. There were a number of inns (*mosāferkhāne*, literally "house of travellers'), in Tehran, and in other large cities, for travellers within the country. These were cheap and dirty places located in the less fashionable areas of cities. The so-called upper classes never stayed in a *mosāferkhāne*. People of position, when travelling to the other parts of the country, which they seldom did, stayed with friends and relatives that they might have had in those parts. There was also the possibility of being invited to stay with persons they did not know, but who offered hospitality because of professional connections.

During the New Year (*Nōruz*) holidays of 1943, my parents and three of the children – my older brother Manuchehr chose to stay at home - took a vacation trip to Ahvāz, the administrative capital of the province of Khuzestān. This province is in the extreme southwest of the country where most of the oil exploration and installations are located. It is the only region of the country that is low lying and is extremely hot and humid in summer time. At *Nōruz* season, in late March, the weather is mild and pleasant. We travelled by train, which, before reaching Khuzestān, traverses some spectacular mountain scenery, and goes through more than one hundred tunnels.

On arrival in Ahvaz train station, we were met by Mr. and Mrs. Shāpuri. Mr. Shāpuri, who was originally from Kermān, was the Head of the Finance Department of the Khuzestān province. Since my father was a highly placed General Director at the Ministry of Finance in the capital, Mr. Shāpuri, having learned of my father's visit to the province, had felt duty bound to come to welcome us and offer hospitality. Although the two men had never met, there was nothing unusual about this gesture; it was perfectly within the expected norms. After some customary verbal refusal on my father's part, not wishing to impose our presence, and the equally customary insistence on Shāpuri's part that he would not hear of it, we ended up by staying at his house for about a week, before heading back home.

The week in Ahvāz passed pleasantly. The Khuzestān province is in many ways different form the rest of the country. It is mostly flat, there are no mountains in sight and even in early spring it was quite warm. I enjoyed my repeated visits to the shores of the Kārun River. It is the widest river in Persia with the most volume of water that runs in a generally southerly direction. A few miles before reaching the Persian Gulf, it merges with the combined waters of the Tigris and the Euphrates and forms a portion of the boundary with Iraq. Kārun is the only navigable, by sizable boats, river in Persia. The population of Khuzestān, particularly in its southern parts, is largely Arabian, but in its northern areas the Iranian tribes of Lors and Kords are dominant.

Our hosts, Mr and Mrs Shāpuri, had three daughters and two sons; the daughters were grown married ladies with their own children. They resided in their native city Kerman; we came to know them at later dates. The two sons, Manuchehr and Cyrus, were unmarried and lived with their parents. Cyrus, who was the youngest of the Shāpuris, was about 3 years older than me.

In the course of the week in Ahvaz, my father and Mr. Shāpuri became good friends; they chatted about the 'old days', smoked and had endless cups of tea together. A topic of discussion that had casually come about, apparently, was Mr. Shāpuri's proposal that, in time, he would like to see Cyrus so honored as to become my father's son-in-law. My sister Fari, at that time, was only 8 years old. This was, of course, meant to be a projection into the distant future and certainly was not entertained, by my parents, as a serious or binding proposition. To them it was a matter to be revisited after the young man finishes his university studies and when Fari was old enough to decide if the idea was acceptable to her.

Cyrus was seventeen at the time of our Ahvāz trip. Two years later, when he had finished with his secondary school studies, he had packed a suitcase, got on the train, and duly appeared at our door. His family was still in Ahvāz. He had come to the capital in order to attend University of Tehran; at that time, there was no university in the Khuzestan province. Although a clear understanding about Cyrus Shāpuri's plan to live with us for the three years of his university degree course had not been reached, presumably some casual remarks to that effect had passed between his father and mine. To cut a very long story short, Cyrus was accepted in our home and lived with us, with full privileges of room and board as if a family member, for three years until he finished his BA in economics. The projected marriage to my sister never took place, particularly since Cyrus was quite a ladies man and, as it came to light, while enjoying our hospitality, he ran around with quite a number of girls. Fari, on the other hand, was too young to fathom the whole foolish arrangement and remained quite detached throughout.

This, however, is not the whole story of my family's entanglement with the Shāpuris. Even after finishing with his university studies, Cyrus remained with us for a few months until he found a job and got his own accommodation. While Cyrus was living with us, we had occasional visits from his parents and his sisters. Mr. Shāpuri had retired a few years after our visit to Ahvāz. He and his wife had gone back to their hometown Kermān, where their three daughters lived. The daughters, their husbands and their children, came to Tehran often for business of holiday and were offered hospitality at our home. I remember with considerable irritation one of the husbands who, whenever staying at our home, displayed uncommon lack of consideration by sleeping until noon; he had to be served breakfast while others were having lunch. The husband of Shāpuri's youngest daughter also came frequently and stayed at our house. I was told that even after my departure for America, long past the breakup of Fari's engagement to Cyrus, this man, Mr. Karimi, had imposed his presence on my family. On one occasion, he had made advances towards my mother. This was the final straw; my father had expelled him from the house for good. And, as I understand it, that was the final chapter of the Shāpuris in our lives.

It is very possible that my family was particularly timorous in their dealings with those who clearly took advantage of their passivity. However, the tradition of opening your house to others, whether or not there was any real obligation, was prevalent among old families. And, perhaps, to a lesser extent, it was common among all strata of the society. It is unlikely, I imagine, with the drastic changes that have taken place in the social fabric of Persian society, that such traditions could still be alive.

❧ 5 ❧

The Romance of the Mountains

Persia is a mountainous country. Except in the southwestern province of Khuzestān, there is no place throughout that country where one could stand and not see high mountains in the distance or nearby. From earliest childhood I felt a kinship with mountains, particularly the Alborz range which crosses the north of the country separating the interior plateau from the Caspian Sea. This mountain range has numerous peaks in excess of 4000 meters in height, with Mount Damāvand, the highest peak, at 5671 meters, located at some 80 kilometers northeast of Tehrān.

In the 1930s, corresponding with my childhood years, Tehran was a city of no more than half a million population. No building in the city was taller than four stories and there was no air pollution. One could see the mountains to the north, only 12 kilometers from the city center, from just about any position in the city. There was not a day that I would not look longingly at these mountains. The peak directly north of the city was called Tōchal; at nearly 4000 meters high it retained patches of snow even through hot summer months. It was common for Tehranis, at summertime, to spread rugs and mattresses on the flat roofs of their houses and sleep the night in the open air. Air-conditioners were not known then and Tehran summers can be very hot with midday temperature often reaching 40 centigrade. The sight of the Alborz mountains, stretching majestically on the horizon, thrilled me as I would wake up in early morning, on the roof top, wishing that I could be right there amid its folds.

I was delighted when, in 1937, my father decided to rent a small cottage, for the summer months, in Darband, a village in a canyon north of Tajrish. Tajrish was the largest in a group of villages, in the foothills north of Tehrān, collectively known as Shemirān. All of these villages – and there were more than a dozen of them - are now suburbs connected to the Capital city that has more than twenty times the population it had then.

The villages of Shemirān were famous for their fruit orchards and their cool and fresh air. The city of Tehran lies at some 1200 meters from the sea level; as the elevation gradually rises from the city to the foothills of the Alborz, all the villages of Shemirān are at a much higher altitude than the city. The temperature, depending on the location of the particular village, on the average is 5 to 8 degrees centigrade lower than in Tehran. Given the dryness of the climate, these villages had absolutely idyllic summers. Some of the capital's grandees owned mansions in Shemirān, and a number of foreign legations, also, had summer residences there. In a vast wooded area, stretching for hundreds of acres between Tajrish and Darband, the Sa'dābād palaces were located. In this compound Rezā Shah had built numerous summer residences for members of his family.

Beginning in 1937, and for the following six years, around mid-June, we moved to Darband and remained there for about three months. The village of Darband is set in a deep canyon on the bottom of which is a riverbed. An uphill road traversed to one side of the river. The houses were built amid tall *chenār* (a tall variety of plain tree) and poplar trees on the two sides of the river in rapidly rising slopes of the mountains. The alleyways leading to these houses and gardens posed steep climbs and could only be frequented on foot. Sounds of rushing water and bird songs dominated the atmosphere. Nightingales sang in the daytime and the unique Persian owl, known as *morq-e haq*, made its melancholy call throughout the night. The air was cool and brisk mingled with the scent of acacia, jasmine and roses.

For my older brother Manuchehr and I, summer time in Darband was a much-cherished break from the harsh world of our over-demanding schools. We were out playing every day. The river that passed in front of our cottage was a favorite playground. Our house was located very close to the far end of the village. About 200 meters further up, the road came to an end. At that point, known as Sareband, the mountain formed a veritable wall. To continue upwards, one had to climb on the side of the ravine that had been cut through the mountain by the rushing water. The trek on the side of the river was steep and perilous; in places one had to wade into the water; at other places, one had to climb boulders that hemmed in the stream on both sides. There were periodic openings in the ravine where one could find space to sit or even to play amid trees and bushes. At intervals large and deep pools were formed in the river. Often, Manuchehr and I would go swimming in these pools. The water was clear and cold, the air warm and dry; it was exhilarating to dive into the icy pools and then lie on the boulders nearby and take in the rays of sun.

I tend to believe that one cannot fully appreciate the beauty of trees, or the melodiousness of running water until one is in Persian mountains. In a country that is predominantly arid and rocky the sight of greenery and the sound of rushing water take on a different meaning; they symbolize life, hope and salvation. At a distance the Alborz range seems hard, barren and forbidding. Once you are close to it, better yet, when you are in the mountains, invariably you find folds that form into canyons where there are springs of cold water seeping through the rocks. They form streams along sides of which there is lush greenery; where wild flowers, trees and bushes abound. They may not be visible from afar, but close by they are little oases of enchanting beauty. These patches of greenery and the running water are indescribably sweet. They contrast so vividly with the aridity the surroundings; they pose a kind of beauty that cannot be found in countries where the landscape is all green anyway.

From Sareband about an hour's climb on the side of the river will bring you to the mountain village of Pasqal'e, at some 2000 meters elevation. In my childhood days, this was a purely pastoral community inhabited by native villagers who, as is true of all rural people in Persia, spoke with distinct accents of their own. The city folk did not own property there; they came and went as hikers. Beyond Pasqal'e, the climb along the river became even more steep and challenging. The next destination, for the determined climber, was the Pasqal'e waterfall, which required at least another two hours hike. We children rarely ventured beyond Pasqal'e; not only was the ascent difficult, it was also time consuming and would have taken us too long to get back home.

On a few occasions, however, when we were older, Manuchehr and I, having received prior permission of our parents, did manage to hike as far as the waterfall.

The river that flows through the ravine and eventually reaches Darband is formed by melting snow and originates high up the mountain. It has greater volume the farther up one goes. In its downward rush, more and more of the river's water is channeled into gardens and orchards in Pasqal'e and beyond. At the level of the waterfall, some 2500 meters elevation, the river has more than ten times the volume of what reaches Darband. This makes for a formidable cascade of water falling a height of, we were told, some 100 meters. The mist created at the base covered a vast area and to approach it one would end up fully soaked.

It was also possible to reach Pasqal'e, from Darband, by bypassing the ravine altogether and climbing the mountain high enough to descend into the village from above. This was much more arduous and took longer. However, at Sareband, the end of the road in Darband, there were mules and donkeys that one could hire to ride the distance. The men who owned these animals would walk up the mountain with their passengers. The journey was not for the faint hearted. The climb was terrifyingly steep; it was not uncommon for the poor beast to falter and fall with serious injury to itself and the rider.

Mountain climbing remained a passion with me into my adult life. In my years in California, I made my way to the mountains whenever possible. One time, with a Danish friend, we climbed Mount San Jacinto, located to the east of Palm Springs, at nearly 3300 meters elevation. This is quite an imposing peak since it rises from a desert area not more than a few hundred feet above the sea level. During the summers that I spent working in Jackson, Wyoming, in the early 1950s, I climbed mountains in the vicinity of the town whenever I had a chance.

In the course of the 18 months of my return to Persia (June 1957 to November 1958), when I conducted research on Persian urban traditional music, in the company of my uncle (my mother younger brother) Abdolrezā and his brother-in-law Shojā, we climbed the 4000 meters high Tōchal peak. This was in early May of 1958 and there was considerable snow above 3000 meters. We had to spend a cold and dreary night in a shelter built of stone for climber at about 3500 meters.

The next morning we managed to make tea by lighting a fire and boiling melted snow. The climb from that point to the top proved extremely tough, not only was it hard to find a foothold in the frozen snow, the air was so thin as to make breathing difficult. Once on the top of Tōchal, however, we felt fully rewarded. The view to the south, overlooking Shemirān villages and the city of Tehran beyond, was breath taking. Moreover, a totally unfamiliar vista to the rear of the mountain opened before us. The view that one has of the Alborz from the south, where Tehran is located, shows the mountains as a veritable wall. From the top, however, looking still to the north, one sees endless mountain peaks, some even higher than Tōchal itself. To the east, towering above them all, is the majestic cone-shaped Damāvand, considerably higher that the Alpine peaks of Europe and any of the mountains in the 48 contiguous States in America. The Damāvand peak, perpetually covered with snow, is one of the cherished symbols of Iran; so much myth and history of the nation is associated with this mountain.

In the years of my return to Iran, from 1968-79, my romance with the Alborz Mountains was rekindled. However, Darband and Pasqal'e area no longer interested me. That vicinity, so close to the capital, had become much too crowded with Tehranis who came there in groups to hike or simply to get away from the bustle of the city. In the gorge above Darband, wherever there was an opening on the sides of the river, flat terraces were constructed. On these terraces cafes had sprung up with table and chairs placed, here and there, among the trees.

In my search for the less disturbed canyons in the Alborz range, I discovered beautiful areas both to the northeast and northwest of Tehran. There are clusters of villages, similar to the Shemirān group, in the folds of the Alborz throughout its length from west to east. These village complexes invariably begin with one large village in the foothills. As one proceeds upwards in the mountain, there are smaller but smaller villages scattered in the canyons above on the side of a river. The highest village in the group would be, like Pasqal'e in the Shemirān group, at probably some 2500 or more meters elevation, with idyllic summers and very cold and snowy winters.

I came to favor two areas. One of these was to the northeast of the city. By driving some thirty kilometers, on the foothills of the mountains from Niāvarān – which is about 4 kilometers east of Tajrish - one arrives at a group of villages collectively known as Lavasan. The first of these villages is Lashgarak. From Lashgarak one can turn left along river Jājrud. This road proceeds through a series of villages, ascending in altitude, terminating in Shemshak, which is a well-known skiing resort. By taking the road to the right at Lashgarak one reaches some very picturesque villages beginning with Nārān and ending with Afje. This is the Lavasān group, one of the many such clusters of villages that are to be found, at distance of some 30 to 40 kilometers from one another, in the folds of the Alborz Range.

The second of the mountain villages I favored begin less than 10 kilometers northwest of central Tehran, again in a canyon, along side of a river. This group, collectively known as Suleqān, begins with the village of Kan, which is famous for its delicious pomegranates. Some 30 kilometers from Kan, at the end of the steep winding road that skirts a number of settlements, is the village of Sangān. The road leading to Sangan goes through some spectacular mountain scenery. Typically the villages along the way were built next to a riverbed. They produce fruits of all kinds, but wherever there is a bit of open flat lands grains are also cultivated. I am told recently that the road from Kan to Sangān has been extended beyond that village and is intended to become another passageway to the Caspian Sea provinces.

Still further to the west, on the way to Qazvin, I knew of two other groups of mountain villages, Bareqān and Tāleqān. Each of these mountain communities begins with a large village in the foothills and by proceeding upward reaches several other villages at increasingly higher elevation. It has come to my attention that the natives of these mountains look physically somewhat different from the city folk. There seems to be a greater homogeneity of physical types; the young in particular seem to be mostly fair skinned and not infrequently blonde. The older they get they are more swarthy and weather beaten. One wonders if the Iranians of the high mountains have remained comparatively undiluted with the invading races that have so often overrun the country. We know for fact that the Arab invaders seldom penetrated into the mountains. The Mongols, also, subdued and devastated mainly the urban centers; they and did not bother with the thinly populated and hard to reach areas in the mountains.

The mountain range that runs from the border with Turkey southeast to the southern province of Fars is called Zagros. This is a much wider range and includes many high peaks of more than 4000 meters. This area is more remote and less explored. Until a few decades ago, nomadic tribes, including the Kurds, the Lors, the Bakhtiāris and the Qashqāi frequented this mountain country. The nomadic ways of these tribes have now changed; they are mostly settled in cities. With the country's growth in population and extensive road building the Zagros region is now better known and is widely visited. I understand that even some skiing resorts have been developed in these mountains.

Unfortunately, I have never had a chance to get to know the Zagros Mountains. The only mountain I have had occasion to climb, other than the Alborz range, is one of the peaks of the Karkas range. This is a range of heights in the central parts of Iran that runs south from below the city of Qom, to the west of Kāshān and Natanz, to the north of Esfahan. The highest point in the Karkas range reaches to above 3700 meters. In the spring of 1968, when I was in Natanz to record the production of a ta'zie, I took the opportunity to climb the peak closest to that city. This was particularly memorable as Natanz, according to what I had heard from my father, is the city from whence, some four generations back, comes my ancestral origins.

As the last chapter of my life has unfolded in Ireland, a country that I love and admire, my romance with mountains has come to an end. What is called a mountain in Ireland, by Persian standards, is no more than a hill. In any event, I have been too old, since settling in Ireland, for serious mountain climbing. However, nature and mountains in particular hold a very special place in memories of my youth. At times, Irish friends have asked if at all I miss my native country. Only the

Persian mountains, I reply, the green oases that lie in their folds, and the murmur of water gliding down through the rocks.

⅔ 6 ⅔

America

A Persian family, even if reasonably worldly and informed as mine was, in the first half of the 20th century, had no reason to know anything about western classical music. Persian music, that is the traditional urban music, was known and appreciated by my family. My father, in particular, knew Persian music well; he had learned how to play one of the leading instruments, the *tar* (six-stringed plucked instrument), quite well; he had studied for a period in his 20's with Qolām Hoseyn Darvish (Darvish Khan), a famous *tār* player. My mother had no formal training but was very musical; she played the *tombak* (goblet shaped drum) quite well and danced beautifully. But western classical music was entirely foreign to them and quite understandingly so. Particularly difficult for them to appreciate was the notion of composition as a profession. Persia had never produced composers since musical creativity has always been wedded to performance, which is highly improvisatory. From late 19th century, as western influence began to make inroads, a few performing musicians did actually compose pieces of music that were written down in western notation. Yet, there was no genuine recognition of composition as an independent field of musical activity, or of a composer as a singular musical figure. Accordingly, my decision to study western classical music with the objective of becoming a composer was met with total incomprehension by my parents.

It took me a long time to bring my mother to my side and convince her that what I aim to do is not to be dismissed out of hand. She was by nature an adventurous and unconventional woman and I gradually managed to obtain her consent to my intention to study music, not to become a performer but a composer, even though she could not fully understand it. In 1947, two years before my departure for America, a French motion picture called *Symphonie Fantastique* was being shown in one of the cinemas in Tehran. The film was based on the life of

Hector Berlioz, and the great French actor Jean Louis Barrault played the part of the composer. I had seen this film, which had made a great impression on me. I decided to take my mother to see it. She was quite taken by the story of this composer's devotion to his art and his struggles to make a living and to be recognized as the genius he was. Although my mother could not understand the music, by viewing this film, she came to appreciate that what I was after was something important.

In the end, I was able to garner my mother's support and my father's submission to my plan to seek musical studies abroad. An understanding was reached, however, that I shall basically manage to take care of myself and shall not be a financial burden on them beyond the first year after my departure. This agreement was not only due to my unconventional, in their view, choice of the subject I wished to study, but because my older brother Manuchehr also wanted to seek further studies abroad. His choice was the eminently respectable field of medicine, which deserved full support. He had already finished two years of medical training at Tehran University and was desirous of further training in America. Clearly our family did not have the means of providing financial support for both of us.

My initial plan was to seek musical studies in France. I was fairly comfortable with the French language and my Armenian violin teacher, who had been trained in France, encouraged me to apply to the *Ecole Normale de Musique* in Paris for admission. Early in 1949, I was overjoyed in receiving a positive response to my application from *Ecole Normale*. Since I had undertaken to manage my life, after the first year abroad, without help from my family, I investigated the possibility of taking part-time jobs while studying. Inquiries soon made clear that in France, and indeed in all of Europe, there was high unemployment and there was no chance of a foreign student finding work. This was only a few years after a devastating war that had destroyed much of Europe; the economies were in ruin; much disorder and insecurity were everywhere. There was no possibility of my being able to work, let alone work and go to school at the same time.

Further investigation led me to believe that the only country in the world that is economically strong and healthy is the United States of America. Moreover, I learned that all American universities offer comprehensive courses in music and that I can study composition there at any of the hundreds of distinguished institutions. In addition, I also learned that many famous European composers, due to harsh conditions during the war in their native countries, or threats to their very existence by the Nazis, had emigrated to the U.S. and were teaching at American universities. More encouraging was to learn that it is not uncommon for American students to take on some part-time jobs while studying. The conclusion I arrived at was to change my plan for musical studies in France in favor of America. In time, I became convinced that the choice of America had been the right one, even if the same opportunities were available to me in France. Had I been much younger, and wanted to study at a conservatory, France would have been a fair choice, but for university level studies in music no country in Europe compares favorably with the U.S. Accordingly, I began exploring the possibility of admission to an American university.

To receive a student's visa from the American Embassy in Tehran the applicant had to prove that he/she has applied and has been accepted as a student by an American University. A young man of my age, whose family we knew well, had recently left for the United States. He had enrolled in a college in northern Utah to study agriculture. I wrote to him and he accepted to submit the transcript of my secondary school records, which I posted to him, to his college's admissions office. In due course I received an acceptance from the Utah State Agricultural College in Logan to begin my studies there in the autumn of 1949. I presented the letter of acceptance to the American consulate and a student visa was issued. Of course, I had no intention of studying agriculture; I had planned to change to another school as a music student soon after arrival.

As to the arrangement with my family, we agreed that I would be given a one-way flight ticket to New York plus enough money to take care of myself for one year. This, as I recall, was about $2,000, which was just about adequate for one year's student subsistence in 1949. My parents were good enough to assure me that if after one year I found myself in dire financial conditions they will send me a return ticket. But I was resolved that such a day would never come.

I flew out of Tehran on Thursday, the 9th of June, and arrived in New York two days later. This was my first airplane ride; the carrier was a DC6 of the Scandinavian Airlines System (SAS). The plane's first stop was in Damascus, Syria, for re-fuelling. From there, after two hours, it flew to Rome arriving at nightfall. From the airport, the passengers were taken, by a bus, to a hotel for the over night stay. In the company of a few of the other passengers, I walked the streets near the hotel. In June of 1949 Rome appeared as a most depressing place. The streets were poorly lit and strewn with rubbish. Men, shabbily dressed, were walking aimlessly or sitting on church steps and around fountains, mingled with young women who were clearly looking for clients with no apparent success.

The following morning we flew from Rome to Copenhagen for a change to another flight. The next stop for refueling was Glasgow in Scotland, which I found rather cold, wet and dreary. The longest stretch of the flight was across north Atlantic. It seemed an interminable night and, as I looked outside, being so far to the north of the planet and so close to summer solstice, the sky remained bright throughout the flight. The final refueling took place in Gander, Newfoundland. The airport was windswept and cold. The contrast with the warm and sunny Tehran of two days before could not have been greater. We reached the final destination and the plane landed in New York around 11 in the morning of Saturday, 11th of June.

A coach took the passengers to the heart of the city in Manhattan. There were two other Persian boys of about my age on the flight to New York and friendship had developed with them in the course of the flight. When we were let out of the bus at the terminal, the two boys and I jointly began to look for a cheap hotel where we might stay for a few nights. As I recall, it was on 54th Street, not far from Broadway that we found a hotel that gave us a room with three beds very inexpensively.

I spent five days in New York wandering the streets being dazzled by
the lights, the bustle and sheer energy of that amazing city. My violin
teacher, Vahe Djingheuzian, had emigrated to the U.S. only six months
before my arrival and was living in the Jackson Heights district; I knew
his telephone number and got in touch with him. He came to see me
every day and showed me some famous sights of New York. One day he
took me to see a movie at the Radio City Music Hall; the showing of
the film was preceded with musical numbers including the dance of the
famous Rockets. He showed me where I could buy food at self-service
restaurants or at automats. The automats – they went out of fashion
long ago - were eating places where sandwiches and pies were in display
in boxes similar to mail boxes in a post office. To receive the chosen
item one had to drop coins in a slot whereupon the transparent cover
could be lifted and the item removed.

Vahe took me to see the Empire State Building one day and; on another day, we went to the Grand Central Station where he helped me
buy a train ticket to Utah. The farthest I could go by train was the
city of Ogden, from there I had to make my way by bus to my final
destination Logan, which was only about two hours ride to the north.
On the fifth day of my stay in New York, Vahe took me to the Grand
Central and I began the long journey west. It took me nearly three days
and nights to reach Ogden, where I arrived at one in the morning. At
the rail station, somehow I was able to ask and receive instruction as to
where I could to find the bus terminal. Fortunately the Greyhound Bus
Station was very close to the train station. The bus made a number of
stops at different towns on the way; it was five in the morning when the
driver informed me that we had reached Logan. Across the road from
where the bus left me was the Hotel Eccles, the best of the few hotels in
town. I took a room at this hotel where I stayed for three days.

On my second day in Logan I made my way to the College. The
Administration Office of the College provided me with a list of rooms
in town available to rent. I had a hard time finding any of the addresses on the list. The peculiarity of the numbering system in American
streets was quite baffling. Everywhere else in the world houses are
numbered in a way that all numbers are used in succession, or all odd

numbers appear on the right side, at the outset of the road, and the even numbers on the left. The American system allocates one hundred numbers to houses between two intersections regardless of how many houses there may be in that block. In fact, rarely would a stretch of a road between two intersections contain more than a dozen houses. If there are, say, only eight houses between the two intersections still one hundred numbers are used at random, odds on the right and evens on the left. For the uninitiated this can be confounding, but once you learn the system it works very well. The advantage is in giving a clear idea as to where the number sought is located. If one is looking to find house number 1628 and you are in the block where numbers are in the 1200 series, then you know that what you are looking for is four blocks ahead; or if the houses are in the 2300 series, you know that your object is six blocks in the opposite direction. A further clarity in the American system is that street signs are displayed, prominently and visibly, at intersections mounted on posts. There never is any problem in seeing the street names; one surely cannot say the same about how roads are named and marked in any European cities, or probably anywhere else in the world.

After some considerable walking and much confusion, I found one of the addresses on the list and rented a room for $8 per week. I remained in Logan, Utah, some eight weeks. Here, I was in a typical western American city with a climate remarkably similar to my own home country. The altitude and the mountainous surrounding were very much like the Iranian plateau. Summer days were mostly sunny, hot and dry. The similarities ended there, however. The streets and the buildings were very different and people in general were much friendlier. On this last point, some clarification is needed. Persians are warm and friendly to those they know; their hospitality is exemplary and their courteousness to guests, family and friends is extravagant. But, the world outside home is seen as basically hostile territory; strangers, if not seen as threat, are certainly treated with caution. Interestingly, Persians tend to be very friendly to a westerner, European or American, but not to anyone of their own kind who is a stranger to them. With that background, I was surprised and charmed to notice that as I walked the streets of Logan, a passerby invariably smiled at me and often said hello. I couldn't quite comprehend, however, when occasionally a passerby would say 'hot enough for you?' I could not figure out what is meant by 'hot enough'. Another common expression that baffled me was that the response to my saying 'thank you' was often 'you bet'. I looked up 'to bet' in the dictionary and the meaning given did not seem to help at all. In shops or restaurants the persons who attended to me always smiled. This too is rather different from what one would normally encounter in Persia. I admit, lest giving rise to the ire of my Persian readers, that there are always exceptions to the rule.

As to the styles of buildings and streets, what impressed me most was the way houses were visible from the road. I liked the space allocated to lawns, trees and flowers that were entirely in view from the roadway. In Persia home are built behind walls or fences; they are shielded from view; privacy is jealously guarded. The homes may be beautiful with spacious gardens and pools, but they are not to be seen form the outside. In America, except in the congested large cities of eastern States, the whole concept of private dwelling is very different. Homes are built on one or two levels; they are spacious and are separated from the next house by vast stretches of grass, flowerbeds and trees. Residential streets, in most cities in America, are quite unique and I was, and still am, totally enchanted by how beautiful they can be. They are mostly much wider than residential streets in other parts of the world; they are lined with trees and have wide sidewalks with a narrow strip of grass separating the paved walkway from the road. Needless to say, once I moved to Los Angeles and saw the residential districts of Beverly Hills, Bell Air and Brentwood, my admiration for the beauty of American residential neighborhoods was greatly magnified.

The eight weeks that I spent in Logan were extremely happy; I was in an unreal world of my dreams, never felt homesick, not for a minute. I spent my time mainly in studying English. I enrolled in a summer course of English for foreign students, at Utah State Agricultural College; the class met for an hour daily and I progressed rapidly. The College, which a few years later was renamed Utah State University, had a small but very good Music Department. Interestingly, the eminent

American composer Roy Harris was there as Composer in Residence. I was too much of a novice to aspire to study with him in 1949. As fate would have it, twelve years later, when Harris was teaching at UCLA, I had the privilege, for three years, of becoming his pupil.

With guidance from the College's Music Department I found a private piano teacher; the Department also was helpful enough to grant me daily access to a piano to practice on. My teacher, a young lady by the name Jean Sorenson, whom I saw twice a week, was pleased with my progress and gave me much encouragement.

There were a few Persian students at the College including the young man to whom I had appealed to for my enrolment procedure. There was also Ardeshir Zāhedi, the future diplomat of great prominence, Ahmad Ali Ahmadi who had a distant family connection with me and who became a good friend much later in my life, and a few others. They befriended me but were rather puzzled by my chosen field of study; also, they quickly decided that I was not a very sociable chap, which was true.

Late in August I decided to move west and register at University of California in Los Angeles, hoping to be able to study, at some point in the future, with the great Austrian composer Arnold Schoenberg who was teaching at that University. I took the Greyhound Bus to Los Angeles. This was a distance of about eight hundred miles passing through the length of Utah, which is an exceptionally scenic state. I recall the stop that the bus made in Las Vegas in southern Nevada, at that time, an inconsequential small town.

Los Angeles, even in 1949, was a huge metropolis. The downtown section was very much the commercial center of the city. I say this because today several business centers, with high-rise buildings, have grown in other areas of the city and the old downtown has become both unimportant and rather shabby. To many visitors, the vast spread of Los Angeles is off-putting; many people equate the amorphousness of this city with absence of character. But I have always liked LA; it has its own character and, given time, can become very likeable. It has a relaxed atmosphere, has some very beautiful neighborhoods and, of course, a near perfect climate. To the far west of the city, by the shores of the Pacific Ocean, are Santa Monica and Malibu. I never forget the exhilaration of my first sight of the Ocean. I stood on the shore and gazed at the sun setting on the waves, thinking to myself of Asia and my own homeland, on the other side of this seeming endless body of water.

On arrival in Los Angeles, for about a week, I stayed at a small hotel not too far from UCLA. With the help of the University's Foreign Students Office, I found a suitable room in a small house owned by a very friendly old lady, Mrs. Saunders, at 1115 Westgate Avenue in West Los Angeles; the rent was $30 per month. My room was small, eight by ten feet. It contained a bed, a small table, one chair and a cabinet in which I stored my clothes. I had no eating privileges, but I had the use of the bathroom and the telephone. I bought a small radio and learned that there was one broadcasting station devoted to classical music to which I listened incessantly when not studying or practicing the violin.

The Music Department at UCLA, where I continued with my violin studies with Dr. Thomas Marrocco, suggested that for my piano lessons I should seek a private teacher. I was sent to a lady pianist with the improbable name of Brabazon Lindsey. She was a very severe taskmaster, just what I needed at that stage. I had noticed that my landlady, Mrs. Saunders, had a garage in the back of the driveway next to the house, but she didn't own a car. After a few weeks I asked her if she would permit me to place a rented piano in the garage. She agreed and I had a piano, rented at 5 dollars per month, brought and placed in the garage where I did my piano practice.

With my limited funds I had to live very frugally. I had breakfast of bread and cheese with coffee that I made in my room. Lunches usually consisted of a sandwich, or soup and crackers, bought in UCLA's cafeteria. Dinners were more substantial at one of the diners in Westwood Village or Santa Monica. The meals, including coffee and dessert rarely cost more than one dollar and 20 cents. On top of such routine expenses, there was the more major expense of University fees, books, and piano lessons.

Also, soon after my arrival in Los Angles I realized that it is very difficult to get around in this city without a car. I paid $300 for a used 1939 Ford Coupe, which served me well for a couple of years. Before taking possession of the car, however, the used car dealer told me that I had to obtain a driver's license. I had learned how to drive and had driven the family car in Iran, but had never obtained a permit; very few did in Iran of those days. The dealer took me to a branch of the Motor Vehicle Department. I passed the tests, including the written part, which was quite amazing since I could not fully understand many of the questions.

In late September, my brother Manuchehr had also arrived in the U.S. He too had been enrolled at the State College in Logan, the courtesy of our mutual friend who was studying there. Soon after his arrival he took the bus to Los Angeles to spend a few days with me. He had been struck by a bout of serious homesickness. He enjoyed his time in LA and returned to Utah in good spirits and high determination. He completed his premedical training in two years, moved to the University of Nebraska Medical School, followed by specialization in neurosurgery in Michigan, and had an illustrious career as a neurosurgeon.

❧ 7 ❧

Odd Jobs

My determination to study music and become a composer, come what may, shaped the course of my life. During the early years in America, in unexpected and at times bizarre ways, this unwavering determination placed me in highly unexpected circumstances. This chapter tells the story of some of the jobs I took on in order to sustain myself while being a full-time university student.

By the end of summer of 1950, fifteen months after my arrival in the U.S., the funds I had been given were used-up; I had to find some work to pay for my expenses. The first job I was able to secure was in the home of a couple, Mr. and Mrs. Goodman, who had a four years old child. As both parents had daytime jobs, I had to be at the house, when a neighbor returned the boy from his kindergarten in early afternoon. My job was to feed him, be with him and take care of his needs until one of the parents came home. In lieu of this service I was given a room free of charge in their house and was able to have dinner with the family. Accordingly, I left the little room at Mrs. Saunders house in West Los Angeles and moved to the Goodman house on 22nd Street in Santa Monica. A few weeks later, I also found a seasonal job delivering telephone directories to homes and offices, which provided me with some spending money.

The work for the Goodman family began well enough but gradually became onerous. Mr. Goodman, who was a pianist and taught at the Los Angeles Conservatory of Music, was rather taciturn, seemed to have little interest in his wife and child, and rarely spoke to me. His wife, a slightly chubby young woman in her mid thirties, after a few weeks, began to show unwanted interest in me. Soon it became clear that, beyond the occasional care of her son, she expected other services. One day, when only she and I were in the house, I heard her calling my name. I knocked on the door of their bedroom where she was. She opened the door wearing a transparent robe but with nothing else on. I tried to look only at her face and asked what she wanted. She asked a very innocuous question and just stood there smiling. As I answered and turned away, she slammed the door behind me. From that time on she was noticeably cool and critical towards me.

With the approach of summer in 1951, I realized that I had to find a fulltime summer job to save money for the school year. A group of Persian boys and girls who were studying at Utah State University in Logan had learned of possibilities for summer jobs in Jackson, in the neighboring state of Wyoming. My brother Manuchehr, who was studying medicine in Logan, was also about to head for Jackson. I decided to join him, quit my work at the Goodman house, and in two days drove from Los Angeles to Jackson, a distance of nearly a thousand miles. This town, also known as Jackson-Hole, in the 1950s, had a sedentary population of about 1200. In summers, however, the population grew much bigger. The town is located about 30 miles south of the Grand Teton National Park and 80 miles from Yellowstone National Park. Large number of tourists (from other parts of the U.S. as in those days hardly any foreign tourists came to America) passed through Jackson on their way to these parks. Restaurants, bars, hotels and motels had a thriving business, which largely came to an end after Labor Day. So, there was plenty of menial work available for the minimum wage of 85 cents an hour.

In order to save money for the rest of the year, some of us took two jobs as I did. I worked full-time as a dishwasher in one restaurant and part-time as fry-cook in another. This amounted to 12 hours of daily work, and I worked seven days a week. The work was arduous and was hard on my hands, but I was very hard pressed financially and had no choice. Manuchehr and I were sharing a rented room in a house owned by a German family. The owner, learning that I was a music student, allowed me to practice on the upright piano in his living room. But working 12 hours a day did not leave me much time or energy to practice. Some days I could manage an hour at the piano. I remember that I was trying to learn Beethoven's First Piano Sonata at the time.

The German landlord was very fond of tittle piece called *Fur Elise* and everyday asked me to play it for him.

By the end of each summer I had saved up enough to pay the university fees and some of the other major expenses. But the saved up funds were depleted soon after the start of the academic year and I had to look for some part time work to make it to the next summer. For a period I found a job in a cafeteria on Wilshire Boulevard as a busboy. I worked from 4 to 8 in the afternoons, four days per week. The pay was again the minimum wage of 85 cents per hour, plus a free dinner not exceeding the same amount; if the cost was more, then I had to pay the extra. As this was a self-service customers did not leave any tips on the table. Ontray Cafeteria was quite large; about a dozen young fellows, mostly Latinos, were my co-workers. The boss was a Mr. McCormick, a well-dressed but unpleasant man. Occasionally he would call on me and give an order; he always addressed me and other busboys as 'Boy', telling us: do this or do that. For this job, at this restaurant, I had chosen to call myself Philip; Hormoz was clearly too much for that ambience. One time when Mr. McCormick addressed me as 'Boy', I gently told him 'sir, my name is Philip, please call me by that name'. He seemed to take umbrage and snapped back, 'Maybe you rather me not call you at all.' I said 'no sir, I rather you call me Philip.' He said no more, looked the other way, but the next time he called me Philip.

Other jobs I had for short periods included a few months of part-time work in a small factory where the plastic shell component of ball-point pens was made. What I remember most about this job was one of the co-workers, a slim young man, who was homosexual. He seemed to have taken a fancy to me and I had a hard time convincing him that I am not of like inclinations. Another interesting outcome of my work in this factory was the acquaintance with a lady co-worker, Valerie, an English war bride. She had married an American soldier stationed in England during the war and had been brought to Los Angeles by her husband after the war. They had a seven year old son, but the marriage had broken-up. Valerie was living on her own; she had custody of the child but the husband had access to his son on weekends when he came and fetched the boy and brought him back late on Sunday afternoon. At some point Valerie approached me with the proposition that she would provide me with a room in her house for the service of being there when the child is delivered, by the school bus, to their home. This was a similar arrangement to what I had the previous year with the couple in Santa Monica. Again, I found the arrangement to my satisfaction; I accepted and moved in with Valerie and her son. Her house was in Culver City, not far from the large compound of Metro Goldwyn Mayer studios.

This set-up, however, proved to be unhappy from the outset. The lady drank a great deal and the boy was a most obstreperous child. The arrangement lasted only six weeks. On a Saturday, when the boy had been taken away by his father, I came to the house around four in the afternoon and went to my room which was at the end of the hallway. As I passed by the living room, at a glace, I noticed Valerie seated in an armchair with her head to one side, seemingly asleep. I took no particular notice assuming her to be perhaps intoxicated and sleeping. An hour or so later, once more I happened to pass by the open door of the living room. Again I saw Valerie in the same position, but noticed saliva that had dripped from the corner of her moth down to her neck. This somewhat alarmed me; I went into the room, called her name and touched her arm. She was cold; there was no sign of life. All I could think of doing was to run to the neighbors' houses. The neighbors came in, the police was notified, and an ambulance arrived. It was all to no avail; she was clearly dead. She had committed suicide. The police questioned me at length, but there was not much that I could tell them. The husband was located and was brought in, but he had been with his son all day. I don't know what transpired in the following days and what became of the child. I left the house on Wagner Avenue, Culver City, the next day, never knowing why and how Valerie had taken her life.

Another interesting experience was the period of a few months I lived with a wealthy family in the Brentwood area of Los Angeles. My room was part of an annex in the back of their mansion. Here, my job was to attend to the care of the large garden behind the house. The owner, Mr. Latta, was a successful patent lawyer. He was a handsome tall middle-aged gentleman; his wife was a very demanding and ill humored lady, a devout Seventh Day Adventist who played the organ in her church, on Wilshire Boulevard in West Los Angeles, on the Sabbath, Saturday. They had two sons who appeared to be in their late teens. This was not a happy home; there were frequent rows, particularly between man and wife. The core of the problem seemed to be the husband's lack of interest in his wife's faith and consequent display of irreverence, which caused her much anguish.

I knew nothing about gardening but Mr. Latta was a patient man and gradually showed me what I had to do. Another duty asked of me was particularly onerous and rather bizarre. He wanted me to substitute for him at 5 in the morning each Sunday by driving to the top of a hill, in the Santa Monica Mountains, to search the skies for enemy aircraft. There was a dirt road that led to the spot on top of a steep rise where a telescope was mounted. This was to assist in ascertaining the identity of the enemy craft. Next to the telescope was a telephone mounted on top of a post; I was given a number and was told to call that number in case I saw an enemy aircraft. To the question: how am I to know if the object in the sky is an enemy airplane, I was told to report any that did not seem to be a passenger plane. When I queried the point of all this some seven years after the end of World War II, Mr. Latta assured me that the enemy – that is the Soviet Union and not Japan which was then under American occupation – is definitely preparing for a war against the U.S. and that the attack is imminent. When I pointed out that Russia is located in eastern Europe and the west coast of America is much too far for them to be able to reach, he said that the attack could be mounted from their Siberian bases. He had a point I suppose, an idiotic one perhaps, but a point! Needless to say, I never saw anything in the skies that would warrant putting a call to the number I was given.

Another part-time job I held for a few months in 1952 was working, two nights a week, Saturdays and Sundays, from midnight until 8 in the morning, the graveyard shift, in a factory where chinaware was made. Dishes of all shape and size were made, painted and glazed during the day. They were placed on shelves on wagons that, like a train, rode on rails. These wagons were automatically moving at a very slow pace, entering a huge kiln where the dishes were baked, and exited at the other end. As they came out of the kiln the dishes were very hot, but gradually they would cool off. My job was to lift the dishes, using heavy canvas gloves, and to place them on assigned shelves in the vast hall of the factory. All the main work of manufacturing the chinaware was done during the previous two shifts, when the dishes were made and placed on the wagons by a large number of employees. At the graveyard shift (midnight to 8 a.m.) there were only two people in the plant to place the finished product on the appropriate shelves; I was one of the two on the weekends. The only thing that broke the monotony of this job and kept me awake was a radio set, which I would tune to the 24 hours classical music station, KFAC. From midnight to early morning this station aired large symphonic or operatic works, which would not be broadcast during the day or early evening. The reason was that daytime broadcasts had many sponsors and had to be interrupted with frequent commercials. Lengthy works were not chosen or were played in segments. Since the midnight to morning broadcasts had very few sponsors, as they had few listeners, large works would be played without interruption, which I found more satisfying. The two nights of graveyard shift work in the ceramics factory gave me the opportunity to hear full symphonies, concertos and operas.

Probably the most ludicrous and the most short-lived job I held was as a salesman. Unquestionably, then and now, the job I am least suited for is being a salesman. But, necessity can bring about strange undertakings. This job required my walking with a briefcase full of Bibles (the New Testament), going door-to-door, ringing bells and trying to interest the person answering the door to buy a Bible. This was a very curious thing for a young man from Persia to be doing in Los Angeles. What made it even more peculiar was the area I was assigned to cover. I was assigned a poor neighborhood in the eastern parts of the city where the residents were mostly Latinos. Nearly everyone who answered the door spoke no English; moreover they were most likely Catholics and a bible brought to their door from an Evangelical Protestant organization was not quite the right sort of thing. Also, since they probably had their own copy of the Holy Book and were quite poor, it seemed highly unlikely that they would be interested in purchasing what I was to sell them. Two days of walking for miles, getting exhausted and discouraged did not yield a single sale. I would most likely have been fired, but I quit at the end of the second day. I received nothing for my efforts as any payment to me had to be as a commission of the sales of the merchandize.

Later, when I moved to Mills College in Oakland, California, for my M.A. studies, I was given part time work in the Music Library that was housed within the large Music Building. In addition, I did some music copying for one of the staff members of the Music Department, Miss Margaret Lyon. She was completing her Ph.D. thesis at UC Berkeley. My handwriting, including music notation, was good. She paid me quite generously for copying musical examples that were inserted in her thesis from old books and manuscripts.

Mills is a wonderful small girls college that admits men only for post-graduate studies. Its campus covers some 150 acres of mostly eucalyptus and pine trees. The college buildings are scattered unobtrusively among the wooded landscape. I had two very happy years at Mills. I was able to earn enough to live comfortably and also attend to my studies with distinction.

In 1955, when I finished my MA degree at Mills College and returned to UCLA to begin work toward a PhD, I found part time work in the Beverly Hills Public Library. That was a most pleasant place to work. In those days the Library occupied a wing of the City Hall building. The building, a lovely Spanish style structure, is still used as the City Hall, and also houses the Police Department. The library was on the north side of building, facing Santa Monica Boulevard. The staff members of the Library were all women, headed by Miss Wallace, a stately middle-aged lady. All the others were also kindly and dignified ladies who seemed well disposed towards me and treated me with deference and kindness. They seemed to think that a young man from Persia with a BA and a MA, working for them at minimum wage was to be prized. My job, however, was very low-grade work; it merely involved putting the books that were retuned by clients back in their proper places on the shelves.

A side benefit of working in the Beverly Hills Library was meeting interesting people. I recall having seen Aldous Huxley who came often to borrow books; also, I met composers Louis Gruenberg, Dmitri Tiomkin and Mario Castelnuovo-Tedesco. A number of famous actors and actresses also showed up at the Library from time to time.

Still I needed full time summer jobs to manage the expenses of the year. In the summer of 1955, for three months, I worked in a factory where various objects were made from fiberglass. They were apparently components of military hardware and the items, by themselves, did not reveal what use they could have, at least not to someone like me. At two dollars an hour this was a well-paid job. The only problem was that by the end of each day my hands and arms up to the elbow were shot full of tiny hair-like strands of fiberglass. I had to use cellophane tape to pull them out of my skin. This did not do my piano or violin practice at night much good, but I had to work to save up money for the rest of the year.

During the summer of 1956 I found work in the Hoffman Television factory. I don't know if televisions are made in America any more, but in those days all TVs sold in America were local made, and there was a Hoffman brand. I worked on an assembly line, putting one screw, with an air gun, on a section of the TV frame as it passed in front of me, moving by the conveyor belt. The job was extremely tedious; however, I was very intrigued by some of my co-workers. These were the kind of people that I knew that, in all probability, I shall never have occasion to meet again. The man to my right on the assembly line, the red-haired Scotty, was an ex-convict. He confided in me at some point and told me that he had served a prison term for armed robbery. At the time I knew him, he seemed quite harmless. He was not in good health and seemed to drag his left leg behind him, which he told me was badly damaged in a chase when he was young. He did not explain further and I did not ask.

The man to my left on the assembly line was Jim Miller, a confessed ex-alcoholic; but I was not sure how ex he was, for he always had a strong smell of liquor about him. Jim was a bitter soul full of hatred for blacks and particularly the Jews. He was generally friendly towards me but I thought it better not to get too close to him; there was something quite menacing about this man. And then, there was Judy who usually worked next to Jim. Someone told me that she had been a call girl when younger, although she seemed no more than thirty years old. They used to call her Bob Hope because she had, like the famous comedian, a long upturned nose.

From early summer of 1957 to the end of the following year, I was back in Persia doing research on Persian traditional music for my doctoral thesis. On returning to U.C.L.A. in 1959, for two years I was granted Teaching Assistantship with a very modest salary. In addition, the ladies at Beverly Hills Library, good friends that they were, offered me a few hours of work per week. This helped me manage my expenses and live comfortably. My first full time academic employment began in September of 1961, when I was appointed Assistant Professor at the California State University in Long Beach. From that time on my career as a handyman, doing in 'odd jobs' was over; I became a fulltime academic in music for the remainder of my working life. I believe that the scattered experience I accumulated with many diversified temporary occupations, totally unrelated to my profession, has enriched my life. I savored the opportunity to get to know the sort of people who would not cross my path ever again. As lowly as some of the jobs might have been, I certainly have no regrets in having done them.

❧ 8 ❧

Musical Developments in 60s and 70s Persia

By late in 1960s, I had lived most of my adult life in the United States. From 1968 to the revolution of 1978 and the creation of the Islamic Republic in 79, I was mainly active in my native country. I was engaged as the Head of the Music Department at the University of Tehran and was Chairman of the Music Council at the National Iranian Radio and Television. In addition, I was commissioned to write music for both the Tehran Symphony Orchestra and the Chamber Orchestra of the NIRT. I was also involved with the planning and provision for the Shiraz/Persepolis Festival, which was a yearly event organized by NIRT. I believe my observations on musical developments in Iran of the late 60s and 70s may be of interest to the reader as such developments were aspects of the accelerated reform and modernization that were in progress. The musical life of the country, in the final years of the Pahlavi monarchy, in no way resembled what I knew in my childhood and teen years.

The two decades preceding the Revolution of 1978-79 represent the peak of reform and westernization in Iran. If the modernization of the Rezā Shah period required his iron will and harsh measures, the reforms of the last two decades of his son's reign were more smoothly processed and seemed to meet with satisfaction on the part of the urban middle class. This was possible as the earlier reforms, however forced they might have been, had developed some roots and were sitting more comfortably with the public. Moreover, by the 1970s the urban society was largely dominated by a well educated and reform minded citizenry. To clarify this point, it is important to appreciate that, only fifty years before, in the 1920s, Persia had no more than 12 million in population of which 80% lived in the rural areas. By the mid-70s the population had grown to some 38 millions, with at least 50% residing in cities.

As concerns musical developments, a great deal of progress was made in the advancement of the cause of native music, and also in greater exposure of the public to western music, both classical and popular. I shall consider developments in native and in western music separately.

Traditional Music

By mid point in the 20th century western popular music was beginning to make a serious impact on the urban youth. The consistent melancholy of Persian music, as contrasted with the rhythmic vitality of western dance music, available in recordings and broadcast from radio, had begun to alienate the younger generation from their national music. Some among the traditional musicians reacted by adopting traits of western popular music and composed pieces in imitation of western popular songs but in Persian modes. This type of hybrid music for the most part had a tinge of vulgarity and was devoid of any artistic merit. Nevertheless, much of this music found favor with the majority of listeners and became a genre of Persian pop music. The more discerning traditional musicians and their supporters came to resent the popularity of this hybrid music and blamed it all on western trends. Inexplicably, they condemned jazz as the source of corruption. For some reason, all western pop songs and dance tunes were identified as jazz, which of course showed a complete misunderstanding of what jazz is.

The exponents of the purity of traditional music found their champion in Davud Pirnia, a gentleman of musical erudition who created a series of radio programs devoted to authentic native music as performed by the best of classical musicians. The programs he produced for radio broadcasts were called *Golhā-ye Rangarang* (Multicolored Flowers). For nearly two decades a weekly concert of *Golhā*, as it was popularly known, was broadcast from Radio Tehran. It had a large and devoted following; it also spun two other programs of similar content: *Golhā-ye Jāvidān* (Everlasting Flowers), and one of mainly solo performances by master musicians called *Barg-e Sabz* (Green Leaf). These radio programs were only concerned with authentic urban music; they also included new composition of songs by master musicians that were free of western influence. These songs were an extension of the *tasnif*s of early 20th century, but now they were generically called *tarāne*. Whereas the poems in the earlier *tasnif*s often had socio-political message, the *tarāne*s of the 60s and 70s were exclusively amorous, written by contemporary poets or were taken from classical poetry.

Further efforts at the preservation and advancement of national music were made by two agencies of the government, the Ministry of Culture and Arts and the National Iranian Television. The Ministry had established a number of orchestras with a combination of native and western instruments; these ensembles gave periodic concerts and also produced programs for radio and television. A large number of musicians were salaried employees of the Ministry; this gave a measure of security and respectability to native musicians, the like of which they had not enjoyed before. The Ministry also produced occasional publications of significance. The most important of which was Ma'rufi's collection of notated *radif* (repertory of classical melody models) of Persian music (1963). This book contains the *radif* of each of the 12 modal collections (7 *dastgāh*s and 5 *āvāz*'s), written in western notation by Musa Ma'rufi, an eminent *tar* player and musician of the old school. This is an exhaustive documentation of all pieces in the 12 groups of modal systems, based on the *radif* of Mirzā Abdollāh, the highly respected musician of the late Qājār period.

The National Iranian Television, was founded in mid-60's, under the dynamic leadership of Rezā Ghotbi, a man of exceptional intelligence and vision. In 1971, the old privately owned TV station, and the long existing state run radio network, were also brought under the aegis of this establishment. The National Iranian Radio and Television, as it was now called, became a huge and virtually independent department of the government with far reaching responsibilities. It employed a large number of distinguished native performers of traditional music, and formed different size ensembles for musical programs of both radio and TV networks. In addition, NIRT established a center for the collection and preservation of traditional music. A number of reputable musicians of the old school were affiliated with this center and were engaged in the training of aspiring young singers and instrumentalists.

Ta'zie Revival

Shiite commemorative rituals in Persia include a type of musical play based on stories related to the martyrdom of saints, in particular the tragic account of events leading to the massacre of Imam Hoseyn, the grandson of prophet Mohammad, and his followers in the year 680 CE. These plays, called *Ta'zie* (lamentation), are enacted in an arena, on a centrally raised stage, with elaborate costuming, sparse staging, and lively acting. The protagonists sing their parts while the antagonists deliver their lines in declamatory fashion. An ensemble of wind, brass and percussion instruments participate, not as an accompaniment to the singing, but for creating atmosphere in the scenes of conflict, and battles, and to enhance moments of great tragedy. The musical instruments used included *zornā* or *surnāy* (shawm), *karnāy* (wooden long horns), *tabl* (two headed drums), *naqāre* (single headed drums), and *senj* (cymbals). As western brass instruments were imported in the 19th century for use in military bands, trumpets and baritone horns also found their way in the *ta'zie* ensemble.

Ta'zie is the only genre of theatre, with music, that has found its way into Shiite religious rituals. Its origins date back to the Safavid (1501-1722) era. The high point of its popularity was reached in the second half of the 19th century during the reign of Nāsereddin Shah. In the 1920s, when Rezā Shah took power, *ta'zie* was banned as all public religious manifestations were discouraged. After Rezā Shah's abdication in 1941, surviving *ta'zie* singers and players made modest attempts at its revival; however, it remained largely a forgotten ritual. Many of the famous *ta'zie* singers had passed away or were too old; moreover, its production required the cooperation of large number of people (singers, actors, instrumentalists, stage managers, etc.). These problems, added to the unavailability of suitable venues with a raised central stage, combined to make the *ta'zie* revival difficult. The tradition was not, however, completely dead. It had survived mostly in small towns and villages.

In the course of my research on Persian urban musical tradition in 1957-58, I had investigated the *ta'zie* in order to find what connections its musical content had with the *radif* of classical music. With considerable effort I managed to contact a number of *ta'zie* singers and musicians. I persuaded them, with adequate remuneration, to mount a *ta'zie* in the house where I was living at the time. This was a private performance, with no attending audience, without acting, staging and costumes. The sound recording I made of the *ta'zie* of Horr (one of the heroes of the battle of Karbala) was, I believe, the first ever recording of this genre of Shiite religious musical drama. A copy of that recording was deposited in the archives of the Near Eastern Studies Department at UCLA.

In 1967 when I was a member of the Music Faculty at UCLA, together with Dr. Amin Banāni, a Persian colleague in the Near Eastern Studies Department, we submitted to our university a research project on *ta'zie*. We requested financial support, and six months sabbatical leave, in order to travel to Iran. Dr. Banāni was to study the texts and I proposed to study the musical (vocal and instrumental) aspects of *ta'zie*. In April and May of that year, we travelled through a wide area of Iran in search of where the *ta'zie* tradition was still alive. Our travels took us to various provinces including Kāshān, Arāk, Esfahān, Yazd, Kermān, Fārs, Gilān and Māzandarān. We witnessed *ta'zie* productions in a number of locations, mostly in small towns. The most impressive that we saw and recorded was in the town of Meybod, in the province of Yazd. We were also present at impressive *ta'zie* performances in Natanz, between Kāshān and Esfahān, and in Shahsavar, in the Gilān province. We also managed to assemble a troupe of *ta'zie* singers and instrumentalists, brought them to Tehran, and produced and filmed a full-length drama. Copies of this film were deposited both in the archives of UCLA and in Iran's Ministry of Culture and Arts.

The research that Amin Banāni and I conducted on *ta'zie* in 1967 set in motion an interest in its revival. Both the Ministry of Culture and Arts, who had given us assistance in travelling within the country, and the Radio and Television organization, that was actively promoting native music, were awakened to the importance of this unique theatrical tradition. The most significant outcome was the inclusion of *ta'zie* performances in the Shiraz Festival in 1977 to great acclaim. Since the revolution of 1978-79 and the creation of the Islamic Republic *ta'zie* seems to be one form of theatre with music that meets with the regime's approval.

Western Classical Music

In the domain of western classical music, both the Ministry of Culture and Arts and the NIRT were active in such an accelerated pace that, by late 1970s, Tehran had become nearly as lively a center of musical activity as some of Europe's major cities. The completion of the Rudaki Hall in 1967 was a significant boost to the musical life of the capital. The Hall had been built as a small opera House with a 1200 seat capacity. Its stage area was large enough for modest operatic productions, and could also seat a symphony orchestra. The Ministry of Culture and Arts was given administrative rights over the Rudaki Hall. At about the same time the Ministry had established both an opera company and a ballet company. By mid 70s the opera season in Tehran included the production of at least eight operas over the span of some eight months (October to May). Standard operatic repertoire was featured, including works by Mozart, Bellini, Verdi, Wagner, Smetana, Gounod, Tchaikovsky and Puccini. The Ministry also commissioned operas by native composers; one of the first Persian operas to be presented to the public was *Delāvar-e Sahand* (The Warrior of Sahand) by Ahmad Pezhmān. The Opera Company's singers and conductors included native and visiting artists. The opera orchestra was composed of both Persian and foreign musicians.

The ballet company of the Ministry was less successful, but efforts were made and occasional ballet programs of interest were staged. Here also works by native composers were presented, notably ballets by Loris Tjeknavorian. A Folk Dance Group was also established at the Ministry of Fine Arts; it also gave occasional presentations at the Rudaki Hall.

The Tehran Symphony Orchestra, whose history goes back to the mid 1940s, had become, by mid 1970s, a full size ensemble with some 100 musicians under contract. They included both native performers and musicians from different European countries. Throughout the 60s, the main conductor was Heshmat Sanjari, who had been with the orchestra since the 50s. In 1972, a dynamic young Persian who had studied in Europe and America, Farhād Meshkāt, was appointed as the principal conductor with extensive authority, and financial support, to reform and enlarge the orchestra. Under his directorship, improvements were such that the orchestra was fully capable of performing very demanding scores as those of Mahler, Richard Strauss, Schoenberg, and occasional commissioned compositions by Persian composers. Works by native composers, such as Samin Bāghchebān, Emanuel Melik Aslanian, and me, were commissioned and performed by the Tehran Symphony.

The Rudaki Hall served, as a respectable venue, suitable for visiting orchestras and artists. The Berlin Philharmonic, under Herbert von Karajan, the Los Angeles Philharmonic, under Zubin Mehta, and the Moscow Chamber Orchestra, under Rudolf Barshai, gave concerts at Rudaki. Violinist Yehudi Menuhin and pianist Emil Gilels were among many famous artists who also performed at this venue.

Western art music was also promoted by the NIRT. Notably, NIRT maintained a chamber orchestra with some15 members. This orchestra was supplemented by any number of wind instruments as may have been required for performances of certain pieces. In its programs, compositions from the baroque era featured strongly; but, also, works of later periods were performed, including commissioned worked by Persian composers. I wrote a number of pieces for this orchestra, as did Mortezā Hannāneh, Mohammad Taqi Masoudieh, and Fowzieh Majd. The NIRT Chamber Orchestra had, over the years, a number of conductors. The versatile Austrian composer, flautist and conductor Thomas Christian David was in charge of the orchestra for a number of years. Among other conductors who periodically worked with this orchestra were the German conductor Thomas Baldner, the American Adrian Sunshine and the Iranian Loris Tjeknavorian. The NIRT Chamber Orchestra gave frequent concerts in the City Theatre. This was a newly built all-purpose hall suitable for chamber concerts, recitals and plays. The concerts of the NIRT Chamber Orchestra were also televised. On one occasion, the Chamber Orchestra went on a European tour and also made an internationally distributed LP recording.

During the 1960s and 70s significant advances were made in the area of music education. The first university music department, with a full time four-year course of study leading to a Bachelor's degree, was instituted at University of Tehran. I have given an account of its formation and its later developments in Chapter 10 to which the reader may wish to refer. Elective music appreciation courses, related to both western art music and to native music, also became available in some of the provincial universities including those in Shirāz, Esfahān and Tabriz. A new university, devoted to the humanities and the arts, called Farabi University, was founded in 1975. Music was to be one of its major concerns. By 1978, when the revolution that toppled the monarchy was underway, this university was still in its formative stages and no course offerings were as yet available. According to my latest information this institution has survived the revolution and is operative, but has been moved to the city of Karaj, some 40 kilometers west of Tehran. Its name has been changed to University of Arts (*Dāneshgāh-e Honar*). It is not clear to me why the name Farabi (one of the greatest Islamic thinkers and writers who wrote, among other things, a monumental work on music in the 10th century) has been removed.

The National Iranian Radio and Television, in 1970s, ventured into the realm of music education by founding a music school for children. This was an important innovation without any precedent in Persia. This school, which quickly became very popular, was headed by Said Khadiri, a specialist in music education with emphasis on children and the young. Khadiri had studied in Germany, had a doctoral degree from University of Heidelberg and was an exponent of the Carl Orff method of music education for children.

Perhaps the most striking move in the promotion of music as a cultural force was the establishment of the Shiraz/Persepolis Festival by the National Iranian Radio and Television. This yearly festival, devoted to music, dance, drama and cinema, ran for eleven years, from 1967 to 77, and made a huge impact particularly among the younger generation. Please refer to chapter 9 where I have given a detailed account of this Festival's activity.

❧ 9 ❧

The Shirāz Festival

One of the most striking moves to promote musical appreciation by the general public was the establishment of the Shiraz/Persepolis Festival, by the National Iranian Radio and Television Organization, in 1967. The idea for the establishment of the Festival originated with Empress Farah who, among the royals, was unique in having interest in music and the fine arts. The Director of NIRT, Rezā Ghotbi, a first cousin of the Empress and his deputy Farrokh Ghaffāri were in charge of the actual creation and management of the Festival. Rezā Ghotbi, an energetic young man of exceptional intelligence, was an electronics engineer educated in France, and Ghaffāri was a motion picture and theatre director with a rich cultural background who had lived most of his life in Europe. Another sympathetic figure, who acted as the chairman of the Board also played a role in the formation and main-tenance of the Festival, was Mehdi Bushehri, the husband of Princess Ashraf, the Shah's twin sister. A very urbane and cultured Dr. Bushehri was more that of a prestige figure who did not have much to do with planning or administering the events. Another important figure was Mr. Ghotbi's wife Ms Sheherazad Afshar. She had received musical training in England and worked tirelessly, as the Chair of the Music Committee, on the last-minute details of the running of the Festival. The Honorary President of the Festival was the Empress Farah.

In its musical programs the Festival emphasized the contemporary and particularly the avant-garde trends in western classical music. The programs that were presented from cultures of Asia and Africa, how-ever, represented the traditional forms, since any 'modernity' in eastern cultures has mainly come about under western influences. The Festival was also concerned with theatre; here, again the focus was on the more innovative styles of western theatre and dance. In this category also, programs from Asia and Africa represented traditional theatre and dance.

In addition to live presentations of music, dance and theatre, there were fringe programs of lectures and of cinema. Lectures were interconnected with music and drama events, usually involving a major personality such as a composer, whose work had been heard in a concert, or a theatre director, or a writer. A series of motion pictures, usually relating to a particular theme, or by a certain distinguished director, were shown every day throughout the life of the festival.

The Festival took place in a period of 10 to 12 days, in late August and early September. Music and drama events took place at night, lectures were scheduled for mornings, and films were shown in the after-noon. Most of the events were placed at venues within the city of Shirāz, nearly a thousand kilometers south of Tehran. Some major events, particularly the opening and the closing presentations, took place among the awe-inspiring ruins of Persepolis, the ancient ceremonial capital of the Achaemenid Empire. The Shiraz venue for most concerts was the auditorium of the Shiraz University. Some dance or theatrical events were placed on a raised platform in the courtyard of Sarā-ye Moshir, an old caravanserai within the bazar of the city, originally built as an inn and for storage of merchants' goods. Concerts of traditional Persian music were late night affairs in the garden of Hāfez's mausoleum. For the Persepolis concerts or dance and drama presentations, a suitable open area among the ruined places was prepared with elevated temporary seating and a raised stage area. Empress Farah always attended the opening and the closing events; sometimes she would stay longer and would attend other events.

The Shirāz/Persepolis Festival ran for eleven years; the twelfth, scheduled to begin in late August of 1978, was cancelled in early summer. The revolution that reached finality on 11 February 1979 had begun in January of 78. By early summer it had picked up momentum and ferocity. The religious faction, that was gradually gaining the upper-hand in the uprising, had already shown marked hostility to the Festival; it was singled out as the most flagrant symbol of western decadence that was polluting the Islamic society. Clearly, the organizers could not

proceed with any certainty that the Festival could take place without
unwanted incidents.

All things considered, the Shirāz Festival, in its short life, made a
tremendous impact on a passionately loyal audience. In the diversity
of its programming, in the high quality of participating groups and
artists, and in its wide range of international participation, the Shirāz/
Persepolis Festival was quite unique. This was a fact widely affirmed by
the foreign critics who attended the Festival's events.

Within Persia, the Festival's influence was significant in both positive
and negative ways. On the positive side, it introduced to native audiences unfamiliar art forms and styles in music and theatre, from both
the west and the cultures of Asia and Africa. I must make clear that
by 'native audiences' I mean the mainly young and educated middle
and upper classes. It would be false to claim that it made any impact
on the population at large. Those who came to see and hear what the
Festival had to offer were a limited group of mostly enthusiastic university age students. The majority of the population, the rural and the
urban downtrodden, were not interested. But, this is perhaps stating
the obvious. Where in the world do the less privileged and the unedu-
cated support the high and the novel arts? In Iran, while perhaps the
urban elite was already reasonably at home with Mozart, Beethoven,
Verdi and Tchaikovsky, they were largely unfamiliar with contemporary movements in music. The Festival actually commissioned works
by modern composers who were present, introduced their works, and
discussed them in lecture sessions with audience participation. Among
notable composers whose compositions were performed were Iannis
Xenakis, Olivier Messiaen, John Cage, Carl Heinz Stockhausen, Bruno
Maderna and Cristof Penderecki. A few of the native composers, whose
work was in line with contemporary styles, were also commissioned to
write new pieces for the Festival. I submitted a Concerto Grosso for
Piano and String Orchestra, called Rhetorics, which was performed in
1977, the final year of the Festival's life.

In the realm of theatre and dance such notable figures as Grotowsky,
Peter Brook, Alvin Nicolai, Maurice Bejart and Robert Wilson were
among the invitees to the Festival who contributed to the program-

ming of events. The innovative and highly influential Iranian experimental theatre workshop 'Kārgāh-e Nemāyesh' also started its life during the Festival through an experimental play by Abbās Nalbandiān directed by Arby Avanessian.

The programming of musical events was not entirely devoted to the most modern trends. Some programs featured famous living performers. For example a giant of 20th century piano, Arthur Rubinstein, performed at Persepolis in 1968; Yehudi Menuhin, Martha Argerich, Christian Ferras, the Melos Ensemble of London and the Juilliard String Quartet and the Moscow Chamber Orchestra with Rudolf Barshai were among the distinguished performers at the Festival.

The Festival, also, opened the way for the public's appreciation of the performing arts of the non-western cultures. Persians have always been a westward looking people. Particularly in modern times, it is the west that is being looked-up to and emulated. To the average Persian, France is closer than the neighboring Indian sub-continent. Even the common man knows more about England, Germany and America than about India, Thailand, China or Moslem Indonesia. The music, dance and drama of Asia and Africa had far greater novelty for the audiences than symphonic music, or ballet, or an Ibsen play. On the whole, as a cultural/educational enterprise, the Shiraz Festival was extremely effective in familiarizing the audiences who came to see and hear the programs with the artistic trends of both east and west.

The Festival was equally effective in promoting the most refined styles of Persian traditional music. The late night programs at Hāfeziye (the garden where Hāfez, the 14th century poet of Shirāz is buried) were very popular. Some of the best performers of urban traditional music were engaged for these concerts. Even presentations of *Ta'zie*, a type of dramatic representation with singing and instrumental accompaniment, based on various accounts of the life of Shiite martyrs, particularly that of Hoseyn, the prophet Mohammad's grandson, were included on two occasions in the Festival. I have given a more extended account of *ta'zie* and its revival in Chapter 8.

On the negative side, the Festival gave ample cause for disgruntlement to the traditionalist and the devout. To them, it stood for blatant

importation of the most objectionable and corrupting aspects of western culture to a society that was already at risk of losing its identity by
rampant westernization. Western dance and theatrical representations
were particularly resented. Programs featuring dance from Asia and
Africa were, also, condemned for their sensuous gyrations and over
fleshiness. The hatred of the Shirāz/Persepolis Festival that the clerics
had stored over the years found its full expression after they took power
in February of 1979. To this day, this Festival is frequently cited as one
of the cardinal sins of the final years of the Pahlavi monarchy.

I became involved with the Shirāz Festival, at the outset of my engagement as the Head of the Music Council of NIRT, in 1968. This
was the second year, in the 11 years life of the Festival. I was one of
a dozen members of the Festival Committee, which met throughout
the year, but at greater frequency as summer approached. Among the
members were writers, theatre directors, set designers, architects and
musicians. The meetings were chaired by Rezā Ghotbi, the Executive
Director of the Festival, or by his deputy, Farrokh Ghaffāri. These gatherings tended to last many hours, with lunch or dinner served on the
premises, as the passage of time may have required. At these sessions,
the content of the next Festival, the central theme, the exact dates, the
needed resources, the venues, and all other relevant issues were discussed. When necessary, specific responsibilities or assignments were
given to individual members. Fortunately, the funding was never a serious problem as the government had undertaken to provide financial
assistance.

Around the World in 65 Days

One of the issues that were decided at these meeting was the theme,
if any, of the next Festival. The chosen theme for the 1969 Festival was
percussion music. Early in the year, it was decided that I should take a
trip, on behalf of the Festival Committee, to various Asiatic countries
with which we had little or no contact. The object was two-fold; one
was to create a liaison with musical and theatrical institutions where
no relations existed, and the other was to make a selection of the type

of program suited to the chosen theme of the coming Festival and to make necessary arrangements for participation.

On the 6th of March, I set out on a two months journey by flying to India. This was my first ever travel to the east of Persia. My first stop was New Delhi where I remained for 5 days, including a day's trip to Agra to see the famed Taj Mahal. In New Delhi, I met with the directors of various music academies, and I was taken to a number of concerts. Next, I flew to Bombay, a hugely congested and oppressively poverty stricken city that is now better known by its correct name, Mumbai. There, the Iranian Consul General, who had been given prior knowledge of my visit, was gracious in organizing an evening's gathering at his place of residence to which a number of local musical figures were invited. The contacts I established with musicians in both New Delhi and Bombay proved useful in paving the way for the participation of numerous well-known North Indian musicians in the Festival.

I remained in Bombay for four days; from there I flew to Madras. There, I made contact with the Music Academy and was most helpfully received by its director. As I knew from my studies at UCLA, and my participation in the South Indian Study Group there, the music I heard in Madras was quite different from the north Indian music that one hears in New Delhi, or in Bombay. This is a musical system of greater subtlety and even more rhythmic complexity. The outcome of contacts I established with musical institutions in Madras was a program of dance theatre of *Katkali* at the Shiraz Festival in the following year, which proved to be one of the most striking theatrical presentations ever seen in Persia.

My next stop, after four days in Madras, was Calcutta, where I lingered for only two days. I was deeply affected by the level of poverty I saw in Calcutta. On arrival, from the airport in the city coach terminal, I was surrounded by a swarm of rickshaw drivers. I could not bear the idea of being driven by a man running and pulling a seat that I was to sit on. However, by declining I soon realized that there was no other means of transport to take me to my hotel. I had to relent and submit to, for me, the embarrassing mode of being carried to my destination. The hotel was an old colonial type grand structure with a delightful central courtyard where tables were set and tea was served in the afternoon.

My two days in Calcutta were depressing and unproductive. I did not manage to make any useful contacts there and, moreover, I was falling behind schedule, so I moved on by flying to Rangoon. Iran had no political relations with Burma (now called Myanmar), and there had been no possibility of receiving a visitor's visa. I had taken a chance on being able to get a visa, on arrival, at the airport. Unfortunately, this proved impossible. The authorities at the airport showed no sympathy for my mission of establishing contacts with musicians and musical institutions in their country. Fortunately, the airplane had to refuel in Rangoon and there was some delay before it took off for Bangkok. I was, therefore, able to get back on the plane, despite the time spent arguing with stone-faced Burmese officials, and proceed to my next stop, Thailand.

I spent five days in Bangkok, a fascinating city of dazzling old temples and palaces and modern high-rise buildings. I made some useful contacts and was taken to three concerts of Thai music. From Thailand on to the rest of south-east Asia the predominant music is orchestral. This is in sharp contrast with the musical cultures of the Middle East and India where emphasis is on soloistic music, or, at best, small instrumental combinations. Dance music, also, features prominently in most south east Asiatic countries; it also has much application in Indian sub-continent, but not in Moslem cultures of the Middle East and north Africa.

While in Bangkok, the Persian ambassador to Thailand offered every assistance and placed one of his secretaries at my disposal as a guide. On my first day, before I had contacted the ambassador, I made the mistake of wondering around in the city by myself. After a while, I came to a waterfront of what seemed like a lagoon or a placid river. A couple of young boys, appearing to be in their late teens, approached and began talking to me in English. They were polite and curious. They wanted to know where I came from and how I liked their country. I told them that I had just arrived and, as yet, had not seen much. They proposed to show me the sights of the city through a boat ride. I accepted and we descended into a long and narrow motorboat. The boat carried us leisurely through meandering waterways that bordered on some truly magnificent, seemingly golden, temples and palaces. This was all fine, the sights were beautiful and the boys were helpful in explaining what we were viewing. However, when we reached the end of the ride, some thirty minutes after having embarked on the venture, the atmosphere changed dramatically. As soon as we disembarked about half a dozen other boys, who appeared to be waiting for us, joined my two companions. I enquired as to the amount I should pay for the services rendered. They responded by asking how much did I have. When I said that is not any of their business, they became quite menacing and repeated their demand to know what money do I have. By this time I was encircled by a large group of youth and there was no police in sight. The situation had clearly become dangerous; I realized that I had no choice but to comply with their demand. Most of the funds I had brought with me for the world tour that was ahead were in traveller checks, which I had fortunately left in my briefcase at the hotel, but I had also some dollar bills in my wallet. As I took my wallet out, one of the boys grabbed it from my hand, opened it and extracted all the dollar bills, amounting to a bit over one hundred and gave me back the wallet. They did not pursue the matter further and without a word scurried away. I was left on my own, feeling and looking quite foolish, but there was nothing I could do; no one was around to whom I could appeal. There I was, a stranger in a strange land, bothered, befuddled and bereft of any money. After a while I hailed a passing taxi and gave the driver my hotel's name. On arrival at the hotel I asked the driver to wait. I went to my room brought some traveller checks to the reception desk, exchanged some for Thai money and paid the taxi driver. When I told the story of what had happened to the people in the hotel they just laughed, as if to say what did you expect! Any suggestion of reporting the incident to the police met with derision; they simply said that what happened was your own fault, this sort of thing happens to 'tourists' all the time and there is not much that the police could do about it.

The next country on my itinerary was Indonesia. I arrived in Jakarta after a short stop at the very modern and clean airport of Singapore.

At the airport in Jakarta, I was met by an official of the Ministry of Culture who drove me to my hotel. This was the only high-rise building that I could see in Jakarta. Now, more than 45 years later, Jakarta has many modern and imposing buildings, but in 1969, the whole city appeared more like a huge, over crowded village.

My ten days in Indonesia were among the most memorable experiences of my entire life. I was already quite familiar with, and had a deep appreciation of, Javanese and Balinese music. During my postgraduate studies in ethnomusicology at UCLA, I had been a member of both the Javanese and the Balinese gamelans. I had played different instruments in both ensembles and had participated in a number of concerts of music from Indonesia. We had even performed, on one occasion, for the visiting Indonesian President Sukarno. It was quite exciting to be in the seat of these magnificent musical traditions and to hear different gamelans, and to see the puppet shows, the shadow plays and various dance groups. Indonesia is huge country made of more than 7000 islands, mostly small and quite isolated, but the two islands of Java and Bali have the most sophisticated and varied musical traditions. It seems extraordinary that Java and Bali have no written literature, but have a most impressive oral literature, which finds its full expression in plays and dances with elaborate musical accompaniment. The music is largely orchestral with the participation of as many as thirty or more instruments. The instruments are mostly percussive of metalophone, xylophone and gong varieties. As an ensemble, the gamelan produces, next to the western symphony orchestra, the most sophisticated and harmonious sound effect of any music in the world culture. The orchestration is highly structured, the pieces that are performed are composed and written in a system of notation, which acts more as aid-memoire, rather than precise notation of every note and rhythm as is the case in western music.

While in Java, I took a side trip, by train, to Magelang in south central parts of the island, where a slightly different gamelan style is practiced. Here also, I was received by officials of the government and was taken to the rehearsal of two different gamelans. Not far from Magelang are located the remains of the monuments of Borobudur. I spent a day vis-

iting these amazing monuments that are among the world's most impressive medieval Buddhist temples. In most of the larger islands of the
Indonesian archipelago, until the 14th century, Buddhism or Hinduism
was the dominant religion. From the 14th century Islam gradually penetrated into some of these islands and replaced older religions. In Bali,
however, Hinduism is still practiced; in most of the smaller islands,
scattered in a vast area, neither religion has a strong hold.

From Jakarta, I flew to Bali for a three days stay. This was perhaps
the very high point of my around the world tour. I know that by now
Bali has become very 'touristy', not so in 1969. I stayed at the only
American run hotel, the Sheraton, located in the outskirts of Denpasar,
the capital of Bali. This beautiful hotel is set amid palm trees and at
a short walk from the beach. In the late afternoon, as I came through
the lobby and walked out into the front garden of the hotel, a gender-
wajong quartet was playing the graceful music that is the usual accompaniment for shadow plays. The gentle breeze, the sight of the ocean
waves a short distance to the front, the swaying palm trees combined
with the sound of the music created a magical effect that made a profound impression on me.

In the course of my three days in Bali I was able to hear a variety of
music and dance and made very useful contacts with local musical institutions. On the basis of these contacts arrangements were made for a
Balinese gamelan and a troupe of dancers to come to Iran for the Shiraz
Festival of 1969. The program they presented was the main feature of
the closing event of the Festival, performed at Persepolis. I believe this
was one of the most strikingly successful events in the 11 years life of
the Shiraz/Persepolis Festival.

My next destination, after Indonesia, was Manila, the capital of the
Philippines. My flight from Jakarta had a refueling stop in Saigon,
where the passengers had to disembark and wait a couple of hours.
At the time America was deeply involved with the Vietnam War.
The Saigon airport did not seem like a regular airport. It was full of
American service men; a few of them were outside the building, in full
view, playing baseball; but the atmosphere was altogether tense. I was
glad to leave and head for Manila.

In the Philippines, I had an old friend, Jose Maceda, who was a composer and professor of music at the University in Quezon City, a short distance from Manila. Jose and I knew each other from the time when he was studying for a PhD in ethnomusicology at UCLA. When I reached my hotel I telephoned him and the next day he came for me and drove me to his home. He showed me his university and made contacts with other musicians who come to see me. Later, I was taken to two musical events. On the whole, my four days in the Philippines were enjoyable, although I found nothing that I could recommend to the Festival Committee for inclusion in the program of the coming Festival. I also found the city of Manila a bit disorderly and the weather oppressively warm and humid.

Hong Kong was my next stop. If I had found Manila a bit disorderly, Hong Kong was down right chaotic. The density of population and seemingly ceaseless commotion were quite stifling. This was a place in which I simply could not feel comfortable. I made contacts with the two major universities in the city but found their music departments rather ill equipped, and the individuals I spoke to did not show much interest in my mission. Moreover, they did not seem to have much to offer in terms of any contributions to our Shiraz Festival. On a personal level, the few days in Hong Kong were useful; I had two suits tailored for me in two days, and bought two quality Swiss watches for very modest prices.

In 1969, in deference to the American policy still in effect at the time, Persia had not, as yet, given recognition to People's Republic of China. The China we recognized and had relations with was the Island of Taiwan (also known as Formosa). They maintained an embassy in Tehran, although Iran had no embassy in Taipei; the Persian ambassador to Japan was also accredited to Taiwan. Their embassy in Tehran had been apprised of my visit to Taipei and the reason for the visit. The government of the so-called Nationalist China in Taiwan, wishing to garner kudos by being seen as the representative of the Chinese people, had decided to welcome ceremoniously the visit of a cultural envoy from Persia to their shores. Accordingly, the reception that I received in Taiwan was quite exceptional. Not only was I met at the airport but a representative of their Ministry of Culture, and a chauffeur driven car, were placed at my service at all times.

My visit to Taipei proved to be agreeable beyond expectations. I was escorted to a number of concerts, two of which had prepared presentations for my exclusive viewing. These were in the halls of two music academies, one of which was structured primarily for training of musicians, singers, set designers, make-up artists, and clothes designers for 'Chinese opera'. What is known as Chinese opera has not come about as an imitation of western opera. The term opera is commonly used because of the resemblance of this particular Chinese theatrical tradition to its western counterpart. As in western opera, the Chinese opera is based on dramatic or comical stories that have protagonists and antagonists; the plots also have elements of conflict and resolution. The characters on stage sing their parts and the songs are accompanied by an ensemble of native instruments. The ensemble is not as large as an orchestra employed in western operas, but it does include different native instruments, winds, strings and percussions. Another difference with western opera is that some of the music in the Chinese opera is recycled and reused in more that one opera. Moreover, it is not a regenerating creative tradition; a set repertoire of some 80 operas make up the pool from which selections are made yearly for production.

I found the music academies to be well endowed and richly supplied with needed facilities. Whereas in the mainland China, at the time, the old traditions were derided and only revolutionary and self-serving music, theatre and dance were fostered, in Taiwan great attention was given to the preservation of national traditions, traditions which, curiously, are irrelevant to the island itself but are those of the bygone days of Imperial China.

While in Taiwan, I was feasted royally. Every night I was hosted by various dignitaries at functions, with sumptuous meals and much toasting to the glory of my king and country. I was taken on sight seeing tours to some of the scenic wonders of the countryside. The island is densely forested and mountainous with some truly splendid natural beauty that I, as a nature lover, was very happy to see. Clearly, the Taiwanese government was taking the visit of a cultural emissary from

Persia very seriously. By 1969, very few countries around the world recognized Taiwan as representative of China. Iran was among the few, which the Taiwanese greatly valued and therefore my visit, however politically inconsequential, was treated as something significant. Sadly for the Taiwanese, following President Nixon's famous visit to China in 1971, and the establishment of political relations with Beijing, Iran also severed ties with Taiwan and sent her first ambassador to The People's Republic China.

Next stop was Seoul the capital South Korea. Those unfamiliar with different cultures of the Far East tend to think of the Chinese, Japanese and Koreans as one race of people. While in Korea, I came to appreciate that Koreans are quite different from the Chinese, as indeed the Japanese, also, are distinct from the other two. Koreans have their own language and their own script. Their music, while bearing influences of the Chinese, is quite distinct. I also discovered that their food is very different from the much better known Chinese cuisine. Although in 1969 South Korea was not nearly as developed and industrialized as it is today, still the city of Seoul seemed like a very busy, congested and polluted place. However, the attention I received and the experience of hearing some very engaging music made my few days there quite memorable. I was met at the airport and was hosted daily by a very distinguished musician who was a professor at the main music conservatory. Through him, I met other musicians and was taken to a number of concerts. Ceremonial and ritual music in Korea have historical and theoretical ties with Chinese music. Korean folk music, on the other hand, is very distinctive; it is rhythmically spirited and has much diversity. The contacts I made during my stay in Seoul resulted in arrangements for the participation of a small dance troupe in the Festival of the following year.

My final Asiatic stop was Japan, an amazing country that seems to stand apart from all others in the Far East. The degree of formality and ceremoniousness that I encountered in Japan had no parallel in other cultures I had visited. Japan, already in 1969, had made great strides towards the inclusion of western classical music in its cultural life. I was told that Tokyo had five functioning symphony orchestras. Tokyo and other major cities had lively concert seasons when noted western artists, pianists, violinist and conductors were engaged to perform. At the same time, the Japanese are committed to the preservation of their own national musical traditions. Much of the Japanese musical genres are allied with ceremonial, theatrical and religious traditions. Gagaku, Bunraku, Noh drama, all are either purely musico-theatrical genres or rites with musical compliments. All these traditions involve both vocal and instrumental music; ensemble playing, combining small group of different native instruments to provide background music to dances and theatrical presentations. In addition there are also purely secular types of music, particularly in the form of chansons that are accompanied by the long-necked lute, the shamisen.

During my week's stay in Tokyo I enjoyed the attention and companionship of the distinguished Japanese ethnomusicologist, Dr. Kishibe. He took me to a number of musical events including a most impressive presentation of Noh drama. I also visited a music academy, where both practical and theoretical studies of various musical traditions of Japan were taught to a vast student body. I was told that there are other conservatories in Tokyo devoted entirely to the study of western classical music.

While In Japan, I also visited the cities of Kyoto and Osaka. I went to Kyoto only for the purpose of seeing this fabulous city, the ancient capital of Japan that contains beautiful palaces and temples. It was April, the cherry blossom time, and the city parks, the grounds surrounding temples, were riots of color. I spent a memorable afternoon walking around Kyoto, and took the train to Osaka the next day. In Osaka I remained for two days and made useful contacts with the director of the music academy, who had already been notified as to my visit.

On my continued eastward journey, the long flight across the Pacific Ocean brought me to Hawaii. I stayed in Honolulu for two nights, which, as far as I am concerned, was more than enough. In Hawaii, I saw nothing that interested me. Next stop was my old stamping ground, Los Angeles. This is a city where I spent many of my young years. It is a vast and amorphous city that many find hard to appreciate.

But, as huge as it is, I know it and like it well. I spent a few days there visiting friends and relatives.

Before reaching the east coast of the United States, I spent a few days in the Midwest. First I visited the University of Illinois in Champaign/ Urbana, where I had an invitation to give a lecture on music and Islam. From there I went to University of Indiana in Bloomington. The object was to visit this University's famous School of Music, the largest such school in the country and probably in the world. One of the music faculty members was George Gabor, a highly respected authority on percussion instruments. Since the central theme of the 1969 Shirāz Festival was percussion music, I invited Professor Gabor to the Festival, which he was very pleased to accept.

From Indiana I flew to New York for a brief stay and arrived in London on the 5th of May. In London I was a guest of the British Council. A meeting and reception had been organized for me with the British Composers' Association. I met a number of composers and was hosted at dinner by Graham Whettam, whose friendship I enjoyed for many years thereafter. In the 1980s and 90s, when I was Head of Music at Trinity College Dublin, he visited me in Ireland on numerous occasions; and, at one those visits, he gave a lecture on his own music for my composition students. Graham Whettam died in 2006, age 79.

Having traversed the globe, east to west, I arrived back in Tehran on the 10th of May, 65 days after my departure. The tangible results of my travels and the contacts I had made were all the events, pertaining to music, theatre and dance from the Asiatic world that were presented at the Shirāz/Persepolis Festival of 1969. These included music and dance from India, Thailand, Indonesia, Korea, and Japan. Early in the summer the directors of the Festival asked me to make another trip, this time to Algeria and Tunisia, in order to assess the possibilities of having musical or theatrical participations from those countries. My few days in Algiers and Tunis were certainly interesting but unproductive. I did not find any material of quality to recommend for inclusion in the Festival.

❧ 10 ❧

Persian Empire, The Final Decade

The 1970s proved to have been a fateful decade for Persia. It culminated in a massive revolution that brought about catastrophic changes to the country with international consequences that, to this day, are plaguing the world. This period and its aftermath have been subject of many scholarly books and a great deal more needs yet to be researched and made public. The Persian Revolution of 1978-79 has been, without a doubt, one of the momentous events of modern times. Had it not been for this Revolution many of the major events of the last 35 years would not have come to pass. The invasion of the American Embassy in Tehran and the capture of 52 American citizens as hostages who were held for 444 days, the failure of President Carter to win re-election in 1980, the Russian invasion of Afghanistan, the 8 years long Iran/Iraq war, Saddam Hussein's conquest of Kuwait and the war to expel him from that country, the presence of U.S. forces in Arabia that formed the pretext for the creation of Al-Qaeda, the Islamic militancy and terrorism, the 9/11 attacks on American soil, the ascendency of the Taliban, the Afghan war, the Iraq war, and the worldwide threat of Islamic terrorism, these events were all ultimately rooted in the rise of Islamic militancy and the eventual theocracy that was established in Iran.

If the Iranian monarchy had remained in place, the Islamic Republic would not have been born and its illegitimate progenies: Moslem fundamentalism, jihadism, and Islamic terrorism would not have followed. This is not to imply that the Islamic Republic was responsible for these developments, rather it was the collapse of the balance of power in the Middle East that was maintained by a stable and powerful Iran that usher in all the problems that have plagued that region to this day. I do not intend, however, to give a chronological or analytical account of these events. That is not in keeping with the premise of the work in hand. I shall only relate personal observations on political events that unfolded in my native country that led to the demise of the age-old Persian Empire.

I have always been committed to the concept of Persia as an empire. This was, perhaps, partly due to having been a child of the Rezā Shah era, when a sense of pride in ancient Persia was reawakened and promoted. Equally important has been my recognition of the fact that this country is made of diverse races, sub-nations, and tribes, its cohesion into a single unit makes sense best in the form of an empire, as it has always been. When a monarch is the head of one nation that is a kingdom, when the reign is over many nations it becomes an empire. It is the unity and continuity that monarchy provides that has kept the greater Iranian nation, made of Persians, Azeris, Kurds, Lors, Gilaks, Turkmens, Baluchis and Qashqais together for all these centuries. The only other alternative is the confederation formation, which is never secure. The very concept of different national units coming together by agreement to form a larger confederated unit implies that, at any time and for any reason, one or more of the parts may opt to leave the union. This, needless to say, I did not wish to see happen in my country. So, I firmly believed in the rightfulness of Persia to remain an empire, as it has been for the past 26 centuries.

My childhood home environment was generally receptive to, not only the acceptance, but also veneration of our royalty. My father, grandfathers and several generations before them, had all been civil servants, which, in effect, meant being in the service of the king. Personally, I was never politically active. In my teens, during the war years and the turbulent years that followed, many of my contemporaries were being drawn into political parties, particularly the left leaning groups. I never joined any party, union or society. In a purely personal way, I was a royalist, but this did not mean that I approved of everything that was done by the king or members of his family. I distinctly recall that even as a child I disapproved of the slogan that we were taught to chant: Khodā, Shah, Mihan (God, King, Fatherland). I thought that the order of the second and third should be reversed.

Except for some 18 months in late 1950s, when I returned to conduct research on Persian traditional music, I was absent from Persia from 1949 to 1968. The most important political events of the years of my absence were: the nationalization of the Iranian Oil Industry, the removal of Prime Minister Mossadeq from office, the creation of the internal security agency (SAVAK), and finally the belated Coronation of Mohammad Rezā Shah in 1967, 26 years after he had succeeded his father to the throne. By that time, the Shah had consolidated powers in his own person and the government, including the Prime Minister, the Council of Ministers, and both Houses of Parliament, were effectively chosen, and performed, in accordance with his will and command.

Nationalization of the oil industry, championed by the Prime Minister, Dr. Mohammad Mosaddeq, a beloved and respected patriot, took place in 1951. His removal from office two years later was a very complicated issue about which much has been written. Usually it is referred to as a combined CIA/MI6 coup d'etat. This is technically incorrect as he was not head of the state; moreover, his dismissal was constitutionally within the king's prerogatives. I should also correct another common misrepresentation. Nearly all sources – countless books and articles – refer to Dr. Mosaddeq as the popularly elected Prime Minister who was removed from office by the intervention of the U.S. and Great Britain. The fact is that no Prime Minister in Persia came to office by popular election. They were either nominated by the Parliament (Majles), subject to the approval of the king, or appointed by the king subject to the approval of the Majles, which was a foregone conclusion. The chosen Prime Minister could be a member of the Parliament, the Senate, or from outside legislative chambers, even high-ranking military officers have served as prime ministers. Dr. Mosaddeq was certainly a popular Prime Minister, but it was the Shah who had appointed him to that post. As to CIA/MI6 involvements, while their role is well documented and cannot be denied, the fact remains that internal conditions had evolved in such a way that their intervention became both possible and successful. If the religious orders had not turned against Mosaddeq, and consequently the business community (*bazaris*) had not withdrawn their support, and if Mosaddeq had not become increasingly reliant on the backing of the communist (*Tudeh*) party, no plan by outside agencies could have succeeded. These were not conditions orchestrated by the outside forces, they were the outcome of Mosaddeq's inability to manage events more adroitly and in a more conciliatory fashion.

The events of 1951-53 led to a turning point in the reign of Mohammad Rezā Shah. From his coming to the throne in September 1941 to August 1953, he had remained largely on the sidelines. This is a twelve year period when the country experienced both a degree of democratic freedom, and a large measure of upheaval and disarray. After the fall of Mosaddeq, the Shah returned from a brief self-exile in Italy and gradually managed to assume powers beyond the limits that the Constitution had vested in him.

The Shah's increasingly autocratic rule, self-destructive in the end, also bore some very positive results. Interestingly, and contrary to popular assumptions, the citizens enjoyed a degree of freedom quite uncommon in standard authoritarian regimes. If one was not involved in political activism against the regime, there were hardly any restrictions on personal liberties. The society was moving rapidly towards secularism and the move was not directed from the throne, as was the case in the time of Rezā Shah. By the late 60s the urban population had grown and had become modernized enough for religiosity to be sidelined, or at least it seemed that way. The urban middle class had become large enough to be at least as dominant as the old time aristocracy. The highly placed figures in the government were young and well educated, not necessarily the scions of the traditional nobility. Above all, a measure of prosperity seemed to have permeated all strands of the population.

The final decade of Mohammad Rezā Shah's rule saw the enactment of significant reforms. Perhaps the most important was the empowerment of women, who received the right to vote and assumed equal status to men in all professions. The Family Protection law of 1968 was particularly important as it gave women equality with their husbands in matters of divorce and child custody. Aspects of this law contravened Islamic Sharia laws and caused serious grievance with the clerics, but their discomfiture was ignored. In the area of reconstruction and development strides were made in road building, installation of dams and extensive hydroelectric projects, telecommunications, creation of institutions of higher learning, and promotion of the arts.

By 1971, the Shah had been on the imperial throne of Persia for 30 years. He had hobnobbed with world leaders, the likes of Churchill, Stalin, De Gaulle, Truman, Eisenhower, Kennedy and Nixon. He was fully in league with European monarchs, whom he visited often and who came on state or private visits to Iran. He was seen not only as the king but a symbol of a modernized and westernized late 20th century Persia. Although the activities of the SAVAK in harsh suppression of any opposition did draw attention and a good deal of condemnation, on the whole, the Shah commanded international respect and, in a world with few remaining monarchies, he and empress Farah were source of much media attention.

Internally, in his early years as king, Mohammad Rezā Pahlavi, was a genuinely well-liked monarch. He was barely 22 when he came to the throne. The public sympathized with him as he faced the problems of securing his position at a time when the country was in the hands of the occupying allied forces. His first marriage to Queen Fowzia, sister of Egypt's King Faruq, was an unhappy arrangement to which neither he nor his wife seemed fully committed. The second marriage to the beautiful Sorayā Bakhtiār who, contrary to Fowzia was well liked by the nation, also sadly ended in divorce, as she was unable to bear a child, and the dynasty needed a direct heir. When he married his third wife, Farah Dibā in 1959, there was unprompted popular jubilation. And, when the heir to the throne was born the following year, the public display of joy was quite genuine. The nation came to love the new Empress who possessed beauty, intelligence and modesty.

Above all, Mohammad Rezā Shah was a patriot, dedicated to the elevation of his country and his people. He was a hardworking monarch who was increasingly at the heart of the decision making process. Any animosity towards the Shah rested on politico-ideological grounds. The communists hated him for obvious reasons: he was a king, and they supposedly believed in the dictatorship of the proletariat. Within the religious hierarchy he had supporters and he also had detractors. In

1963 and 64, Ruhollāh Khomeini, then a fairly junior Āyatollāh, had taken issue with some of his reforms, mainly opposition to land distribution to the peasants (including vast land endowments in possession of religious institutions), and women's rights. He had mounted demonstrations against the monarch, but the uprisings had been successfully quelled. Khomeini had been arrested and eventually exiled first to Turkey and, a year later, to Iraq. By early 70s, with Khomeini out of the way, no serious religious opposition appeared as a threat.

As the Shah increasingly assumed the role of decision maker, effectively he became the dictator of policies. The legislative and the executive branches of government acted according to his directions. If things went wrong the blame was his, but no one dared to point that out. The only reason why the government of Premier Amir Abbās Hoveidā remained in office for 12 and half years – unprecedented in Persian modern history - was that he and his ministers only performed the will of the monarch. The Shah even occasionally summoned the cabinet to have its meetings in his presence. This was the sort of hands on monarchy that nurtured its own vulnerability. When decisions were proven to have been flawed the blame rested with the king and not with his ministers who could be chastised and removed.

Perhaps it was the sense of security combined with increased international prestige that gave the Shah, in his final decade on the throne, an air of grandiosity bordering on the bizarre. This was manifested most glaringly in the celebrations, in 1971, of 2500 years of the Persian Empire. These celebrations became a source of public grievance on various grounds. To begin with, the correct date of the founding of the Achaemenid Empire is 550 BCE, the year of Cyrus the Great's accession to the throne of Persia; 2500 years after that date would have been the year 1950. Having missed that date and still wishing to celebrate 25 centuries of the Empire by approximation, one could understand that a series of conferences and lectures by recognized scholars, plus publications would have been eminently acceptable by all, both internally and internationally. Instead, the celebrations became a costly extravaganza that the majority of the population came to resent. The lengthy parade of soldiers, dressed to represent different periods of history, put on at Persepolis, appeared slightly vulgar and risible; it was a show only worthy of a Cecil B. DeMille production. The whole affair was viewed internally as a display of profligacy that the nation could ill afford.

The most objectionable aspect of the celebrations, to the Iranian nation, was the large number of invitees and the luxury that surrounded the ceremonies. Although the hoped for participation of all heads of states – kings, queens and presidents – did not quite materialize, still there were too many of them to meet with the approval of the common man. The sumptuous way they were treated became a source of much public scorn. The public's perception of the cost of the celebrations was undoubtedly exaggerated, but enough evidence existed to give way for hyperbole. Food flown from Maxim of Paris, the large quantity of consumed liquor and champagne, foreign waiters, and most of all, the tent city that was imported and erected at Persepolis, at great expense, for the residence of the dignitaries, were all deeply resented. Whether true or not, the common believed that millions of the nation's wealth was wasted in feasting a bunch of second-rate international figures, at a time when a large segment of the population still lived below poverty line.

Two years after the 2500 years celebrations, in 1973, the so-called Yom Kippur war between Egypt and Israel, resulted in a sudden four fold rise in the price of a barrel of oil. Since the Arab countries, for several months, ceased exporting of oil to the west, the Iranians became the beneficiary of the rise in the cost of fuel. Not only they continued their export at the high price, they increased their production. Paradoxically, this huge increase in income was one of the major contributors to the revolution of 1978. The sudden wealth had an unsettling effect; people's expectations, in receiving benefits from this wealth, rose unrealistically. Incomes did grow significantly, but that was easily swallowed by high inflation. Moreover, the higher income did not match the level of hopes and expectations. Equally upsetting was the rampant corruption and the widening gap between rich and poor. To be sure, Persia never had an egalitarian society; however, there had existed a traditional pattern to which the nation was accustomed.

The wealth, land ownership and power rested with the aristocracy who formed a small minority. This was not a fair set up, and certainly not democratic, but it had time honored-roots; in fact, that is how societies were structured everywhere, even in Europe, until not so very long ago. It is only natural that, once this pattern is upset, and is upset suddenly, upheaval will soon follow.

The over-night wealth generated by income from oil exports was more than the country could sensibly absorb. Quite suddenly Iran, by all accounts still a developing third world country, was giving foreign aid to other countries, was building a university in Senegal, giving loans to some European countries, and, of course, buying every modern weapon in the U.S. arsenal. As the country did not have adequate means of transportation, the goods arriving at southern ports were piling up on the docks, rusting and spoiling in the hot sun. Waste and pilfering became endemic; well-connected contractors sold contracts they had won to sub-contractors and made huge profits without having lifted a finger. Because of vast construction projects villagers from all parts of the country headed for the big cities for jobs, jobs that supposedly paid better than working the fields. In consequence, the country's agricultural production suffered a decline.

The rise in revenue due to the higher income from oil exports did filter down to nearly everyone in the country. However, this was upset by rampant inflation. Housing, in particular, due to the flood of workers from the rural areas to the cities, became a crippling problem. The rental costs went up astronomically and acquisition of property became out of reach for the average income earner. The fact that there was a lot of money and jobs around did not help; what was earned was never enough to balance against the cost of living. If, say, an average earner was making three times as much as he did ten years ago, he had to manage against a cost of living that was four times higher. So, the newly found wealth of the country did not bring greater satisfaction to the majority. To make matters worse, everyone was aware of corruption that, more than ever, was plaguing the system; they could see how some crafty individuals were getting grossly rich; they could see palatial mansions that were going up in northern suburbs of Tehran.

Businessmen and industrialists from western countries were arriving in Tehran by plane loads, seeking new contracts. There was something unreal about Tehran of the mid-70s. The city had grown and doubled its population since the 50s and was becoming singularly shapeless and chaotic. Tehran of my childhood was an unpretentious but attractive city with character and style. By the 70s, it was fast becoming the world's most unattractive capital city. It was unsightly because it lacked form and order. One could see a high-rise building next to an old stately home, or a modern structure next of an empty lot covered with weeds and rubbish. Many of the new urban developments in the outskirts of the city were shoddily built with narrow streets. In a country as vast as Persia with unlimited available space, it was puzzling to me why new housing developments were laid with narrow roadways, as if land were too precious to be wasted on roads. The traffic had become agonizingly congested and frenzied. Tehran looked pretty much like the affairs of the nation, disturbed and confused.

Altogether, conditions in Iran of the last few years before the Revolution had become somewhat unreal. By the mid 70s, the Shah was speaking of Iran as being on the verge of 'the Great Civilization'. What exactly he had in mind as evidence of this Great Civilization was not clear. He was also projecting that by the end of the century Iran will be the world's fourth greatest power. One may only speculate as to which would have been the first three at that point.

One of the strangest and most disastrous moves by the Shah was his unexpected speech in March of 1974, broadcast to the nation, in which he spoke of the need to abolish the two political parties and to form a single party to which, as he declared, all must belong. In the early 60s, the Shah had published a much lauded little book called *The White Revolution*. One of the main points raised in this book was the importance of the two-party system whereby one party, on the basis of public's vote, gains the majority of parliamentary seats and forms the government, while the other acts as the loyal opposition. The model, presumably, was the two major parties in the U.S. or in Great Britain. In accordance with the tenets of this thesis, two political parties, *Iran Novin* (New Iran) and *Mardom* (People), had been established. The former had gained most seats in the parliament or *Majles* and had formed the government, and the latter was the opposition party. In reality both parties were subservient to His Majesty's directions.

   In the days following the king's speech, of the many people I spoke to, I could not find one person who could claim to understand why the man had suddenly reversed himself and had come up with the idea of one party system. Even more bewildering was the way he sprung the notion on the nation. The speech sounded almost spontaneous and improvised. He even said: (I am paraphrasing) we'll perhaps name the party *Rastākhiz* (resurgence), if that name has not been used for a political party before. The most objectionable part of the announcement was a peculiar commandment to the effect that 'everyone must join the party or we'll give him/her a passport to leave'. This was an astonishingly arrogant remark, highly insulting to the free citizens of a nation. Not even the most ruthless dictators of the century, the likes of Stalin, Hitler, Franco or Mao had given such a directive. I know that many royal apologists have tried to rephrase the Shah's remark so that his command to those refusing membership to leave the country is made more palatable. Some have even denied that he made such a statement at all. But, this loyal royalist begs to differ; I heard what the Shah said with my own ears.

   Why did the Shah, reversing his professed admiration for the two party system, suddenly opt for the single party model? Was it the Leninist or the Maoist models that had captured his imagination, or had the fascism of Mussolini era or the Nazism of Third Reich suddenly appeared as good models to emulate? But all of these were outdated models that had been fully discredited. The two existing parties were servants of His Majesty anyway, why would their merger into one make any difference? Why should a king who should be above petty politics give such political directions anyway? Perhaps there are some who have answers to these questions; I don't.

   In practical terms, the idea of a single party, the *Rastākhiz*, never got very far. As an example, at the University of Tehran, in each faculty, a large notebook was laid open for the academic staff to sign their names as indication of their intended membership in the *Rastākhiz* party. I never did put my name down in that notebook and I know that many others also declined to sign in their names. By a year later, even though the *Iran Novin* and *Mardom* parties were nominally amalgamated into the *Rastākhiz*, in real terms nothing momentous had happened. No new policies, no change of directions, and no sense of national unity behind the one flag were in evidence. Even, more surprisingly, the new government that was formed, after the old *Iran Novin* cabinet had resigned, with very few changes, consisted of the same ministers back doing the same job as before. Mr. Amir Abbas Hoveidā was the Prime Minister before and remained in that post after the formation of the single party.

Some consider the change of calendar from Islamic to Imperial as another major blunder. I do not subscribe to this view, but admit that it was done too abruptly and, at a time of mounting dissatisfaction, it did exacerbate the problem of disharmony between people and the governance. Although the Persian calendar, from the time of Rezā Shah, was changed to solar, with *Nōruz* as the first day of the year, and all months bore ancient Persian names, the year one, however, still remained the date of Prophet Mohammad's flight from Mecca to Medina. The new calendar, announced in 1975, moved the starting date to the supposed establishment of the Persian Empire. At the same time, the date apparently was calculated so that the beginning of Mohammad Rezā Shah's reign would be the year 2500. Having just celebrated the 2500 years of the Empire in 1971, now that date was moved to 1941. This was to be, henceforth, the nation's official calendar. Religious holidays and commemorations were to remain, as before, according to Islamic lunar hegira dating. (In Islamic dating Prophet Mohammad's flight from Mecca to Medina, year 622 of Roman calendar, is year one, and years are calculate on 12 lunar months, which fall short of the correct solar year by about 11 days.) I was rather astonished at the degree of resentment created by this issue. Not only the religiously devout seemed to protest but the young and well educated people also showed disapproval. There was such hue and cry that, in the course of the revolution, in 1978, as one of the many concessions in the hope of pacifying the public, the change to the Imperial dating was rescinded. This and other concessions, were not only made too late to bear fruit but was taken as a sign of the regime's weakness, which only served to embolden the revolutionaries. Had the calendar change been done during the reign of Rezā Shah, when the solar and purely Persian calendar was introduced, it would have met with no effective protest and no move to reverse it would have been needed.

In light of the events of 1978, it is easy to see where the system had failed and how conditions had ripened for the clerical take-over of the country. Subsequent to the fall of Mosaddeq and assumption of ultimate power by the Shah, no genuine political party with popular mandate was allowed to take form. The two parties, and eventually the one and only party, were shams. They did not resonate with the nation and they did not enjoy any real public support. At least the Two Party System had some democratic pretense; the *Rastākhiz* was totally bereft of all legitimacy. Moreover, since the removal of Prime minister Mosaddeq, no political personality had emerged who could capture the public's admiration and support. I have heard it claimed that as soon as someone with any charisma had appeared on the national scene, he would be neutralized by being demoted or removed to an inconsequential position. Whether true or not, the fact remains that by 1978, there was no national figure that the public could look up to as someone remotely resembling a leader. There was only the Shah.

Meantime, Āyatollāh Khomeini in Iraq, still largely unknown to most Iranians, had been rising in stature among a growing band of followers. His vituperative sermons against the Shah were tape recorded, brought back to Iran, and disseminated through mosques, in cities and towns around the country. Thus, religious institutions began to function as political organizations, and an absent figure loomed as the opposition leader. At the same time, a new American president, Jimmy Carter, was applying pressure on the Shah to liberalize his policies. The Shah, who regarded the maintenance of good relations with the U.S. essential to the safety of his realm, reacted by instructing relevant agencies of the government to allow the public greater freedom of assembly and of expression. The SAVAK was also directed to refrain from harsh treatment of detainees and to forego any exercise of torture.

I was on sabbatical leave from University of Tehran for two years, from the summer of 1976 to the end of August 1978. On my return, I learnt that during those two years considerable change in allowing greater liberalization had taken place. New publications sprung up, large evening gatherings for poetry reading were allowed, intellectuals and academics were given greater freedoms, political assemblies and even some protests were tolerated. As more liberal policies came into effect the relationship between the Shah and President Carter was improved. In early autumn of 1977, the Shah had been received, with much fanfare, in the White House by the President, followed by a sumptuous state dinner. Only a few weeks later, on the eve of the New Year, Mr and Mrs Carter returned the Shah's visit to the U.S. by coming on a state visit to Persia. They spent the last day of 1977 and the first day of 1978 with the Shah and Empress Farah. At the New Year's Eve dinner in the Niāvarān Palace, President Carter, while toasting the king, gave an extravagantly panegyric speech about the Shah, praising him for his wisdom and counsel. He complemented the Shah for his rule over a stable country in the midst of the most troubled region of the world. The effusiveness of Carter's speech surprised even his own entourage.

On the 8th of January 1978, an article, prepared by the SAVAK, was published in the daily Ettelāʾāt. It contained deprecating remarks about Āyatollāh Khomeini and his son Mostafā's activities abroad. Seminarians at religious institutions in Qom took to the streets in anti-government demonstration. This had led to riots and confrontation with security forces resulting in a few fatalities. Many commentators date this event as the starting point of the Iranian Revolution. By tradition Iranians hold commemorative ceremonies forty days after the death of a loved one. A cycle of 40th day commemoration of those who had perished in demonstrations followed, with ever increasing public participation and attendant violence and casualties. It quickly spread to other cities. By the spring of 78, the news of mounting revolt in Iran was making international headlines. When I returned, from my two years long sabbatical abroad in early September, soldiers in armored cars were on the streets of Tehran. The situation was tense, yet ordinary people went about their business, more or less, as usual.

In late September, there was a major confrontation between a vast crowd of demonstrators and the armed forces in the *Jāle* Square, northeast of central Tehran, in which possibly dozens perished. This tragic event, in its much magnified version, became a rallying point after which the Revolution became massive and unstoppable. By this time, the religious faction in the uprising had taken the upper hand. Although the seminarians in Qom had triggered early demonstrations in January, by the summer's end, participants in the revolution were young and old, male and female, of diverse persuasions. For the communist sympathizers this was naturally an opportunity to reappear on the scene. The well-educated young, with their high-minded ideals of liberty, including many from high-income families, also joined the movement. It is important to appreciate that the uprising in 1978 was not a purely religious movement. However, as the revolution progressed and gained volume and momentum, the only participating faction that had organization and leadership was the religious one. In the end that faction won the day and registered this monumental event to its own calling, hence the "Islamic Revolution".

I do not intend to give an account of the progress of the Revolution, the departure of the king on 16th of January 1979, the arrival of Āyatollāh Khomeini from Paris on the 1st of February, and the collapse of the Bakhtiār government ten days later. These are among the most important events of recent history, about which much has been written. I only wish to comment on how the Revolution continues to be perceived by an overwhelming majority of Persians who are not in sympathy with the Islamic Republic.

Most of the Persians who have been hurt by this revolution, whether they live inside or outside the country, appear to remain in a state of stupefaction. In their assessment of how and why the revolution came about, they persistently begin with a conclusion as unquestionable fact and then proceed to look for ways of proving it. The absurd but persistent conviction is that the revolution was brought about by western, primarily American but also possibly British, powers in order to remove the Shah. Why? Because he was becoming too independent, and, also, for having led the rise in the price of oil. In other words, they believe that western leaders plotted to remove a trusted friend and ally, a leader who only a few months ago was praised to high heavens by the U.S. President, in order to punish him for being too independent. And, whom did they trust in his place? A cleric who had repeatedly vilified the Americans and the British, who had expressed hatred for Israel and who was fundamentally and quite vocally anti-western. They had supposedly placed faith in, and had supported, a man who decried the western world for being the source of all 'corruption' that is poisoning Iranian society. The invasion and ransacking of the American embassy in Tehran, the hostage taking and break-up of diplomatic relations with the U.S., America's not so covert assistance to Saddam Hussein during eight years (1980-88) of Iran/Iraq war, unremitting hostility to America's closest ally Israel, undermining America's position in Iraq, and countless other active expressions of the Islamic Republic's confrontational policy towards the U.S. and Britain would not deter many Iranians from placing blame on them for having brought about the 'Islamic Revolution'.

Iranians search far and wide for evidences that can somehow prove this absurd conspiracy theory. Recently, a high minded former president of Tehran University, who has written a number of books about the Revolution, and now resides in Belgium, in a TV interview for BBC Persian Service, claimed that in 1974, in a White House meeting, Henry Kissinger had stated that the Shah has to either change his ways or we shall have to remove him. This is supposed to prove that the Americans were behind the Islamic Revolution and that they brought Khomeini to power. This risible claim ignores the fact that Dr. Kissinger was a steadfast supporter of the Shah to the end. He was one of the few American dignitaries who attended Shah's funeral in Cairo in July of 1980. He could not have possibly said anything like 'we shall have to remove him (the Shah)'. If such a thing had been said, it would not go into official minutes of any meeting, for the removal of the head of a state, by a foreign power, is an illegal act. Moreover, Dr. Kissinger was the Secretary of State in the Republican presidents Nixon and Ford administrations, what does any remark of his have to do with the policies of the Democratic president Carter who came to office later? A further relevant question is: just how does an American administration go about removing the Shah of Persia? By causing a revolution? How would they do that? The whole proposition is too preposterous to deserve scrutiny. The Americans have not been able to remove the communist leader of Cuba, Fidel Castro – and not for lack of trying - from an island that is only 90 miles from the U.S. shores, an island that, before the January 1959 take over by Castro and his revolutionary followers, was practically owned and run by the Americans. Now we are to believe that Kissinger said, in 1974, that the Shah must go and the administration of the opposing Democratic Party, in 1978, did just that, by mounting an Islamic Revolution.

A much cited piece of 'evidence' by the adherents to this 'conspiracy theory' goes as follows: BBC, in its Persian language programs, daily reported, in detail, the revolutionary clashes that took place in Persia. When Khomeini, in the final four months of his 15 years of exile, ended up in Neufle le Chateau, in the outskirts of Paris in autumn of 1978, BBC reporters covered his movements and reported his pronouncements. These are supposed to testify to the British having had a bias in propagating the revolution and identifying Khomeini as its leader. Persians simply do not accept that BBC News is an independent organization, even though its foreign language broadcasts are funded by the Foreign Office. They firmly believe that the content of its broadcasts are dictated by the British government. That the Iranian Revolution, as it picked up momentum, had become a major event of international interest, and not only the BBC, but all news media were giving it daily coverage, somehow did not come into consideration. The fact that when Khomeini moved to France the world media found access to him – the 14 years he was in Iraq, a dictatorship, he was out of reach of the press – and, all news media including BBC were focusing attention on him does not enter into the argument.

Another 'explanation' that has had wide circulation is speculation on the decisions made, by western leaders (U.S., Great Britain, France, Italy and Germany), in January of 1979, at a conference in the island of Guadeloupe, a French possession in the Caribbean Sea. This theory sees the western leaders at that meeting deciding that the Shah must go. Although we have no published documentation of discussions that took place in Guadeloupe, it is safe to assume that the critical situation in Iran was on the agenda. No doubt the leaders concluded that the Shah could not survive the sweep of the revolution, and that the west had no choice but to come to terms with this reality. Therefore, they must have concluded that to safeguard their interests they should make contact with the Ayatollah, who was in Paris at that time, in the hope of establishing a working relationship with him and with what was to follow. The common argument by Iranians, either deliberately or un-knowingly, omits the date of this Guadeloupe conference, which was January of 1979. By that time, the Revolution had become massive, and the Shah had demonstrated near paralysis in his ability to quell the uprising. By early December, based on any informed assessment, the situation had passed beyond the stage of repair and compromise. Sadly, the end of the Pahlavi regime had become unavoidable. It was only logical for western leaders to face reality and try to cope with what was to follow in a manner that would bring about some rapprochement with the regime that is likely to follow.

The question that arises is, why do so many Persians search for ways, however unreasonable, to prove a western design in the fall of the Shah? As I see it, there are two basic reasons for this aberrant tendency. One is the lingering belief that the British, and more recently the Americans, run the world as it pleases their interests. Their mentality is stuck in the colonial days of the 19th century. They still believe in the hidden hand of the British, and now the Americans, who manipulate and control international affairs. The second is their unwillingness to credit the *mollā*s, subjects of perennial derision, with the ability to have mount-ed a revolt to the extent of destroying the age-old Persian monarchy. Curiously, many of the exiled Persians who persist in maintaining these conspiracy theories participated in the uprising, which, as said earlier, did not begin as an Islamic Revolution. Intellectuals and left leaning educated classes were very much involved in the uprising; they deserve much credit for the fall of monarchy, if 'credit' is the right word. But now that they have lost the ground to the religious faction and find themselves discredited, ousted from positions of power and persecuted, they prefer to forget the crucial part they had played in mounting the revolution and call the whole thing a western plot. By this logic, if they were not the winners, then those who won must have been in the service of western powers.

The memory of the British colonial supremacy in the 19th and early 20th centuries is very much alive with Persians. They have heard and have read about the British near omnipotence, a century ago, to manipulate destinies of other nations to their own advantage. Although Persia was never an outright British colony, from the mid 19th century, their influence increasingly dominated the internal affairs of the country. By the time First World War got underway, all effective power rested with the British and the Tsarist Russians, who even maintained armed forces in the country and fought the Ottomans within Persian borders. Only in the 1920s, after Rezā Shah took power he did manage to steadily curtail British influence and meddling. Even so, the mistrust of the British had found a deep niche in the Persian psyche. I recall distinctly that, in my childhood and youth, adults spoke of the British as if they were responsible for any momentous event that happened in the country. Later, after America entered into the Second World War and became the senior partner in vanquishing the German and the Japanese foes, they gradually captured the imagination of Iranians as the master manipulators. The CIA's complicity in the removal of Dr. Mosaddeq's government in the summer of 1953, became the final proof of America's ability to alter the course of history everywhere to their advantage. From that point on most Iranians could not conceive of any major upheaval in their country without American involvement, no matter how harmful the outcome might be to America's own interests.

The second reason rests on the prevailing contempt that upper class Persians have always had for the clerics. To them the idea of the emergence of a theocratic regime was so absurd that it had to be at the instigation of foreign powers. Again, the fact that an Islamic theocracy is inherently anti-western, and therefore cannot be sponsored by western powers with any hope that it might serve their interests, somehow does not come into the equation.

Within a few years after the Revolution, I learned that the conspiracy theorists had even involved me in the plot against the monarchy. In the early 1980s I was confronted with an oblique insinuation to the effect that I was personally one of the operatives of the American government in undermining the Pahlavi regime. This curious allegation was brought to my attention by some friends and relatives in the course of a trip to Nice in the south of France. It was put to me as a joke, so any protest on my part would naturally be met with: of course we know it is all nonsense. And, if I simply laughed it off as a jest, it could be taken that I was really not denying it.

I was never involved in politics but was known to be a royalist, how was it possible to link me with a plot to bring down the Persian monarchy? The basis for the bizarre notion of my complicity turned out to be a paper that I had presented at a conference, with the participation of the Aspen Institute for Humanistic Studies, about Iranian development programs, held in the autumn of 1976 at Persepolis. The article was later published in a book containing all the papers read at that conference. A review of that conference appeared in the New York Times with reference to only a few of the articles, including a few quotations from my paper which was given particular prominence. My article was about the importance of two social issues, truth and justice, without which, I maintained, no meaningful social progress can be achieved. Admittedly, I had obliquely made reference to the Shah's recent heralding of what he called the dawn of 'the Great Civilization', and had subtly suggested that no civilization, let alone a great one, can be built without truth and justice.

Needless to say, I had written the article in all sincerity as a loyal citizen. No one had questioned my intentions at the conference, which, by the way, was attended by the Empress Farah. Any comments that I received from colleagues at the conference were highly complimentary. Had any malicious intent been detected in my statements, I would have surely been called in by the SAVAK for questioning. Now, some years later, the conspiracy buffs, in their convoluted mentality, had construed that if I had covertly criticized the Shah's pronouncements, and had suggested that the Iranian public was not given the truth nor treated justly, then I must have been part of a plot to bring down the monarchy and was doing so at the instigation of the Americans. It did not occur to them that perhaps I had expressed my convictions out of loyalty and in good faith.

Even at the writing of these lines, in 2013, when confrontation between Iran and the United States is at its peak, the diehard believers in the 'hidden hands', refuse to abandon their position. I suppose this line of thinking finds its parallel in other conspiracy theories such as: 9/11 destruction of the World Trade Centre and attack on Pentagon having been designed by the American Government or by Israel; or, the massacre of European Jews by the Nazis being a lie; or, the Egyptian pyramids having been built by aliens, etc. These are self-indulgent and mindless fantasies that capture the imagination of some people where rationality seems to find no space.

My grandfather Mohammad Reza Rais (Salar Moazzam).

My parents, Sediqe and Ebrahim Farhat (Amjad el-Molk), circa 1942.

Author at age 17.

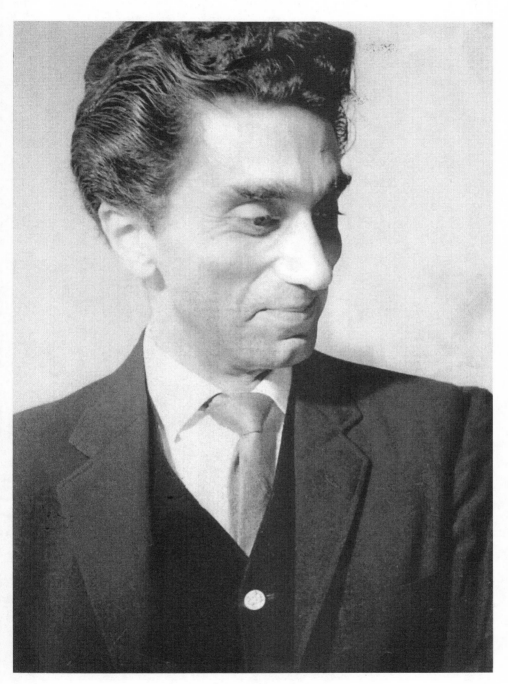

Author, circa. 1965.

Author at UCLA, 1959.

Judge Farhat.

Mantle Hood.

John Blacking,
1989.

With Slovenian musicologist Prof. Andrej Rijavec in Lublijana.

With ethnomusicologist Prof. Bruno Nettl in Dublin.

With my sister Fari and brothers Saeed, to my right, and Freydoon, to the left.

In New York City with pianist Alfred Brendel and philosopher Paul Boghossian.

With my long time friend, Romanian pianist Julien Musafia.

With Prof. Mantle Hood and Prof. Josef Pacholczyk at the
University of Maryland.

With former teacher and later colleague and friend Prof. Jan Popper in Dublin.

With my cousin composer Shahin Farhat, Gotenborg, Sweden, 2011.

With pianist Soheil Nasseri in New York.

With my wife Maria and Jamshid Khabir in Nice, 1980.

With my son Robert, 1999.

With my wife Maria, 2006

In Dublin, 2008.

With my wife Maria.

At home, 2014.

❧ 11 ❧

Exceptional People

In a long life lived across three continents, I have met and been friends with people of many backgrounds and peculiarities. On reflection, there have been five individuals who have carved indelible impressions in my memory for the uniqueness of their personalities. Two of them were close relations and three were among friends and colleagues. Not every aspect of their traits was necessarily praiseworthy, but their overall individuality posed the sort of distinctness that made them exceptional and memorable. I believe they have a place in this selected memoire and hope that the reader will find them of interest.

The Honorable Judge

My father had only one brother, Qolām Ali, who was his junior by 11 years; they had no sisters. In their personalities, the two brothers were very different. Father was basically gentle and retiring; his brother was rather severe and imperious. In his educational upbringing, my father Ebrāhim had followed the usual upper class Qājār period pattern of being taught mostly by tutors, and had entered into civil service in his late teens. He rose gradually to the high office of Director General in the Ministry of Finance. My uncle Qolām Ali had a more formal schooling, and had obtained a third level degree in law from an institution run by French professors in Tehran. He was employed by the Ministry of Justice, began as a public prosecutor and eventually rose in judicial ranks to become a member of Iran's Supreme Court.

Qolām Ali was a man of unimpeachable integrity. In a country where bribes, favoritism, nepotism, shirking responsibility and evasiveness were the norms of operation at all levels, he was a beacon of unwavering honesty and bluntness. Up to his forced early retirement in 1955, when he was only 58 years old, he had maintained an impeccable reputation as a judge, but also had made many enemies. Judge Farhat knew the laws of the country inside and out, he had a thorough command of the French language, had most beautiful hand writing, and was meticulous in his personal appearance. My uncle was of average height, light skinned and svelte; he was not a handsome man but was strikingly elegant. He had a collection of beautiful ties, wore well-tailored clothing and was always perfumed; as he passed by on the street for several meters the fragrance of his perfume permeated the air.

In the late 1930s Qolām Ali Farhat was the Chief Prosecuting Attorney of the Tehran Province. He had acted as the State's Counsel in the trial of the leaders of the outlawed Communist Party who had all been convicted and jailed or exiled. The Communist Party of Persia, called Tudeh (Masses) Party acted under direct Soviet instructions. When the British and the Russians invaded in August of 1941, and the country came under the occupation by the allied forces, he rightly feared some form of reprisal against his person by the Russians. Fortunately nothing came of this, despite the fact that the Tudeh Party came into open at that time and became an overt instrument of Soviet machination.

After the war had ended and the allies had abandoned their occupation of Persia, my uncle was appointed a member of the Supreme Court. In August of 1953, the government of Prime Minister Mohammad Mosaddeq, who had nationalized the oil industry, was brought down with a coup engineered by the CIA and MI6. Dr. Mosaddeq, who had defied the royal *farmān* dismissing him, was arrested and was to be tried for treason. The case against him was prepared by the prosecuting attorney and had eventually landed on judge Farhat's desk; he was to preside over the eventual trial. My uncle, who had spent considerable time studying the documents, evidently had remained ambivalent as to the legal force of all the evidence. In various meetings with the state's prosecutor he had posed certain questions that placed doubt on the outcome of the trial. I was in the United States at the time and I learned of the circumstance surrounding this case, years later, from my cousin Shāhin, one of my uncle's four sons. The State had been determined to prove Mosaddeq's guilt. Apparently, in order to appease judge Farhat and secure a guilty verdict, in private, he was offered all sorts of inducements, including the ambassadorship to France. He had refused and had remained adamant as to the weakness in the prosecutor's case, in seeking death penalty for treason. Consequently, the only way out was for my uncle to be induced to take early retirement. Eventually Mosaddeq was put on trial and was sentenced, in 1955, to be execut- ed. However, the Shah intervened and the sentence was commuted to lifetime house detention; he lived for another 12 years in his country estate and died in the autumn of 1967.

It was regrettable for the country to be deprived of the services of a highly capable and honest judge, but my uncle bore no resentments and lived the rest of his life attending to his two hobbies, a keen devo- tion to France and love of Persian music. He died peacefully of a sud- den heart attack in July of 1978 at age 81.

From the days when he was a student at the School of Law run by the French, Qolām Ali had developed an all-consuming admiration for all things French. In Persia, from the mid-19th century, French cul- ture and language had gained a position of prominence. This was in line with the general perception, in the 18th and 19th centuries, that French culture and language were the high points of European civiliza- tion. In the Russian Imperial court, and among the nobility in Russia, French was widely spoken. The same was true of the Prussian high society; even Frederick the Great spoke and wrote in French fluently. The smaller European powers all looked up to France as the source of scientific innovation and cultural advancement. French influence in Persia began with Nāsereddin Shah's first visit to Europe in 1873. This monarch, who ruled from 1848 to 96, was the first king of Persia to travel to Europe on official state visits. He had visited various European countries on three separate occasions. The Shah, and his courtiers, were impressed by France above all others. From that time on many children of aristocratic families were sent to France to be educated.

So my uncle's admiration for France was not unusual, but his attach- ment and loyalty was rather excessive. Prominent on the wall of his study was a map of France. On his desk, under a sheet of glass, was a map of Paris. He had a whole library of French books and read French novels all the time. From the time that I can remember – and that goes back to mid-1930s – he had a subscription to the glossy French magazine *L'Illustration*. This was a very posh weekly magazine; it was printed on magnificent paper; in addition to article on serious subjects it contained beautiful color pictures of paintings of the masters. These photographs were mounted on heavy grey paper, which could be lifted out of the magazine and placed in frames.

During the Second World War, most people of means had short wave radios and listened to the news as broadcast by either BBC or Radio Berlin; my uncle only listened to news from France. Both BBC and Berlin had daily news programs in Persian language. The French had no broadcasts in Persian language; that did not pose any problem as he understood French perfectly. The problem was that the French transmitters were not powerful enough to be heard in Tehran through ordinary radio sets, so he found and bought a very rare and powerful radio that could tune to Paris. Sadly, by the summer of 1940, less than a year after the war had begun, France succumbed to the might of Germany and was occupied by Nazi forces. To my uncle this was a calamity; from that time to the liberation of France in 1944, he would tune in the broadcasts from Radio Brazzaville in French Congo, which was held by the forces of the Free France and, for some reason had a very powerful transmitter.

From childhood I looked up to my uncle and loved him dearly; he also had a soft spot for me. Our homes were side by side in an alleyway just off of Shāhābād Avenue, very close to the Parliament Square. When I was a teenager, I used to go next door almost every day to spend some time with him. He asked me once if I would assist him in translating a book from French into Persian. He wanted my help merely to write down as he dictated his translation, which I was only too glad to do. I think I was no more than 14 at the time. The book was one of the lesser works of Jules Verne called *Un Hiver dans les Glassier du Nord*. (Most of Verne's more famous fiction were already translated and published in Persian.) I went to him every day for about an hour, he dictated and I wrote; we finished the book in about three months. For all I can remember, he never attempted to have his translation published, and I do not know what happened to the manuscript of this translated Jules Verne book that was in my handwriting.

Judge Farhat was a collector. He would take a fancy to a certain object and proceed to acquire a variety of that object, certainly beyond the numbers that could be seen as reasonable to anyone else. At one time he was collecting watches. Within a couple of years he had bought about a dozen quality Swiss watches: Longines, Omega, Universal, Patek Philippe, and Zenith were among his collections. For a period the interest in watches moved a step further and was focused on clocks. Numerous clocks of different shapes and sizes appeared in his house. Then, there was the long lasting fondness for elegant fountain pens. He was particularly fond of Mont Blanc pens that are among the finest and most expensive to this day. He also had the best of Parker and Shaffer pens. Altogether he came to possess more than a dozen beautiful pens, which he used alternatingly. He imported a special ink of unusual color from France the like of which I have not seen since. It had a unique color, something between mauve and brown. His handwriting, both in coursing Persian and in French, always stood out, not only for its beauty but also for its unusual color.

From a young age, my uncle bought perfumes from France by mail order. In those days, I don't believe there were any special men's perfumes or colognes. He simply purchased perfumes, if they were meant for women, it did not matter to him, he used them just the same. By the end of his life, his perfume collection, most of which I imagine had spoiled because of being too old, numbered in scores. I remember having heard the names of companies like Guerlain, Coty, Jean Patou, Lanvin and Lancome since childhood. My uncle's love of beautiful fragrance extended to cultivating roses. For a period he took interest in planting rose bushes in his garden. He was not interested in roses that were common to all gardens; he wanted roses of unusual colors. I was no more than ten years old but remember distinctly when he was showing my father an array of different colored rose bushes he had planted. There were red ones so dark as to be called black roses. There were roses of one color with fringe of a different color; also those with petals that were curled. He admired roses not only for their shape, size and color, but also for their splendid aroma that in the dry Persian air can be almost intoxicating.

Qolām Ali was a man of unwavering discipline. He woke up unfailingly at 5 in the morning. He would shave, check the thermometer at the end of his garden, write down the high and low of the temperature of the preceding 24 hours, and proceed to make himself the morning cup of coffee. He drank his coffee while listening to the radio. By 6.30 others in the household would be up and breakfast would be served. By that stage he was dressed and after a light breakfast of bread, cheese, soft-boiled eggs and tea, he would be on the way to his office. After retirement, he still followed the same routine except, instead of walking to the Ministry of Justice, which was at a distance of about two kilometers from his home, he would simply go for a walk lasting an hour.

My uncle's devotion to France and all things French bordered on the obsessive. When he made some extensive renovations in his old ancestral home and had his garden remodeled, he designed an ornamental pool for the garden in the shape of an F. This looked downright peculiar, particularly since the letter F is not symmetrical. I asked my cousin Shāhin one time about the pool, wondering if the F stood for the initial of our common surname; he said no, it stands for France.

In the spring of 1949 I was preparing to begin my journey to America to study music. The idea of overseas travel, apparently, had not occurred to my uncle; I was the first family member to do so. He was very intrigued by what I was about to do, which must have seemed an exceptionally adventurous move. Within a year of my departure, my uncle made his move to travel abroad; needless to say, his destination was France. Thereafter, at least once every year, he travelled to Paris. I do not believe that he ever went to any other city. He adored Paris and who can fault him for that. There was a hotel very close to the Etoile, off of Avenue Wagram, where he always stayed. One time, in June of 1970, when I was back in Persia and was living in Tehran, I took a vacation and travelled with him to Paris. We stayed at his customary hotel, which had a most disagreeable female concierge. I tried to convince him, on that trip, that he should try other hotels on his next visit. I doubt if he took my advice. Fortunately, a few years later, his youngest son Ali, moved to France for his university studies and rented a flat in Vincennes, just outside the eastern parameter of Paris. From that time, when my uncle came for his visits to Paris, he stayed at his son's flat and was immeasurably happier. On these Parisian sojourns, every day he took the metro to different destinations within the city, walked the streets and savored the beauty of that wonderful city in its every district. He went to the Louvre every Sunday and admired the treasures of this vast museum.

In the 1950s tape recorders had become widely available for sale. Within a few years my uncle had acquired half a dozen recorders of different size and quality. Tape recorder collection was an aspect of his love of Persian traditional music. He never took any interest in western music. My commitment to western classical music did not seem to impress him very much. When in 1960s his own son Shāhin took to the study of western music, my uncle still remained disinterested. But he had an abiding love of Persian music and proceeded to build a vast collection of recordings made from radio broadcasts. For many years the local radio station had daily programs of Persian classical music as performed by the most famous instrumentalists and singers. A program that was highly regarded went by the name, *Golhā-ye Rangarang* (multi-colored flowers). This was an immensely popular evening program, with the participation of distinguished artists. By the end of his life, my uncle had recorded hundreds of hours of *Golhā*, as it was endearingly called. He had a filing system where every detail of the content of each program was meticulously registered. They were classified by names of the participating artists, the particular *dastgāh* (modal system), and the date and length of each performance.

There were a few other habits that my uncle cultivated throughout his life, some of which had nothing to do with either France or Persian music. He kept a record of Tehran's daily maximum and minimum temperature, without fail. He had a very elaborate thermometer mounted on the back wall in his garden, where it was at no time exposed to sunlight. The thermometer had two connecting tubes with small needles sitting on the mercury on both sides. As the mercury rose on one side the needle would be pushed up and stay up when the mercury descended. On the other panel the needle would go down and remain on the lowest point of mercury's reading. Every morning, he went to the thermometer, read the highest and the lowest of the previous 24 hours temperature, as indicated by the position of the needles, and wrote them in notebooks. There was a tiny magnet hanging from the side of the thermometer with which he would move the two needles back in position on the two ends of the mercury. Once more the thermometer was ready for the reading of the high and low of the next 24 hours. For all I know, these highly accurate records of Tehran's daily temperature, from mid 1920s to his death in 1978, exist and are in his son Shāhin's possession. I doubt if the Iranian weather office has a comparable record going back to mid-twenties.

In the years after the end of World War II, somehow my uncle became a film buff. I am not sure how this came about but I must have had something to do with it since I loved movies from childhood and used to talk with him about the pictures I had seen. At some point in the mid 1940s, he ventured to a cinema to see a film with me and he was hooked. I remember summer afternoons when he and I would walk to one of the nearby cinemas to watch a movie together. He came to know the names of many movie stars of that era. He was particularly fond of beautiful actresses like Rita Hayworth, Maria Montez, Hedy Lamarr and Lana Turner. There was something a bit bizarre about sitting in a cinema with one of the most respected of the country's judges watching something like *Bathing Beauties* with Esther Williams and Red Skelton. But he was very comfortable about it and I enjoyed his company.

In the period of my return to Persia, from 1968 to 79, the close bond between my uncle and I was renewed. I used to visit him mostly on Friday afternoons. He had sold his old ancestral home in central Tehran. This was the house next door to my parental home where I had lived during my childhood and teen years. He had built a new house, on a property owned by his wife, in Farmāniye, in the Shemirān area in the foothills of the Alborz Mountains. This was a modernish sort of a house but furnished in a fully traditional way. As always I felt that he enjoyed my visits when we had congenial conversation about music, politics and France. By that stage he had developed a grudging admiration for America. I say grudging because my uncle basically resented the fact that France was no longer a major player on the world stage. That America had now overshadowed France and the rest of the European powers grieved him. Nevertheless, he appreciated that only America could stand in the way of soviet expansionism, which he deplored.

The last time I saw my uncle was in June of 1978, in Paris. In Persia, the revolution was in progress, gaining momentum by the day; my uncle was on his usual French holiday, staying with his son Ali a resident of Vincenne. This was near the end of my two years sabbatical leave from the University of Tehran. I was to return to Tehran by the summer's end. While in Paris, I saw my uncle every day; we walked the streets, visited art galleries and went to cinemas together. He returned to Tehran in early July; I remained in Paris. Only a few days later, a telephone call from his wife gave us the sad news of his sudden death. In retrospect, I feel that perhaps this very special man had died at the right time; he did not remain to see the grotesque outcome of the revolution in his beloved native country.

The Fallen Aristoctrat

Jamshid Khabir was my father's first cousin; his father and my grandfather were brothers. Jamshid was a slightly portly man of fair complexion and hazel green eyes with a permanent air of warmth and joviality about him. The Khabirs were wealthy and carried their aristocratic lineage with style. This was particularly true of Jamshid who was of a generous disposition, whereas some of his siblings were known to be exceptionally parsimonious. Although he had a rather limited formal education, in some respects, he was a cultured man and had impeccable good taste. He knew both French and English adequately and was reasonably familiar with Persian literature and music. His palatial home in Niāvarān, within a short walk of one of the Shah's palaces, nestled against the mountain foothills to the north of Tehran, was filled with beautiful rugs, paintings and other art objects.

Before my departure for the U.S., I knew Jamshid only slightly. He had been born in 1910, was much older than me and there had been very few occasions that we could have had any meaningful contact. The enduring childhood memory I have of Jamshid is of the trips we made to the family property in the Shahriyār region, some six kilometers south west of Tehran. This was a farming village with its surrounding land that had been jointly owned by my grandfather and his two siblings. After my grandfather's demise the joint owners were my great-uncle Kabir Saltane, my great-aunt Nimtaj Dowle, my father and uncle Qolām Ali. The property was quite sizable, estimated as 4 square kilometers. Within the village there were large tracks of vineyards, fruit orchards with apple, pear, fig, almond and walnut trees. In the fields around the village vegetable and melons, but most of all wheat, were cultivated.

Once or twice a year, the absentee landlords, my father, uncle and the Khabirs, would pay visits to their property. The ladies of the respective households would never accompany the men in these inspection visits, but the male teenagers of the families were permitted to join the party. I have vivid memories of these trips to our village Saidābād and remember Jamshid as the life of the party. He was a joy to be with, full of good humor and joviality, his presence was half the fun of going on these junkets. For my brother Manuchehr and my cousin Parviz, Jamshid's youngest sibling, and I there was the added delight of playing in this vast village that we figured to be our own, and the unlimited grape, fig and melons to eat. Saidābād was sold in the early 1950s and the memory of my childhood visits to 'our village', seems no more than a distant dream.

In the 1970s, when I was back in Persia, I came to know my cousin Jamshid well and saw him at least on weekly basis. By that time, he was in his early 60s; he was widely known as one of the capital's celebrated hosts. Every Friday, without fail, he had an open house where as many as forty guests would be wined and dined. There were regulars, some of whom were family members, but also included was a number of friends who had become permanent fixtures at these parties. In addition to the Friday dinners, there were occasions such as Nōruz (Persian New Year, 21st of March), his own birthday (5 May), his wife Marina's birthday, which coincided with Christmas, and any number other holidays that created an excuse for festivity. Most dazzling of all were the Christmas/ Marina celebrations when as many as 200 guests were entertained with live music, dancing and lavish food and drinks.

Among Jamshid's friends who frequented his parties were a large number of foreign diplomats. It was at these gatherings that I came to know ambassadors from the U.S.A., United Kingdom, Argentina, Norway, Greece and Italy, among others. I recall having long conversations with Richard Helms, former Head of the CIA, who was the American envoy to the Iranian Imperial Court in mid 70s, and with Sir Anthony Parsons, his British counterpart. I was rather surprised to find Ambassador Helm very interested in classical music, which he discussed with me at some length. Some very prominent local politicians also were often seen at Jamshid's parties including both serving and ex ministers of the government, parliamentarians, senators, etc. One of the Shah's brothers, Prince Ahmad Rezā and his wife, also, were occasionally present.

In his younger days, Jamshid had worked in the Ministry of Finance where my father who was a high official of the Ministry had found him a suitable post. By the time he was in his late 40's, due to his aristocratic lineage and connections, he had been appointed as the Chief Secretary to Prince Abdol Rezā, one of the Shah's other brothers; he was also one of the king's civil adjutants. These were positions of prestige and influence without any significant stipend; to the adjutancy, in fact, no salary was attached.

Most wealthy Persians, over the years and particularly during the prosperous 1970s, had placed some of their fortune in banks outside the country. To my knowledge, Jamshid had never done so. Although he did occasionally travel abroad, contrary to most other Persian grandees, he did not particularly enjoy travelling; to him there was no place more comfortable and desirable than Tehran where he lived a life of luxury among family and friends.

In the early autumn of 1978 Jamshid and his wife Marina had a number of invitations to visit friends and relatives in the U.S. They left Tehran in early November with every intention of returning after two months. Meantime the revolution, which had begun in January of that year, had grown in momentum and scale; by autumn it had become massive and inextinguishable. After their visit to America, on their way back home, the Khabirs had come to France. As the news from home steadily indicated worsening conditions, they decided to remain in Paris and to see how the events would unfold. On the 16th of January 1979, the Shah left his kingdom, and two weeks later, on the 1st of February, Āyatollāh Khomeini returned from exile to triumphant reception by a tumultuous public, who by that stage had championed him as the leader of a revolution in which he had had no physical participation.

Jamshid believed that he had no reason to fear a return to his home and property. Yet, other Persians in Paris at the time judged the situation back home as volatile and unpredictable; they persuaded him to wait and see how things would turn out. Meantime the country was witnessing a hideous convulsion. The last government of the monarchy under Prime Minister Shapur Bakhtiār collapsed on the 11th of February and Āyatollāh Khomeini emerged as the virtual dictator. Major personalities who had been in positions of power in the fallen monarchy were being arrested, submitted to cursory trials and summarily executed. Lists of individuals, purportedly having taken huge sums out of the country, were daily published in the papers. Some of them had been wealthy and powerful figures and might indeed have had large assets abroad. Others were possibly quite innocent of the charges brought against them in the papers. Jamshid's name also appeared on a list one day as having transferred out of the country the sum of $40,000,000. Every one who knew Jamshid also knew that he did not have that kind of money; I don't believe that his entire assets amounted to a quarter of the amount he was alleged to have moved abroad. In fact, soon it became clear that he had no bank accounts outside Iran. The claim was a sheer calumny but those were not the times one could expect fairness and honesty.

Aside from the spurious accusation of having moved a fortune abroad, the charge against Khabir, were he to return home, would have been his well-known life style. On that score, according to the thinking of the clerics who had taken charge of the country, he was undoubtedly guilty. To them, he was the very personification of 'mofsed-e fel arz', (the corruptor of the earth). In fact, within a few days of the clerical ascendency, all his property, his magnificent home in Niāvarān and the belongings therein were confiscated; his bank accounts and even his stately Cadillac were impounded. There was no question that, had he returned home, he would have been immediately incarcerated and sent to the firing squad shortly thereafter. So, Jamshid and his wife Marina remained in France. They had some funds with them for their travels, and relatives in Iran were able to send them, by circuitous means, small amounts, from time to time. A couple who had enjoyed a princely life-style in their own country were reduced to poverty over night.

After a few weeks in Paris the Khabirs moved to Nice. There, they found a one-room apartment to rent on the Premenade des Anglais. The room was provided with a bed that came down from a closet in the wall; they also had a small kitchen and a bathroom. For them, this was a descent of biblical proportions. Nevertheless, they managed to remain cheerful; they never complained. Their tiny apartment was on the ground floor of a large building; it faced the sea and had a small garden in front, which they kept full of flowers. By the mid 80s, a large community of self-exiled Persians had gathered in and around Nice. Among them were some old friends of the Khabirs whose little garden had become the hub of the expatriates' congregation.

Marina was the daughter of the industrialist Dr. Ossip Friedlieb, the patriarch of a very distinguished German family. He was a corporation lawyer and entrepreneur who had been active in pre-revolutionary Russia and was married to a Russian lady of nobility. He had travelled far and wide and was known and respected even in America. In the 1930s, Dr Friedlieb was brought to Persia, by the government of Rezā Shah, in order to take charge of a project for the establishment of the national tobacco monopoly. Later, he was also responsible for the creation of the first insurance company in Iran. His children, including Marina, had lived in the lap of luxury from the day they were born. Now she and her aristocratic husband lived their remaining years, without rancor, in a one room flat. Marina died of a heart attack in 1984, at age 66. Jamshid lived on and managed on his own until December of 1994.

He was 84 when he died. He went to sleep one night and did not wake up the next morning, a peaceful end of a courageous man whom extreme adversity could not defeat. He did not deserve the harsh fate he endured in the final 15 years of his life. But if fairness and just rewards were meted out in this life, then surely men would not have thought of inventing heaven and hell.

I went to Nice three times to see the Khabirs. On my first visit in the summer of 1980, they were very hopeful that the Islamic Republic, which had just been proclaimed in Iran, would not survive the year; they expected their exile to be short lived. When, in the September of that year, Iraqi forces under Saddam Hussein invaded Iran, the Khabirs, and most other Persians who had fled the beloved homeland fearing for their lives, were sure that Iraq had started the war at the instigation of the Americans, and felt certain that it would end with the destruction of the Islamic Republic. But that was not to be. In fact, the eight years of this war consolidated the tenuous hold that initially the clerics had on the country. Disunity and fractiousness that existed within the structure of the fledgling theocracy, in the face of aggression by the enemy outside, were replaced by unity of all competing elements. The suffering and destruction that Persia suffered in that long war, with no less than half a million in fatalities, was God sent for the clerics to whom death and destruction paved the road to paradise.

The second time I visited Nice was in the spring of 1986. Marina had died two years before. Jamshid, at 76, was living alone but gave every indication of managing his precarious existence cheerfully. His little garden remained the hub of Persian expatriates' gathering. The last I saw him was in the spring of 1991. His son Teddy, his daughter Vicky, one of his sisters, a niece with her husband, and some old friends were in town. He invited them all to a dinner party in my honor; he cooked the meal himself. Warmth and good humor never left him. This was a man of superior strength of character; some faulted him for his frivolity and worldliness, but no one doubted that Jamshid's presence, at all times, exuded happiness.

The Tempestuous Greek

Of all the people I have known in my long life, undoubtedly the most peculiar was Philip Kalavros, a dermatologist of Greek origins whom I first met in 1959. It was in the spring of that year, a few months after my return from Persia, where I had spent a year and half for research on traditional urban music. One afternoon I received a phone call from a man with a heavy accent who introduced himself as Dr. Kalavros. He said that at a gathering, the night before, he had learned about me from a mutual acquaintance and that he wished very much to meet me. Naturally, I asked in what connection had he become interested in getting to know me. He explained that he is a medical doctor and was very keen to learn about the life and works of Avicenna (Ebn-e Sina) and that he thought I could help him. I told him that his interest in the 11th century Persian physician was, I imagine, related to the great scholar's writings on medical science, about which I knew nothing. Moreover, I informed him that I only knew of Avicenna's writings on music theory and on music therapy. I made it clear that I was no authority on this renowned medieval sage. Nevertheless, Dr. Kalavros insisted that since he knew that I had just returned from Persia he would like to meet me as he planned to make a trip to that country very soon. I accepted and we agreed on a date for the meeting. As to the place, I proposed that we might meet, for a cup of coffee, in UCLA, where I spent most days working both as a Teaching Assistant and a doctoral student.

Dr. Kalavros suggested that instead, if not inconvenient to me, he would like to have me go to his house for lunch on that date. I accepted and on the agreed date drove to his house, whose address he had given me. At the appointed hour, which was one in the afternoon, I arrived at his house in Encino, a suburb of Los Angeles. I rang the doorbell a few times, but there was no response. On a calling card I wrote that per your invitation I was here at one o'clock, but you were not at home.

That night, Dr. Kalavros telephoned and offered profuse apologies. He went on to explain that an emergency call had come through and he had been summoned to hospital for an operation; he had instructed his secretary to telephone and inform me accordingly, but that regrettably she had failed to make the call. It was a satisfactory explanation as I felt that the life of a medical doctor is such that understandably this sort of emergency can arise. We made another arrangement for our first meeting, this time in coffee shop close to UCLA, and I finally did meet Philip Kalavros.

It was much later, when I had come to know him well, that I learned that he was actually a dermatologist; the likelihood of someone with his expertise being called to hospital for an emergency was very remote indeed. By that time, I knew Philip Kalavros for what he was, a well-meaning but absentminded and thoroughly unreliable man. Nevertheless, there was something very engaging about this man who, in his early 40s, was handsome, opinionated and passionate with an explosive temper. He seemed infatuated with fantasies about my native country, which to him was a place in the fabled world of A Thousand and One Nights. Persia of his imagination was not very realistic but was touchingly romantic, which I found quite endearing.

Unfortunately, Philip was also a man of far reaching prejudices; he disliked blacks, Jews, Catholics, Baptists, Mormons, and most of all he hated the Turks. He used to say the Turks have given nothing to the world but misery. They have produced no culture of originality and have had no great men. Of course I disputed all these claims, but he would not yield. Once I said that he surely would accept that Mustafa Kemal 'Ataturk' was a man of vision and a great leader for his country. He shook his head, smiled sardonically, and said: 'Hormoz, you obviously don't know that Mustafa Kemal was in fact by origins a Greek'. Philip also seemed to disapprove of everything about America, which made it difficult to understand why he had chosen to come to live and work there.

In time, I learned that he had been born in 1918 in the island of Rhodes, a Greek possession off the coast of Turkey. Rhodes is a Greek island but for centuries it had been part of the Ottoman Empire. It was ceded to Italy following the brief Turko-Italian war in 1912. The island was finally united with Greece in 1947. Philip had his childhood during the period that Rhodes was under Italian administration. Later, he had gone to Italy and had received his medical training at the

University of Pisa. He had come to the U.S. in mid 1940s and had his internship and specialization training in Texas. When I first met him he had a partnership practice in Beverly Hills. According to him, some of his clients were movie stars.

The friendship that developed between Philip and me was riddled by mishaps and down right bizarre events. Two years after our first meeting, when I received my first full-time academic appointment in 1961, at California State University in Long Beach, he insisted that he wished to throw a party to celebrate the occasion. He telephoned one day, proposed the idea of a party at his house and suggested Saturday night in the following week. I was engaged on that night and told him so. He then suggested the Friday night, which was acceptable. He also indicated that he was going to invite a number of Hollywood starlets to the party.

On the appointed evening, I drove to his house in Encino, which appeared to be in total darkness. I rang the bell; there was no answer. By that stage in our friendship, I was familiar with Philip's habits and knew that he spent much of his time in his vast orchard behind the house, where he also kept a goat for its milk. I went to the side door, which led to the orchard and knocked several times on the door. Finally, I heard footsteps; he opened the door. Looking rather disheveled, with surprise mixed with display of joviality, he asked me to come in. I kept saying that evidently he did not expect me. After the initial denial, eventually he said, it is great to see you but it is a pity that the party is arranged for tomorrow night. I had to remind him of our telephone conversation and the fact that we had agreed on Friday night, as I was unable to accept the invitation for Saturday. While cheerfully disputing the outcome of that conversation, he kept saying that he is always glad to see me and that I am very welcome but sadly his other guests are going to come tomorrow night. Not much time had passed, as we argued, before the doorbell began to ring and guests began to arrive. In fact, he had invited a large number of people for Friday night, but had forgotten all about it. The poor man kept running to the phone to call a nearby restaurant ordering food to be delivered to the house.

In maintaining a relationship with Philip, this sort of mishap, unfortunately, became quite routine. He had been married at some point in his younger days, but the marriage had been short lived. He had no real friends and was a lonely man. Countless times he would telephone and practically invite himself to my home for dinner, but would not show up. He would never bother to explain, and if the matter would come up later in conversation, he would deny the whole thing.

Early in 1962, Philip made a trip to Persia. I had given him names and whereabouts of a number of people in Tehran who would be able to assist him with his research project on Avicenna. I gave him, also, names and addresses of my parents and a few other relatives whom he could meet and receive any help that he may require. He had spent a few weeks in Persia, had been lavishly entertained by some of my relatives, had travelled to different cities within the country, but had done absolutely nothing in respect of research on Avicenna. On his return to California, I found him more than ever in love with Persia, but none the wiser about Avicenna.

In 1963, Philip Kalavros was in a romantic relationship with Linda Darnell, the popular movie star of the 30s and 40s. By the early 60s Miss Darnell's popularity had waned and her movie career was in decline. According to him, they were engaged and were to marry soon. One day he telephoned and said that he would like me to meet Linda. They both arrived that night at my house in the town of Bellflower, close to Long Beach, where I was living at the time. I found Miss Darnell to be a modest and very friendly woman; she was only forty years old and very attractive. We had a pleasant evening together. Sadly, the marriage did not take place; she had serious drinking problems and he was tempestuous and domineering. Two years after the night Philip brought her to my house I heard from the news broadcasts that she had perished in a fire at the home of a friend she was visiting in Chicago.

Philip was an avid reader; he knew major Italian, French and Russian literary works; he was particularly fond of the writings of Balzac, Turgenev and Dostoyevsky. He was also interested in philosophy and in 1963 published a small volume of philosophical essays titled *Pose and Jealousy*. The essays were mainly about pretentiousness and envy, replete with personal observations and conclusions drawn by a highly intolerant and prejudiced mind. This book was published by the New York Philosophical Library, but I don't believe it received much commercial distribution. He kindly presented me with a signed copy of it. About classical music Philip knew nothing but he loved Argentine tangos. He asked me repeatedly why I didn't compose some tangos; my explanation that I was not in that line of work never seemed to satisfy him.

From 1968 to 76, when I had returned to Persia, and was active as the Head of the Music Department at University of Tehran, my contact with Philip Kalavros was largely broken, except for rare correspondence. He was no good at letter writing. Occasionally he sent me a photograph of the sunset over the Pacific Ocean with some illegible writing on the back. For two years, from early summer of 1976 to the September of 78, I was on sabbatical leave; part of that period was spent in Europe (Britain, Holland and France), and for several months I was back in the U.S. I lived in a small rented flat in Long Beach, California, and was working on two commissions, for compositions, I had received for the Tehran Symphony Orchestra and the NIRT Chamber Orchestra.

While in California, my contact with Dr. Kalavros was re-established. All evidence indicated that his medical practice had declined; he was not working in any hospital and he had no private practice. The man who used to be quite dapper appeared poorly and untidily dressed. His house in Encino was gone; he was living in a rented bachelor apartment, adjoining a garage, in the back of a house in Santa Monica. He seemed quite lonely and wished to see me often, although I lived at a considerable distance to him. Unfortunately, not only did old habits persist, he had become even more eccentric. Frequently he would ask to see me, specify the place and the time, but would not show up. Repeatedly he stood me up in the coffee shop of the Miramar Hotel in Santa Monica, where I had to drive some 40 miles to reach. At times, humble apologies and fabricated excuses would follow, at other times no explanation or acknowledgement.

It was in April 1977, Philip telephoned one day and insisted that
I take a break from my work and go with him to the northern parts
of the State and see a property he had bought in the vicinity of Santa
Cruz. The arrangement was for me to meet him in Santa Monica at the
Miramar Hotel Coffee Shop at 12 noon. If we were to start our journey to Santa Cruz at about that time we should reach our destination
by early nightfall. He did not show up at noon. About an hour later,
a waiter came and told me I was wanted on the telephone. Philip was
on the line with apologies about some emergency that has kept him
and assured me that he will arrive within the hour. I ordered lunch and
waited. It was 3.30 when he appeared with profuse apologies and sat
to have a cup of coffee. It was clearly too late to begin the trip which
would have lasted about eight hours. When I proposed that we should
abandon the project he was offended; he insisted that I could spend the
night at his apartment nearby and that we could begin the trip in early
morning. Foolishly I accepted.

I left my car on the street near the Miramar and we drove to Philip's
place of residence in his car. Dr. Kalavros's rented apartment, in the
back of a garage of a house, turned out to be a single large room filled
with countless boxes. What all these boxes contained I don't know,
but many of them seemed to be filled with books. They were piled on
top of each other and covered, waist high, so much of the surface of
the room that only narrow irregular pathways remained leading to the
small kitchen and to the filthy bathroom. Moreover, I noticed, here
and there, trails of ants crawling over the boxes. There was a bed in
one corner with crumpled and unclean beddings strewn over it; and,
somewhere between the boxes there was a folding type cot for me to
sleep on. Clearly, I was trapped in a highly unsavory situation that I
had to endure till morning. We had agreed to an early departure. After
a most uncomfortable sleepless night, I was up and ready to go at 7 in
the morning. But Philip was asleep; it took two hours before we got
on the road.

The trip north was interrupted by two stops for breakfast and lunch
and by a traffic policeman who stopped him at some point on the highway for driving too slowly on the left lane, which is designated for pass-

ing. In fact, I had already pointed out to him a number of times that he was driving in the wrong lane, which he chose to ignore. He argued with the policeman and received a citation as a result. For several minutes afterwards, I heard nothing but his angry monologue lambasting America and the Americans. We arrived in Santa Cruz at dusk. Philip drove to a motel where, evidently, he always stayed when visiting that area; he asked for a room with two beds and I spent a second uncomfortable night in the company of my irascible friend.

The next day Philip took me to see the property he had bought outside the city of Santa Cruz. This was ostensibly the whole purpose of the trip. What I saw was a track of land overgrown with a variety of bushes and weeds. That was it. When I asked what he intended to do with this land, he said that he has not yet decided. After this pointless viewing of his property we headed back south towards Los Angeles. About one in the afternoon we had reached the vicinity of San Luis Obispo, which is midway between the San Francisco Bay area and Los Angeles. At that point he veered the car away from the highway onto a side road, then turned to a narrow dirt road that climbed a hill. After a few miles the track ended at a wired fence, nestled in the folds of steep hills sparsely covered with tall cacti. On the fence, at intervals, there were placed 'No Trespassing' sings. He stopped the car and told me with some apologies that he always comes to this spot to pick some prickly pears, a kind of fruit that grows on some cacti. He asked to be excused for a few minutes, assuring me that he will be back shortly. He opened the trunk of the car and took out a large bucket, a knife and some thick gloves; he climbed over the wire fence and disappeared into the undulating hills beyond.

As minutes passed, and his absence seemed inordinately long, I began to worry if something had happened to him. Could he have fallen through some gully; perhaps beyond the fence is private property, what if he has gotten into some sort of trouble for trespassing. I sat in his car becoming increasingly vexatious and anxious as to what could have happened to him. Exactly an hour and half later a sweaty Dr. Kalavros reappeared carrying the bucket full of prickly pears. When I told him that instead of a few minutes he had me waiting for 90 minutes, he

simply denied that it had taken that long. As to the fruit he had picked
– filched for I could tell – they were coved with very sharp thorns. It
was enough to touch them to have one's hand pierced by countless
furry needles that remained in the flesh. He proceeded to peel a few,
using his heavy gloves and a knife. He ate them heartily; I refused to
have anything to do with his prickly pears.

Philip and I continued to meet occasionally during the spring and
summer of 1978. Increasingly, he displayed ever more eccentric behavior. I had not known him to be miserly; now he was showing frugality
bordering on mania. When we went to a restaurant to have a meal he
would order only a cup of soup or a small plate of salad. When I would
ask why he is so abstemious, he would say he had just eaten before
coming to see me. At one time he raised a fuss, in a coffee shop, about
the cost of a cup of coffee. On a number of occasions, in a restaurant,
he took left over items such as crackers or buns that were left uneaten at
the table next to where we were sitting, after the party at that table had
departed. His sudden cat-like pounce to take such items from a nearby
table both amazed and embarrassed me. But he thought nothing of it
and gave no explanation. He always asked the waitress for sachets of
honey for the tea he would order. He never used the honey in his tea
but placed the sachets in his pocket.

A few years later, when I was living in Belfast, Northern Ireland, and
was teaching at the Queen's University in that city, Philip wrote to me
that he was going to visit his sister in Greece and that he intended to
come to London for a few days on his way back to the U.S. I wrote to
him asking him to fly to Belfast from London, if he could, and spend
a couple of days there as my guest. He seemed delighted with the idea
and promised to come. On the day he was to arrive I went to the airport to receive him. He did not show up. There was no phone call,
no letter, and no explanation of any kind. A few days later a parcel,
the size of a shoebox, arrived by post in my name. Inside, there were
about a hundred or more little sachets of honey with the names and
addresses of different California coffee shops printed on them. Some of
the little containers had been torn and the whole box was a gooey mess
of honey and plastic. This was a gift that Philip had brought all the

way from California, presumably taken to Greece and then to London, from whence it had been mailed to me in Belfast.

I did not see Philip Kalavros again. For a few years, after I had moved to Dublin, I received occasional postcards from him, the last one of which was received in 1991; thereafter there were no further communications. In summer of 93, when I was in Los Angles, I made every effort to find him without success. His telephone was cut off and his post box address was no longer in his name. More recently, attempting to find out something about him through the internet, I have learned that he has passed away, which deeply saddened me. He was the most eccentric person I have ever known. Although totally unreliable, I liked him for his individuality. He was a passionate, opinionated and angry man. This is not a happy combination, but it did make him a peculiarly interesting man.

The Creative Pioneer

In September of 1955, after two years at Mills College, where I earned an M.A. in Musical Composition, I returned to UCLA to begin work toward a PhD. At that time, very few universities conferred PhDs in composition; that degree had to be obtained through research and not creative work. For the topic of this thesis, which had to be done at some point in the future, I was entertaining the idea of research on the works of one of the Spanish composers of the Renaissance (Morales, Cabezon, or Guerrero) whose music I found particularly appealing.

Within the first few weeks of the academic year 55-56, I met Dr. Mantle Hood who was one of the new members of the music faculty. He had received a BA degree and an MA from UCLA only a few years earlier, after which he had gone to Holland and had finished a doctoral degree under the supervision of Jaap Kunst, the eminent authority on Javanese music. His dissertation on the modal concept of *pathet* in gamelan music of Java had been published and had received much praise. On coming back to UCLA as a faculty member, he had set about to create courses on non-western musical traditions, a branch of musicology that was becoming known as the field of ethnomusicology.

In the course of numerous conversations I had with Dr. Hood he convinced me that it would be far more valuable for me to do research on the music of my own native country than to produce a thesis on 16th century Spanish music. His argument rested on the fact that there already were recognized authorities on Spanish music, whereas not much was known in the western world about Persian music. Appreciating the reasonableness of his argument, I made extensive investigation as to the availability of sources for research on Persian music. Surprisingly, it came to light that virtually no books had ever been written on this music in western languages. The few encyclopaedia and dictionary articles on the subject were risibly brief and erroneous. For example, Groves Dictionary of Music and Musicians, 1955 edition, had a two columns article written by Henry George Farmer, who was a scholar of Arabian music and viewed Persian music as subsidiary to Arabian music. Moreover, his article was essentially descriptive of medieval theories and was irrelevant to contemporary practices.

As I became convinced that I should do research on Persian music for my doctoral thesis, I moved into Mantle Hood's orbit. There were a number of other postgraduate students who had settled on research projects on the music of different cultures, notably Indian, Indonesian, Thai, Chinese and Japanese musical traditions. We formed a group of about half a dozen students, the earliest pupils of Mantle Hood, with whom the beginnings of the ethnomusicology program at UCLA were founded. Within a few years some members of this group made field trips to the countries whose music they wanted to study. In time, they returned with research material they had collected and contributed to the formation of the Institute of Ethnomusicology, in the 1960s, of which Dr. Hood was the Director.

The institute, under Hood's direction made remarkable progress. By mid 1960s there were a number of eminent scholars affiliated with its program. Notable among them was Charles Seeger, a towering intellect with a multi-faceted musical background as composer, musicologist, organizer, and all around music activist whose contributions went back to the pre-First World War era. There was also the striking figure of Colin McPhee, Canadian composer and authority on Balinese music.

His orchestral *tour de force*, Tabu Tabuan, remains one of the most effective blends of modern composition with elements of Balinese gamelan music. Another important figure among those who conducted seminars for ethnomusicology students was Professor Klaus Waxmann, an eminent scholar of Indian music. The assembly of this remarkable group of scholars, and their contributions to weekly seminars at the Institute, were entirely due to Mantle Hood's industriousness.

In addition to staff members, some of the students who had returned from fieldwork were contributing to the creation of courses on the music of their areas of expertise. They organized lectures as well as workshops where practical lessons were given on the performance of musical instruments from different parts of the world. There were workshops on music from India, Thailand, China, Japan, Ghana, Greece and Mexico. My own involvement with the Institute's program, after returning from Iran in 1959, was in the establishment of a Persian music study group. My study group, composed of 6 members each playing a different instrument, participated in UCLA's Festival of Oriental Music in 1960, by presenting a whole concert of Persian traditional music.

The most important of the Institute's Study Groups were those of Javanese and Balinese gamelans. In late 1950s, Mantle Hood had taken a sabbatical leave from teaching and had spent a year in Indonesia. On his return to the U.S., he had imported a large array of gamelan instruments from both Java and Bali. In addition, he had also brought to UCLA a number of professional native musicians from Indonesia. A vast area in the basement of the Music Building (The Schoenberg Hall) was taken over by the Gamelan instruments, both Javanese and Balinese. The total number of instruments exceeded one hundred. The activity of the gamelan ensembles involved dozens of members who participated in weekly rehearsals and occasional concerts. These were the real showcases for the Institute of Ethnomusicology and attracted a great deal of well-deserved attention.

Mantle Hood attended every rehearsal and played different instruments in both the Javanese and the Balinese gamelans. Most often he played the *rebab* (spiked fiddle), which, with a flute, are the only two sustained tone instruments in the gamelan formation. The *rebab* is difficult to master and its role is to improvise on the main theme as played by the ensemble. Not all the members of the gamelans were music students. The enchanting sound produce by both Javanese and Balinese gamelan had attracted a number of interested individuals from the community at large who attended rehearsals without fail. Individual instruments are not difficult to learn; it is the ensemble participation that requires skill and produces a glorious sound. There were about thirty people, students and non-students, the membership of the two gamelans. They rehearsed once a week each, between 8 and 10 at night, and gave frequent concerts.

By late 1960s, Mantle Hood had developed the Institute of Ethnomusicology into a position of prominence that almost overshadowed the Music Department of which it was supposed to be a mere appendage. This was certainly true given the number of postgraduate students who were in the ethnomusicology program. The work of the Institute was receiving more national attention than other activities within the Department. As of 1968, I was back in Persia and had no more affiliations with UCLA, but I had learned that by early 1970s Mantle was facing considerable opposition and even hostility from his colleagues in the Music Department. More than any member of the music faculty, he had given the Music Department of UCLA international recognition. This had no doubt caused some unease among his colleagues, some of whom had little regard for his area of musical interest. Some of the hostility was no doubt rooted in resentment for his close relation with the University's administration, the preferential treatment he was deservedly receiving, and the rapid growth of the Institute under his leadership. He had been given two accelerated promotions; within eight years, from a beginning as an Assistant Professor in 1954, he was a full Professor in 62.

In 1973, Mantle Hood took early retirement and, for a few years, moved to Hawaii. From that time the Institute of Ethnomusicology at UCLA began its steady decline, which to some extent was the unspoken wish of some members of the Music Department. The Institute was abolished in the 80s and the ethnomusicology program at UCLA no longer has the high reputation that it once enjoyed.

I remained in contact with Mantle after his retirement from UCLA. In 1971, as a member of the Music Committee of the Shirāz Festival, I instigated an invitation to Dr. Hood to attend the Festival of that year as one of our distinguished guests. I invited, also, another ethnomusicologist friend, Jose Maseda of the Philippines. Mantle enjoyed his time in Shirāz, was greatly impressed by Persepolis, and took part in a round table discussion on the importance of ethnic studies in contemporary musicology. He was also interviewed on television. With his distinguished grey hair and moustache, he was a great hit. His stylish presence and command of the English language, as I had known from years ago, impressed his audience. He even had occasion to have a brief discussion with Empress Farah about the creation of a center for the study of world music in Iran.

When I moved to Dublin as the Professor of Music and Head of the School of Music at Trinity College, I was able to invite Hood to our School for a seminar which was well received by the staff and students. Late in the 1980s, I saw him once when he was Regis Professor at the University of Maryland. On that occasion he had reciprocated by inviting me to give a seminar at his university. In the 1986, the Government of Indonesia honored him with the title of Ki, which I understand is something equal to knighthood, and in 2002, the University of Koln bestowed on him an Honorary Doctorate.

The last time I saw Mantle Hood was in October of 2004. I was visiting friends and relatives in the Washington D.C. area. He was then 86 years old, was living with his wife Hazel in Ellicott City, Maryland, not far from D.C. I drove there and spent 24 hours with them. We had a grand time reminiscing about the old days at UCLA. There were faint signs of Alzheimer in his speech and behavior, but on the whole he seemed to be in good form. For a few months after that last meeting he kept in contact by sending me occasional emails. Early in 2005 the emails stopped. In May I telephoned to see how he was; he simply could not understand who was on the line. Hazel was not at home and Mantle was totally incoherent. Two months later the news reached me that he had passed away.

Mantle Hood was a very remarkable individual. His appearance made an immediate impression; he had a presence. He was not handsome but was very striking. From the first time I saw him, when he was 37 to the last at 86, he looked more or less the same. He always had grey hair, the same British lordly moustache and mischievous blue eyes. He wore distinctive clothes that invariably caught the attention. His shoes were always different from what most men wear; he favored tan colored suede half boots. He was a smoker and had a collection of beautiful of pipes. Mantle never showed ill-temper, always spoke in a measured manner. He had an admirable command of the English language and wrote beautifully. When he took early retirement and left UCLA to spend a few years in Hawaii, and particularly during his final years in Maryland, he devoted his time to writing fiction. He published half a dozen very readable novels; he also published an autobiography. I am very pleased that in our last get together he gave me copies of all these books, souvenirs that I cherish.

In his youth, Mantle Hood had been interested in jazz. He had told me that he played the clarinet as a teenager and participated in jazz ensembles in his native Springfield, Illinois. Later, he had also tried his hand at composition. Before being attracted to ethnic music he had aimed at a career as a composer. For a number of years he had studied with Ernest Toch, one of many well-known German composers who fled their homeland, after the Nazi take over, and ended up in the U.S. I had heard a very impressive string quartet that he had written as a student. I also heard an orchestral piece of his called *Vernal Equinox*, performed, in the early 1960s, by the UCLA Symphony Orchestra. But, as he had become increasingly involved with the cause of ethno-musicology, composition no longer was at the forefront of his mind.

Mantle Hood had his detractors. At UCLA, he moved fast and created waves, to the discomfiture of some who envied him. His books and articles on ethnomusicology were highly original; as such, they were not universally endorsed. But he had a creative mind; he was a pioneer and an effective organizer. He made immense contributions to the advancement of ethnomusicology as an academic discipline. The Institute of Ethnomusicology at UCLA was entirely his creation and at its high point, under his directorship, was the world's liveliest center for research and study of non-western musical traditions at university level.

On a personal level, Mantle was one of the very few who made an impact on the course of my life. He persuaded me to study Persian music in which I had no particular interest. By so doing my musical horizon was expanded. Moreover, my research, as published in my writings, I believe, has made a contribution to the clarification of major issues on the theory of scales, intervals and the modal system of this music. And, if I am right in so believing, then it is all owed to Mantle Hood.

The Magnificent Englishman

In the spring of 1973, when I was the Head of the Music Department at University of Tehran, I had a visitor in my University office. He introduced himself as Dr. John Bailey, a lecturer in ethnomusicology at the Queen's University of Belfast in Northern Ireland. He informed me that his University was in the process of creating an extensive program in ethnomusicological studies within the Department of Social Anthropology, headed by Professor John Blacking. I had heard John Blacking's name but knew nothing about his work and had not read his writings. Dr. Bailey himself was interested in Afghan music and had come to Persia for a brief stay, on his way to Afghanistan, where he proposed to remain for six months in order to do research on the traditional music of that country. He had read some of my writings on Persian music and, knowing that Afghan music is bound to have fundamental connections with Persian sources, wished to have a few sessions of discussion with me.

John Bailey and I met a few times and then he proceeded to move to Afghanistan. About a year later, I received a letter from Professor Blacking inviting me to his University in Belfast in order to conduct a series of seminars on Persian music. He had proposed a full term of teaching which, given my obligations in Tehran, I could not accept. Further correspondence resulted in my consenting to a four weeks long engagement, involving presentation of three seminars per week, on all aspects of Persian traditional music. The date we agreed on was January of 1975, after the Christmas/New Year holidays. This invitation, from a man I had never met, was clearly as a result of the contact that John Bailey, a member of John Blacking's department, had established with me during his visit to Tehran.

Early in January of 1975, I arrived in Belfast and was met at the airport by the very tall and handsome Professor Blacking. He was very warm and friendly and I felt immediately comfortable with him. Over the following weeks, as I got to know John better, I found him to be an extremely well informed person. He was interested in everything and had vast musical knowledge. He had in depth familiarity with many non-western musical cultures; but he was equally well informed in western classical music. In time, I learned that he was a highly ac-complished pianist who gave periodic piano recitals. From the first en-counter in the Belfast airport John and I felt close to one another and in the course of the four weeks I spent in Belfast we became very good friends.

In the evenings, John frequently entertained me at his home. I came to know his lovely and accomplished wife Zureena, a South African medical doctor of Indian origins. Also, I became friends with a num-ber of his academic colleagues including the excellent Cyril Ehrlich, an Economics Professor and a serious music scholar. Some years later, Cyril published an important book on the history of piano and an-other one on the history of music as a trade. Another friend of John, a man of exceptional quality with whom I formed lasting friendship was Professor George Huxley, a classics scholar of international standing. Some years later, when I came to Trinity College Dublin as Professor of Music, George Huxley, having taken early retirement from the Queen's University, also became active at TCD, as a Visiting Professor. This gave us the felicitous opportunity to continue with our friendship. Through John, I also met David Greer, who was Professor of Music and Head of the Music Department at QUB. David was not exactly a member of John's circle; we became good friends some years later when I was at Trinity College Dublin and he was our External Examiner. In the 1990s, when he moved to northern England and became the Head of the Music School at University of Durham, he invited me to act as the External Examiner for his School.

My four weeks in Belfast, thanks to John Blacking's kind attention and his stimulating company, became one of the most memorable periods of my life. This is particularly remarkable since the January of 1975 was among the harshest periods in the so-called 'troubles' in Northern Ireland. At its roots, these 'troubles' originated with Ireland finally gaining independence in 1922, at which time six counties in the north of the island chose not to become incorporated into the Irish Free State and elected to remain within the United Kingdom. The majority of the population in these counties was of Scottish and English stock and was protestant; they did not wish to become a small minority in an independent Irish state that was overwhelmingly, and committedly, catholic. A significant minority in the six counties, however, was catholic and was desirous of union with the newly independent Republic. This led to decades of conflict, at times violent, in both sides of the community.

In 1975, the conflict, involving terrorist activity, bombing and assassinations, precipitated by the IRA (Irish Republican Army), and its 'loyalist' underground counterpart groups, was at its height. Almost daily acts of violence and sabotage were taking place within major cities of the six counties of Northern Ireland. The city of Belfast, the capital of Northern Ireland, had an air of being under siege. Parts of the central downtown were cordoned off; there were inspection points of entry, where one had to submit to bodily search before being admitted. Despite all these hazards, I found my stay in Belfast in every way enjoyable, largely due to the friendship and kindness of John Blacking. I had a very comfortable room in the Building known as the Common Room, ate my lunches there with other colleagues, and spent my evenings with John and friends.

My lectures, three two-hour periods per week, in the seminar room of the Department of Social Anthropology, went very well. There were some twelve students who attended my lectures. John Blacking attended every one of the lectures and took copious notes. John Bailey and a few other staff members involved with the ethnomusicology program were usually present.

The more I came to know John Blacking, the more I recognized that he was a man of exceptional qualities. Above all this was a thoroughly positive human being. He possessed the sort of enthusiasm about life and people that lit up the surroundings. I never heard him say a mean thing about anyone. His students loved him and he looked after them in every way he could.

John Anthony Randoll Blacking was born in 1928; he had studied the piano in his youth but at Cambridge University he had chosen to read social anthropology for his BA degree. After a period of service in the armed forces in Malaya, he had spent a good portion of his young years in South Africa. For a period he was assistant to Hugh Tracy, the famous scholar of African music. He received his PhD at Witwatersrand University of Johannesburg where he also taught for a number of years. In Africa, he had done field research on the music of the Venda tribe and had a major publication on the subject. In 1971, John Blacking was appointed to the Chair of Social Anthropology at the Queen's University of Belfast. At the time, there were no courses on ethnomusicology at the Queen's, and the Music Department had no interest in non-western music. Accordingly, John set about creating a postgraduate program in ethnomusicology within his own Department. By 1975, when I first met him, this program had become quite extensive, with courses on Indian, Middle Eastern, Chinese and African music on offer. There were about a dozen students both from the U.K. and from the overseas enrolled for higher degrees. By the time John Blacking passed away in 1990, the ethnomusicology program at the Queen's University of Belfast was the most extensive of any university in the British Isles and probably in Europe.

My visit to Northern Ireland and my close friendship with John Blacking, in time, proved pivotal to the rest of my life. By the end of January I was back in Tehran, but my contact with John continued through correspondence. At the end of summer of 75, on my return from a holiday in America, I stopped by in Belfast, and stayed a few days with John and Zureena. There was some talk of my revisiting the

Queen's University, at some point in the future, for a more extended period of lectures, but nothing definite was decided.

The uprising that led to a massive revolution in Iran began in January of 1978. It steadily assumed momentum and force. A year later the monarchy collapsed and the clerics took charge of the country. (For a more detailed account please refer to Chapter 10.) By the early spring of 1979, the Iranian Revolution had concluded with the establishment of an Islamic Republic through a referendum in which a large percentage of the population had participated. At that point, knowing the Moslem clerics' negative attitude toward music and the arts in general, I concluded that it was best to seek continuance of my musical and academic career elsewhere. I wrote a letter to John Blacking (telephone contact in those days, from Iran to the outside world was difficult) indicating my desire to leave the country. Upon receiving my letter John had gone to see the Vice-Chancellor of QUB and had made a case for needing my services. Within a day or two he had secured the offer of a Visiting Professorship at the Queen's and sent me a telegram stating the offer and the salary pertaining to it. This was done so swiftly, and seemed so generous, that I unhesitatingly accepted and forwarded my assent by telegram. In July of 1979, I left my native country for the last time. I spent the summer in the U.S. and arrived in Belfast in early October.

With John's support, the one year Visiting Professorship at QUB was extended to two. However, there seemed to be no prospect of a permanent position and I really had to seek a secure future elsewhere. In 1981, I had responded to a notice about the creation of a Chair of Music at the University of Hong Kong. I was invited to attend an interview by a board, acting on behalf of the University, in London. The committee that interviewed me in London had been sufficiently impressed for me to be flown, at a later date, to Hong Kong. There I met the ranking officials of the University, was interviewed and eventually, when I was back in Belfast, was offered the job. I turned down the offer; Hong Kong, both at the time of the interview and when I had visited that city in 1969, seemed like a very strange place. For my taste the city is oppressively overcrowded; the climate is uncomfortably warm and humid, and the life-style is hectic, overly geared to commerce and all-together alien to my nature.

Early in the summer of 1981, John brought to my attention an advertisement in the *Irish Times* stating that the Chair of Music at Trinity College, University or Dublin, was becoming vacant, as the current Professor was to retire at the end of summer 1982. The notice had specified the prospective applicants' qualifications and the job responsibilities and when and how to apply. He pressed me to apply for the post. I demurred as I thought it unlikely that the preeminent university in a small country would appoint a total outsider to a prestigious Chair. I believed that the advertisement has been placed as a matter of form and, in all probability Trinity had already an internal candidate picked for the job. John disagreed; he assured me that Trinity was a very international minded institution and that he is sure that I would be given serious consideration. It was through his guidance, and later his supporting letter of recommendation that I came to Dublin as Trinity's Professor of Music and Head of School of Music. As I write these lines, I have lived in Ireland, north and south, now for nearly 34 years. My wife's higher education and eventual academic career, the birth of our son Robert, and the peace and happiness we three have enjoyed in Ireland, have all been consequences of John Blacking's friendship and support.

I had cherished our daily visits and lively conversation with John during the three years I lived in Belfast. I was saddened that the move to Dublin in September of 1982 had placed a distance of one hundred miles between us. I made a point of driving up to Belfast at least once every month and John occasionally paid us visits in Dublin. At one time, I organized for him to give a seminar for our music students at Trinity College. The lecture he gave was on 'bi-musicality', one of the important subjects in his late research and publications.

In early December of 1988, I received an agitated telephone call from John's wife Zureena telling me that John has been suffering abdominal pain of late and that he had been diagnosed as having pancreatic cancer. She added that he has been hospitalized where he was to remain for needed treatment. Being a medical doctor, in response to my distraught query, she had to be forthright and informed me that there is not much hope for recovery. I cannot imagine that I have ever received a more upsetting telephone call. The next day I drove to Belfast and directly to the hospital where I was told John is staying. It was a great shock to see this man of great verve and vitality in a hospital bed. He was cheerful, however, and full of hope of beating the dreaded disease.

Thereafter, at least once a week I went to see him. In the course of the following year, 1989, for long periods, John was at home or at work at the University, but as the year wore on, more and more, he had to be hospitalized for longer periods. By the end of the year he was but a shadow of himself. I could not bear to see this wonderfully exuberant, handsome and energetic man so emaciated and listless. The last I saw him was three days before death took him on 24 January 1990. He was only 61 years old, much too young to die; he had so much yet to give. I have not mourned more anyone's passing.

John Blacking was a man of keen perception with an incisive mind. In his writings, particularly in *How Musical is Man*, he broke new grounds in the assessment of musical values. In his lectures, and his papers read at conferences, he made a point of being provocative with the intention to jolt the minds of his audience and to make them re-examine the accepted norms. Also, John was a man of extraordinary warmth and goodwill; always cheerful and positive, he delighted in helping others. Aldus Huxley was asked in an interview - I saw on television years ago - what makes for a superior man? 'Equal measure of intelligence and benevolence', he responded. He didn't know it but he was describing John Blacking.

❧ 12 ❧

My Composition Teachers

By the time I was in the final year of high school I was resolved to devote my life to music. My passion for western classical music was all consuming and composition was the focal point of this obsession. I did not know much about the rules of harmony or counterpoint, yet I was composing little pieces for my instrument the violin. I would show them to my violin teacher who would play them for me, much better than I could, and gave me both encouragement and suggestions as to how to improve them. When the move to America for my university studies became a reality (please refer to Chapter 6) and California loomed as the final destination, I entertained the idea of studying with Arnold Schoenberg, who had been engaged as Professor of Composition at University of California at Los Angeles (UCLA). I did not understand nor particularly liked his music, but I knew that he was recognized as a great composer; moreover, he was known to be a very attentive teacher and had written some excellent textbooks on harmony and counterpoint. Unfortunately, when I finally made it to UCLA in 1949 Schoenberg had retired from teaching and passed away two years later.

In the course of my studies for a B.A. in music at UCLA, followed by two years at Mills College for an M.A., and several years back at UCLA, I studied composition with a number of distinguished composers. From each of them I was able to add new ideas, methods and devices that have been pooled into the technique of composition I have employed in my works. What I have written definitely does not resemble the works of anyone of the masters I have studied with. Had I studied with only one of my four composer teachers, in all probability, my style would have been in line with the style of that one person. As it has turned out, it is the accumulation of ideas drawn from lessons and recommendations I was given by all of them that have become, for me, tools of creative process. As all four of my teachers were accomplished composers, and certainly three of them were among major figures of the 20th century, I shall devote this chapter to a brief account of my associations with them.

Boris Kremenliev

Although my first composition teacher was not as renowned a figure as were the next three, he was also a composer of considerable accomplishments. Boris Kremenliev was born in Bulgaria in 1911. He had emigrated to the U. S. just before the Second World War, had studied with Howard Hanson at Eastman School of Music and had earned a doctoral degree in music. Kremenliev was a member of the Music Faculty at UCLA, from the late 1940s to the end of his teaching career. I had classes with him in composition and orchestration during my undergraduate years. Later, when I was appointed to a teaching post in the same Department, we were colleagues and good friends.

From my student days I had found Kremenliev to be a kindly and modest person. He was always helpful and supportive. In his teaching method Boris was rather cautious, never criticized anything that the student produced in a decisive manner; he only made suggestions. He encouraged me in my pursuit of composition and led me to believe I had a future as a composer. For that above all else, I was grateful to him, even though I cannot claim that I learned a great deal by attending his classes. Boris had a number of large and ambitious works to his credit; his music was clearly influenced by Bartok and had similar rhythmic rigor. He was also the author of a book called *Bulgarian and Macedonian Folk Music*. Because of his research on music of the Balkan region, in the 1960's, Mantle Hood persuaded him to accept affiliation with the Institute of Ethnomusicology, an association that Boris never took very seriously. I have always regretted having lost contact with Kremenliev, when I left UCLA and returned to Iran in 1968. Years later, I learned from a mutual friend that he had often inquired about me. Boris died in 1988 at age 77.

Darius Milhaud

Mills College in Oakland, California, was founded in 1852 as a very exclusive girls' school. Men can only apply for admission to post-graduate courses. In the period I studied at Mills (1953-55), the College had about 600 full-time students, only about a dozen of whom were male. Mills is a liberal arts college that has maintained very high standards throughout its long history. This is particularly true of its Music Department. Since the Second World War, the famous French composer Darius Milhaud had been teaching there, and that was the reason for my decision to do my Masters degree at Mills College. Other notable figures who were members of the music faculty included the great Dutch pianist Egon Petri and the musicologist Margaret Prall. In 1955, Leon Kirchner also joined the staff, and a few years later Luciano Berio and later Yannis Xenakis were among the famous composers of avant-garde tendency who taught there.

When I first met Milhaud he was 62 years old; he was wheelchair bound, neither in good health nor in a cheerful state. There were six of us composition students, 4 men and 2 women, who went to his on-campus apartment for our lessons. He only came to the Music Building on rare occasions, particularly to attend student concerts. His wife Madeleine always accompanied him to wherever he went and one of the male students helped in wheeling him around. On one occasion, when I was wheeling him through the downward slopping isle of a concert hall, I had much difficulty in controlling the chair as he was a portly man and his weight, plus the weight of the chair proved hard to control. As I was beginning to lose control and Milhaud and the wheelchair were beginning to pick up speed, his wife Madeleine who was nearby came to help and the great man was safely deposited in the front of the hall. He told me afterwards: "you should eat more, you are too puny", which was true.

Darius Milhaud was one of the most prolific composers of the 20th century; he wrote well in excess of 400 works. He had developed a personal technique that, aided by his fertile imagination, resulted in creation of compositions with remarkable ease. He wrote in every genre including a vast corpus of orchestral music, concertos, a great deal of chamber music, and a number of large scale operas, among them, *King David* and *Christopher Columbus*. At one time, when I was in his private office, I noticed on his desk the score of a cantata for chorus, soloists and orchestra; the date on the opening page was 18 February and on the final page 2 March. That was a work of considerable duration for a large assembly of forces, written in less than two weeks.

Milhaud was an excellent teacher who was well versed in every conceivable idiom. He was quite indifferent as to the style that a student chose to follow. He would make apt remarks about the music regardless of its style. Barbara Harris, one of the two girls among the students, was writing show type music in the style of William Rogers or Jerome Kern. That did not concern Milhaud; in fact, he seemed to like what she was doing and made suggestions as to how to improve the piece. One of the other students was Ezra Sims, who later developed a career as a composer. At the time, Sims was writing a serial composition. Milhaud had no problems with this either, even though it was so radically different from his own taste and style. However, he had very sharp words with Sims one day, when he had produced more than 70 pages of music that was intolerably meandering and boring. Too many repetitions, lengthy developments, and ponderousness in music were anathema to Milhaud.

Initially, I had the feeling that Milhaud did not like me. In my compositions, he detected faint traces of what he called 'orientalism', for which he had no taste. He gave me a hard time about the string quartet that I was writing; he wanted alterations in the main theme of the first movement, which I resisted. The second and the third movements he approved, but the fourth movement was decidedly not to his liking; it was too thickly contrapuntal. To satisfy him, I made a lot of alterations. My final Masters project was a Sinfonia Concertante for a seven solo instruments, soprano and string orchestra. I had a lot of problems with Milhaud about this composition before getting his final approval. I made a two piano arrangement of this work for a concert performance at Mills, which Darius Milhaud attended. On hearing this arrangement, he seemed very pleased and he complemented me for it.

During our lessons, invariably famous composers' works and stylistic traits would come up for discussion. Milhaud had great admiration for the music of Debussy. Among his own contemporaries, he had much respect for Bartok, as composer and even more so as a pianist. He particularly admired the music of his friend Francis Poulenc, an admiration that I very much shared with him. Of 19th century composers, he thought highly of Berlioz, even though he clearly thought him too much of an individualist who did not, and could not, have been the founder of any stylistic trend. He disliked the music of Cesar Franck and his followers, on that score I found myself, then and now, in total disagreement with him. Among the Germans, he had respect for Beethoven, no patience for Wagner, and contempt for Brahms. Once, when the San Francisco Symphony Orchestra scheduled a performance of his *Creation du Monde* on a program that also included Brahms' 2nd Symphony, after the intermission Milhaud, who had been invited to attend the concert, left during the break; he could not bear to sit through the Brahms symphony.

Milhaud was such a renowned composer, and had been around for such a long that he knew personally all other great contemporary figures. Discussions, during our class sessions, would at times warrant inclusion of anecdotes about other composers whom he had known as friends. Arnold Schoenberg was mentioned often. One story that Milhaud liked to tell was about having told Schoenberg, shortly after war, that his twelve-note technique has found quite a large following among young French composers. To which, Schoenberg had responded: 'Ach so, but do they put any music in it!'

Another story about Schoenberg concerned his friend and pupil, Anton Webern. According to Milhaud, Schoenberg had said that Webern is like the little bird that jumped out of the mountain climber's hat, once the climber had, after much labor, reached the top of the mountain, and sang a song saying that he has reached an even higher peak.

Lukas Foss

In 1955, Lukas Foss was a mere 33 years old composer who had captured the imagination of the musical world with a number of remarkably beautiful and original compositions. His cantata, *The Prairie*, on a poem of Carl Sandberg, an exceptionally engaging work, had been sensationally received and had won the New York Critics' Circle Award. Despite his relative youth, he had been appointed as a full professor of composition in the Music Department at UCLA.

Since Mills College had no doctoral program, I returned to UCLA for my PhD studies in 1955. For two years, I was a composition student of Lukas Foss. There were no more than six students in his class, none of whom, to my knowledge, has emerged as an internationally known composer.

Foss had extraordinary abilities as a musician. He was an all-round genius whose range of musical talents was in the class of Leonard Bernstein and Andre Previn. He was an outstanding pianist with a commanding technique and expressive powers. He was a very good conductor and, above all, he was a truly gifted composer, brimming with fresh ideas. However, he seemed not to have much interest in teaching. His comments on composition assignments that were written by students lacked consistency. What he had recommended one day might be ruled as the wrong thing to do the next. Continuation of a project, from one meeting to the next, often met with conflicting reactions from him that showed he was unaware of his own previous recommendations. Nevertheless, I found his classes stimulating, because of his overwhelming musicality. He played on the piano anything that we wrote, at sight. Whether it was an orchestral piece, a choral work, a piece for brass instruments, woodwinds, anything at all; he would sight read it, at the right tempo, with no difficulty. I wrote a fair amount of music under his, be it inconsistent, guidance, among them my first Piano Sonata, which was dedicated to him.

In 1956, Ravi Shankar, the famous Indian sitar player, gave a concert at Royce Hall in UCLA. Moreover, he gave a lecture about North Indian music and the importance of improvisation in that musical tradition. I believe it was the influence of this concert and lecture, which Lukas Foss attended, that led to his interest in the infusion of improvisatory elements in compositions that he wrote from that period onwards. In fact, shortly after Shankar's presentations, Lukas organized an ensemble of students, playing different instruments, as a workshop, experimenting with composed pieces interwoven with improvised passages. I participated, for a few sessions, in the ensemble playing the violin. The first major work that Foss produced based on this 'aleatory' style was his *Time Cycle*, a highly praised work that also received the New York Critics Circle Award.

Among the memorable experiences of my Foss years was a concert at UCLA, when he conducted and played the solo piano part in Bach's Brandenburg Concerto No. 5. He played the lengthy and demanding solo part in the first movement with amazing fire and brilliance. Equally memorable was another concert at UCLA, of compositions by Stravinsky, conducted by the composer. The program included *Les Noces*, which requires four pianos plus percussions. Foss played one of the pianos, Ingolf Dahl and John Crown were at two other pianos; I do not remember who played the fourth piano.

Foss was friends with Igor Stravinsky and visited him, from time to time, at his house in Beverly Hills. One day he brought the manuscript of the Great Russian's *Canticum Sacrum* to the class. This was one of the first major compositions of Stravinsky employing the serial technique. As Lukas went through the piece on the piano, there was not much that either he or any of the students could say about it. It certainly had no relation to other Stravinsky works that we had known, yet there were unique touches of the master in terms of precision and finesse of craftsmanship. In his remaining 14 years (he died in 1971), Stravinsky cultivated this new style of composition without really succeeding to equal his earlier achievements. The music of the great man's late period remains largely under performed.

Lukas Foss did not remain at UCLA for long, by early 1960s he resigned his teaching post and took up the conductorship of the Buffalo Symphony Orchestra. For a period he also conducted the Brooklyn Symphony Orchestra. However, Foss did return to teaching when in

1991 he was appointed as Professor of Composition and Theory at Boston University. He remained active as a composer throughout his life and died at age 86 in 2009. Foss is rightly recognized as a major figure in 20th century composition.

Roy Harris

Beginning in 1961, for several years, Roy Harris was the Composer in Residence at UCLA; he taught composition only to advanced students. Although I was engaged with my full time teaching responsibilities as Assistant Professor of Music at the Music Department of California State University in Long Beach, I signed up for Harris's composition class. I was still nominally a postgraduate student at UCLA; my thesis was not completed until 1964, at which time I was transferred from Long Beach to UCLA as a member of the Music Faculty.

By late 1930s, Roy Harris had been recognized as one of the major figures of American music. His expansive yet highly concentrated *Third Symphony* had established his position as a composer whose music expresses the grandeur of the American landscape. His other works, symphonic or choral, had consolidated his position as the American Composer par excellence. That he was of English stock, born in humble circumstances in the Lincoln County, Oklahoma, on Lincoln's birthday in 1898, added to this recognition as a uniquely American figure.

For three years (1961-64) I took sporadic composition lessons from Roy Harris. The arrangement was for me to go to his place of residence on appointment. These were one to one meetings; no other students were involved. As I recall, Harris always lived in rented accommodations and moved house a number of times. The first appointment he gave me, after I had spoken to him on the telephone, was at 8 in the evening. He had just moved to the Los Angeles area and was living in a house in Pacific Palisades. I took a number of my recent compositions for him to see and to decide if he would accept me as a pupil. Of the pieces he looked at, he particularly liked a recently written Woodwind Trio. From that first meeting we became friends and for the next three years I visited Harris on pre-arranged appointments.

The sessions I had with him were concentrated on the particular piece I was writing at the time. He had very clear ideas as to what he wanted me to do, quite a contrast from Milhaud's approach to teaching. He liked long notes; he preferred 4/2, 6/2 or 9/2 time signatures, rather than 4/4, 6/8 or 9/8. He also favored thematic material that moved in a grand manner, covering many measures, perhaps covering two or more octaves. At times, he would cross out something that I had written and make changes in his own handwriting. For the most part I was acquiescent and we got along very well. After our lessons he would always ask his wife Joanna, who was an accomplished concert pianist, to bring us a drink. His favorite drink was bourbon whiskey mixed with ginger ale.

Harris was a cheerful and unaffected man, plain spoken and rough-hewn. Often, I had stimulating, at times illuminating, discussions with him. We got into an argument once about Stravinsky. I have been always an admirer of the Russian composer's inventiveness and precision; Harris thought highly of his early symphonic works; however, he disparaged Stravinsky's Neo-Classical period, and particularly the late serial efforts, which he characterized as bereft of original ideas. For Schoenberg and his followers he had no patience at all. Hindemith's music he found well written but utterly arid. He had high praise for some of his own countrymen, notably Aaron Copland, Samuel Barber and David Diamond.

When I was appointed to the Music Faculty of UCLA in 1964, Harris and I were colleagues; I took no more lessons from him but visited him from time to time at his home. For a period he lived in a house on the beach in Malibu. He enjoyed living next to the sound of the Pacific Ocean's crashing waves and the rays of setting sun shimmering over the water. He used to say: I need to live next to something primeval.

It is very rare, particularly for a man of my background, to have had the privilege of studying with such important composers. I benefited greatly from the instruction I received from all of my composition teachers. At the same time, I was aware that these were composers of distinctly different persuasions. Moreover, I have had my own natural instincts and inclinations, as indeed all creative artists must have. In the end, I have developed my own style; it cannot be identified with that of any of my teachers, but is surely informed by the guidance they have given me.

❧ 13 ❧

Music at Universities: U.S., Iran and Europe

This chapter has a two-fold purpose. One is to compare the way musical studies are covered in third level education in Europe with the same in America; the other is a review of my own experiences at the various universities where I have taught.

The approach to the inclusion of music in third level education is significantly different at American colleges and universities from similar institutions in most European countries. I believe that I am in a position to comment on these differences, and point out the strength and weakness of each system, for the following reasons. I did all of my university studies in the U.S., and also taught at American universities for several years. In addition, I have been guest lecturer at a number of universities in the United States including Illinois, Princeton, Harvard, Michigan, U.C. Berkeley and Swarthmore College of Pennsylvania. From 1969, for some ten years, I was Professor of Music and Head of the Music Department at University of Tehran. The music curriculum that I instituted there was modeled on the American system with the addition of some courses on Persian traditional music. In midlife, after three years as Visiting Professor at the Queen's University of Belfast In Northern Ireland, I moved to the Republic of Ireland as the Head of the School of Music at University of Dublin, Trinity College, a post that I held for 13 years. I have also been associated with a number of universities in the U.K., as Visiting Professor and acted, for three years, as the External Examiner for the School of Music at University of Durham. I have been a guest lecturer at universities in Koln, Copenhagen, Ljubljana and Warsaw. It should not seem boastful, therefore, to say that I know something about the way music figures in third level education in some European countries, United Kingdom and Ireland in particular, as well as knowing the American system well.

Old European universities were mostly founded in or near large cities; many of them were, in their inception, affiliated with religious institutions. These universities catered to the needs of the upper classes. Their courses were primarily concerned with religion, classics, philosophy, natural sciences, law and medicine; also, they trained clerics, lawyers, and medical doctors. European universities were not concerned with practical arts such as music, theatre, painting and sculpture. As with the other arts, musical studies were in the domain of schools expressly concerned with music. These were music academies, conservatoires, hoch schules, and the like. The same was true of the visual arts, architecture and drama studies for which specialized institutions were founded. In a few cases, at major universities, Chairs of Music were created, but only aspects of philosophy and history of music were taught. As a rule, in Europe, one did not go to a university to learn harmony, counterpoint, composition or orchestration; nor did one seek further studies in piano repertoire, violin, clarinet, voice and the rest. Accordingly, European universities either had no Music Departments as such, or they merely had some lectures on non-technical aspects of music literature and philosophy.

In America, many of the major universities were built in small communities that, in time, grew around the university. They were often founded on land grants given by the state government, or were funded by an individual philanthropist, for the creation of an institution of higher learning. Often, universities were built within large campuses in sparsely populated locations, where separate establishments to cater to other needs, such as music, were not practical. From the outset, music was seen as important enough to be included in the university curriculum. Moreover, America was free of the notion of a hereditary aristocracy, and political power did not rest with a traditional ruling class. Accordingly, not only the wealthy but also the common people of diverse backgrounds, and with varied interests, had access to higher education. By the end of the 19th century there were far more institutions of higher learning in the U.S. than in any comparably populated area even in the most advanced of European countries.

There have been some old and reputable music conservatories in major American cities such as the Oberlin Conservatory of Ohio, Curtis Institute of Philadelphia, Peabody School in Baltimore, New York's Juilliard School of Music, and the New England Conservatory in Boston. However, universities and colleges throughout the U.S. – and there are thousands of them – effectively contain conservatoires within themselves. Their course offering includ all subjects related to the technique of musical composition (harmony, counterpoint, analysis, instrumentation and orchestration), all periods of music history, courses on individual major composers, subjects pertaining to the methodology of music education, and instruction of all musical instruments and voice. American Music Departments invariably maintain student symphony orchestras, marching bands, and choral groups; some universities also have active opera workshops. Courses in ethnomusicology, a comparatively recent area of interest, have been also added to the curriculum in nearly every large institution.

By comparison universities in Europe have much smaller music departments. They have far fewer staff members and their course offering is more limited. Some European universities, in the last fifty years, have upgraded their music program and have become closer to the American system. Nevertheless, the scope of what is on offer is comparatively small. At UCLA, where I taught in 1960s, we had some 40 full-time, and 18 part-time, academic staff. In recent visits to the same department, I have noted that at least twice that number are currently engaged as members of the music faculty. A British university would have an inordinately large academic staff in music if there were 15 of them. As to the continental universities, they are generally modest in their staffing and their program is more limited as compared with similar institutions in Great Britain or Ireland.

Another important difference between British/Irish universities and institutions of higher learning in America is in the way staff attain tenure. Although universities in Britain and Ireland have rigorous procedures for the appointment of a lecturer, which includes careful scrutiny of the applicants' credentials, short listing and interviews, once a candidate is employed, even when the appointment is technically on probationary basis, it becomes practically impossible not to make the employment permanent, regardless of how poor the provisional lecturer's performance has proven to be. In the U.S. an Assistant Professor (equivalent to a Lecturer in the European system) can be dismissed on evidence of poor performance, without much fuss. He/she must prove suitability as a university teacher within seven years, both in terms of teaching abilities and research activity leading to publications, before being promoted to Associate Professorship, which is a tenured post. Failure to have done so, even after seven years, may result in dismissal. In the British/Irish universities there is less emphasis on research; an academic member of staff may fail to produce, year after year, any significant publication; he/she may not be promoted but can stay on in a junior rank indefinitely. Unions have a powerful presence and any attempt on the part of an academic department to rid itself of an incompetent member, regardless of justification, will result in confrontation with the union and can end up in the courts. Usually, universities shy away from any entanglement in court cases, particularly since they often end up with heavy costs and doubtful outcomes.

There are points of strength and weakness in both the American and the European approach to education as a whole. The European third level student invariably has had a far more comprehensive 12 years of schooling before being admitted to a university. The primary and secondary school curricula in the U.S. are flimsy by comparison. It is for that reason, perhaps, that a BA course in America, regardless of the major field of study, includes other subjects such as history, foreign languages, science courses, and a number of electives from a prepared list of possibilities. This is to compensate for the inadequacy of schooling prior to the third level. In other words, some of the subjects that the European student has had in the secondary schools, and were absent from the American students background, are included at the university level.

This may seem to put the American university's BA degree in a poor light. However, there are mitigating factors to be considered. An American BA is a four years degree; in Europe, generally, it requires only three years. (This does not include degrees in sciences, engineering or medicine.) The length of the academic year in the American pattern is usually longer, in some cases by as much as eight weeks. Also, the number of contact hours, or required attendance in classroom, for a student in the U.S. is significantly more. On the average, a BA student in an American university, throughout the four years, has 15 hours of lecture attendance per week; a European student's required contact with lecturers, including tutorials, on the average, would not exceed 10 hours.

The requirements for postgraduate degrees in the American system are decidedly more demanding and better structured than any comparable program in European institutions. The American universities require attendance in a number of courses that involve research and passing of examinations. Also, there are the so-called comprehensive examinations before the submission of the final thesis. For a PhD degree, many universities quire the candidate to pass examinations in reading knowledge of two foreign languages (usually French and German). This is to prove ability to do research in sources beyond those that are available in English. The thesis is prepared under the guidance of a staff member and is finally read and approved by four others, two from the Music Department and two from the outside. In the European system postgraduate degrees are granted fundamentally on the strength of a thesis written under supervision of one staff member. It also has to receive the approval of an external examiner. Although usually no taught subjects were figured in the postgraduate programs at European institutions, in recent times a trend to include some taught courses has come into effect. This is to bring about a greater conformity with the American system so that students may adjust more easily when moving from one country to another. There is also a growing intention to bring about greater uniformity in the content of degrees in order to improve access to the job market on the international scene.

The above points of comparison show that the two systems are conceived differently. The old world maintains the traditional pattern of providing the necessary broad education to the young, so as to prepare them for a vocation, in the twelve years of pre university schooling. In its origins, the third level education was designed for a small elite who would be trained for more professional occupations, i.e. law, medicine, the sciences, engineering, divinity, and politics. In the American approach, that broad education is spread over a 16 years period; but, in its final four years, it also lays the ground for a specialized profession, the full accreditation for which is to be achieved by postgraduate studies. Indeed, postgraduate studies in American universities are taken far more seriously than in their European counterparts. In most continental institutions, until recently, the Masters degree, as a midway between Bachelors degree and Doctorate, did not exist. It has now been introduced in many countries, in line with the American system. Still, a postgraduate degree usually involves very few taught elements; class attendance is minimal and there are often no examinations other than the oral defense of the thesis at the very end.

As concerns music, European universities are not in the business of training composers and performers; they are more geared to producing scholars. This is not to say, of course, that among the music graduates from these schools there are no future composers or performers; it is simply that the course structure, in its conception, is not designed to educate performing artists or composers. The American model, particularly on the postgraduate level, is very much concerned with the creative and the practical side of the music profession, as well as to promoting scholarship and research. (I should add that the British and Irish universities, in recent times, have made striking moves to include the training of future composers.)

❧ ❧

In the second part of this chapter I should like to recount my personal observation on four music departments with which I have been closely associated in the course of my academic career. These are the Music Departments at California State University in Long Beach, University of California in Los Angeles (UCLA), University of Tehran, and the School of Music at University of Dublin, Trinity College. The following are reflections on my experiences at these music departments with reference to some of the personalities I have known at each institution.

California State University in Long Beach

My first full-time academic appointment came about in 1961. Two years before, my very close friend, Julien Musafia, had been employed at California State College at Long Beach, a city some 30 miles south of Los Angeles. At that time this institution was one of 14 state colleges throughout California; it was elevated to university status a few years later. Julien, a Romanian by birth, had established a reputation as a brilliant young pianist in his home country. He had arrived in the U.S. in 1948 and had spent a period at Juilliard School of Music, followed by a move to California. Although he gave a number of recitals to rave reviews, the recognition he deserved did not quite materialize, which only attests to the over crowdedness of the field. He enrolled at UCLA for postgraduate studies and received a Masters degree in 1958. In 1959, Julien was appointed to a Lectureship in Piano at California State College in Long Beach. There, he gave regular recitals and added much luster to the reputation of the College's Music Department. It was through his recommendations that I was invited to give a lecture there and subsequently was offered an Assistant Professorship. My assignment was teaching courses in musicianship, harmony and counterpoint.

Although CSULB, was only a few years old its Music Department was housed in a new well-equipped music building, attached to a handsome theatre that was used for concerts as well as for other cultural events requiring a large hall. At the time of my appointment the Department had 19 full-time academic members, plus a librarian and an executive secretary. From the outset, it was clear that the academic staff of the Department was divided into two opposing camps. The animosity between members of the two camps was palpable; they hardly spoke to one another. For me to have been considered at all for the appointment I had to be favored by the larger group, to which my friend Julien also belonged. Since I was the choice of the majority I had to put up, from day one, with the hostility of the minority group. As time went by and I came to know my colleagues, I found very few, in either camp, whom I could admire. The most respectable musician in the majority group was easily Julien Musafia. Also, among the majority was Frank Pooler, a choral conductor of considerable accomplishments with a nationwide recognition. He was also a composer of a large number of published choral pieces. Frank was a very warm and genial person and we quickly became good friends. None of the others in the majority group was particularly distinguished in any area of musical scholarship or performance.

The opposing camp had one notable individual, Leon Dallin who, from all evidence, was a competent composer and author of several books, including one on the technique of musical composition. The rest were less than mediocre as personalities or musicians. The frosty ambience in faculty meetings, and the general demeanor of supposed colleagues, was quite disconcerting. But that was the reality of the situation and I could not alter it. Throughout my three years at Long Beach I received nothing but expressions of resentment and disapproval from the opposing camp. Despite support and camaraderie from most colleagues in the majority group, my years in Long Beach did not pass happily.

Early in the third year of my service an episode involving the election of a new Chairman for the Music Department sadly darkened my relationship with Julien Musafia, which, added to the wretched atmosphere all around, and led to my decision to terminate my engagement at CSULB. Our longstanding friendship was one of the few rewards of being in the midst of a strife-prone group of mostly non-entities. With that anchor removed I became resolved to seek employment elsewhere.

At the start of the academic year 1963-64, the Chairman of the Music Department, an ungainly tall fellow named John Green, whose specialty was in music education and who also ran the College marching band, announced that he has accepted a job offer at a university in Texas and that he was to leave Long Beach at the end of the year. The headship was subject to election, and the rules required that the candidate must receive at least two thirds of the votes of the members of the Department. To my surprise, Julien, who always derided administrative work, suddenly got fired up with the idea of running for the headship of the Department.

There were at least three reasons, I thought, why it was a bad idea for Julien to compete in this election, and I told him so. One was that, although he was highly respected as a musician and pianist, I knew that our colleagues regarded him as uncooperative and haughty. I was sure that he would not receive even one third of the votes, so why lose face by competing? The second reason was that he was not suited to administrative work; he was a pianist who needed to devote his time, as much as possible, to practice and performance, not to sitting behind a desk and pushing paper around. The third reason, which I had to explain with much delicacy, was that he would not make a good Chairman; he tended to be aloof and opinionated; he did not easily get along with people; he was bound to create much disharmony and friction, and that was not conducive to the wellbeing of the Department already plagued with factionalism.

Long discussions failed to persuade Julien not to put his name forward; equally they failed to convince me to cast my vote for him. In the end, of a staff of 19, he had the assent of 6; the other candidate, also from the majority group, received 13 votes and was elected. To my great chagrin, this episode caused a rift in our relationship, which fortunately was fully repaired within a few years. I could appreciate his disappointment with me in not having supported his desire to become the Chairman for a few years, but I was convinced that the idea was utterly foolish. The following year, 1964, my own Alma Mater, UCLA, offered me a full time appointment in theory and composition, which I was glad to accept. The bond of friendship between Julien and I was too strong however and within a couple of years after I left Long Beach, we re-established contact and saw each other form time to time. In 1977-78, when I was on sabbatical leave from University of Tehran, and was occupied with composition of a number of commissioned works, I rented an apartment in Long Beach and spent a great deal of my free time in his company. To this day, we remain very close; we talk on the telephone frequently and I make a point of visiting him whenever I travel to California.

Music Department at UCLA

My years at UCLA, both as student and later as a member of the Music Faculty, extend from 1949 to late 60s. I finished my BA in Music there in 1953. I retuned there, to begin work towards a PhD in September of 1955, after completing my MA at Mills College in Oakland, California. Two years later I went back to Persia to do research for my thesis. I was back in UCLA, from 1959 and continued with my studies for two years, but was also employed as a Teaching Assistant. I was an assistant to Dr. Mantle Hood in his ethnomusicology courses, but was also in charge of some classes in harmony and musicianship. In 1964 I was appointed to a fulltime Assistant Professorship at UCLA. I taught courses in harmony, counterpoint, composition and orchestration. I was also active in the Institute of Ethnomusicology, which had been created by Mantle Hood a few years earlier. In that context, I established a Persian Music Study Group and had a number of pupils, who studied both the theory of Persian music and learned how to play some of the instruments.

UCLA's Music Department, in the mid 1960s, had an academic staff of nearly sixty members. This was a very well equipped music school, housed in a purpose built new building, the Schoenberg Hall, with one large and one small concert hall, many class rooms, practice halls for the university band, for the symphony orchestra and for the opera workshop. There were about forty practice rooms in the basement; offices for the academic and administrative staff were located on the top floor of the building. The Music Library was also housed in the Schoenberg Hall. With the enlargement of the ethnomusicology program in the 1960s, a portion of the basement was turned into practice rooms for different Study Groups. A very large area was taken by the vast collection of Javanese and Balinese gamelans where regular practice sessions were conducted by Mantle Hood, involving as many as 40 student – and non-student - participants. Smaller rooms were taken by the Chinese, Thai, Indian and Persian instruments, where related study groups met and practiced.

The academic staff of the Music Department included a number of distinguished scholars, composers and performers. Sadly, the assembly of these notable musicians, on the whole, did not project a warm and congenial atmosphere. There seemed to be a great deal of disharmony and rivalry between various members of the staff. Faculty meetings were often fraught with tension and occasional display of antagonism. The Chair of the Department rotated between the tenured members on the basis of internal election. The Chairperson served for three years, subject to re-election. The strength of the Music Department was in its musicology and composition components. In time, with Mantle Hood's tireless efforts, the ethnomusicology program developed into the most comprehensive in all American universities. I have written about Dr. Hood at some length in the chapter of exceptional people. Here, I will discuss other areas of the Department's strength and will underline the more interesting personalities among my colleagues, some of whom, only a few years before, were among the professors with whom I had studied.

In the area of western musicology, undoubtedly, the most remarkable figure was Robert Stevenson. Dr. Stevenson was a world authority on the music of Latin America. His interest primarily centered on church music in the New World and on Latin American composers. He was a singularly prolific scholar with a staggering array of publications in both books and articles. His writings on Iberian and Latin American music are considered as seminal. Stevenson was also an excellent pianist; he had studied with, among others, Arthur Schnabel, and gave occasional piano recitals. He was also a composer of considerable accomplishments, and had studied with Howard Hanson and Stravinsky. He had several published compositions for piano and had also written a sizable corpus of chamber and orchestral music. Stevenson was a solitary, Lincolnesque figure, tall and gaunt. No one seemed to know much about his private life except that he lived alone. In faculty meetings he spoke little, but when he did he tended to be acerbic and contrary. One had a feeling that he had very little regard for his colleagues.

I remember a piano recital that Robert Stevenson gave at UCLA in 1964. The program was quite demanding and included one of his own piano sonatas. As usual there was a 15 minutes interval separating the first half of the program from the second. When the last piece before the interval was played the audience, as is customary, expected that he would exit the stage and return after the interval to perform the remainder of the concert. He did not exit. After acknowledging the applause and taking a perfunctory bow, he sat back on the stool at the keyboard. The audience hesitated and wondered if he intended to disregard the interval and continue with the second half of the program. But he just sat at the piano with his arms folded. After a few minutes some people got up to go to the lobby for a chat; others remained ambivalent as to what to do. He just sat there and looked straight ahead. After 15 minutes, as the audience had begun to take their seats again, he resumed playing the second half of the program.

In my undergraduate days at UCLA, I had a counterpoint class with Dr. Stevenson; he was rather remote as a teacher but fortunately seemed to like me. Years later, when we were colleagues, I had occasional conversations with him. These were not social occasions – he did not socialize with anyone – but chance meetings in the corridors of the Music Building (Schoenberg Hall). He often had negative comments about what was happening in the Department, and sometimes made asides about one or another of our colleagues. Years later, when I was at the University of Dublin as the Head of the School of Music, I wrote to him and invited him to visit Trinity College as our guest and to give one or more lectures. He did not respond.

Robert Stevenson died in December of 2012 at age 94. He wrote and published to the very end.

Among other major figures in western musicology was Walter Rubsamen, a very arid and conceited man who had studied in Germany during the Nazi era. He was mainly known for a number of very incisive articles on the music of the early Renaissance. He was a very hardnosed lecturer, unsympathetic to students. However, when he served two terms as the Chairman of the Department, he proved to be very fair and efficient. Robert Tusler was another musicologist member of the Department whose area of expertise was late Renaissance and particularly the music of composers from the low Countries. Frank

D'Accone was a newer member of the musicology section who was appointed about the time I also joined the staff in 1964. He rose to considerable prominence in his area of interest, which was early Italian opera. An excellent teacher of theory, harmony, counterpoint and analysis was Robert U. Nelson. Although rather aloof, he was meticulous and conscientious; he wrote detailed comments on assignments submitted by students.

There were a number of prominent composers on the staff of the Music Department. In the 1940s, Arnold Schoenberg had taught at UCLA. He was one of the most celebrated composers of the early 20th century, one of the many great musicians who had arrived in the U.S. from central Europe, subsequent to the Nazi take over in Germany and other countries they over ran during the World War II. Schoenberg had retired, however, a few years before I came to UCLA in 1949 and passed away in 1951. His replacement was the Bulgarian composer, Boris Kremenliev. He had joined the music faculty in 1947 where he remained to his retirement in 1978. He died 10 years later at age 76. Boris was a gifted composer and had written a large corpus of music, but, in the long years of his service at UCLA, he became increasingly inactive. He did not have very good relationship with other staff members. With me, on the other had, he was always kind and friendly, both when I studied with him in my undergraduate days and later when we were colleagues. The oldest of the composers on the staff was John Vincent. He had been born in 1902 and had studied, for a period in the 1930s, with Nadia Boulanger in Paris. He was a good composer but seemed increasingly disillusioned and inactive.

In chapter 12 I have written about my composition teachers; with three of them, Boris Kremenliev, Lukas Foss and Roy Harris, I had studied at different periods at UCLA. Foss was brought to UCLA, as a full professor in 1954, when he was only 32. He did not stay long, however, and left after a few years to become the conductor of the Buffalo Symphony Orchestra. Roy Harris who came in 1961 as Composer in Residence stayed well into 1970s. Two other composers among the staff, Henri Lazaroff and Roy Travis, were very active and became nationally important figures. Other composers in the Music Department, in addition to myself, were Paul Chihara and Paul DesMarais.

Most of those who taught practical courses on different instruments were part-time lecturers, some of whom were prominent members of the Los Angeles Philharmonic Orchestra. For piano instruction, however, there was always at least one well-known figure as a member of staff. In my undergraduate days it was Guy Meyer and in the 1960s it was Aubi Tzerko. A noted violinist among the teaching staff was the Hungarian Feri Roth who in earlier decades had formed the well-known Roth String Quartet. When I knew him he was one of the least remarkable men in the department, nobody seemed to have much regard for him. Thomas Marrocco was another violinist who was also a highly regarded scholar of medieval Italian music. In my undergraduate years Dr. Marrocco had been my violin teacher. Those who taught wind and brass instruments were mostly members of the Los Angeles Philharmonic Orchestra; they were engaged on part-time basis. The conductor of the Department's Symphony Orchestra was Mehli Mehta, the father of Zubin Mehta, who happened to be, at that time, the Principal Conductor of the Los Angeles Philharmonic. Roger Wagner, the famous conductor of the Wagner Choir, was in charge of the Department's Chorus.

One of the most versatile musicians at UCLA was Jan Popper. Dr. Popper was a native of Prague who had had the beginnings of an illustrious career in his native Czechoslovakia. In his twenties he had been the assistant conductor of the Prague Opera and had conducted in Hungary and Germany before escaping to the U.S. when the Nazis descended on his homeland. He was an outstanding all around musician. I had a course on Richard Wagner with him in my final year of my undergraduate studies in 1952-53. He infused so much enthusiasm in his discussion of Wagner's music that made every student fall in love with the German master's music. He not only discussed Wagner's operas, he played portions of each opera at the piano and even sang bits of the arias. That was the most enthralling music class I ever had.

Jan Popper created an Opera Workshop at UCLA and trained numerous singers some of whom achieved international fame. One of his pupils who began a career as a singer, and later opera producer, of was the Persian Lotfollāh (Lotfi) Mansuri. Lotfi was a contemporary of mine, also an undergraduate student at UCLA, but not in music; he was studying psychology. At some point he had discovered that he had a good tenor voice and had come to see Dr. Popper for advice. Popper took him under his wing and gave him voice training. Lotfi became a member of the Opera Workshop and sang in some of Popper's productions. He gradually moved to stage direction and production. In time Mr. Mansuri became a highly regarded opera production manager of international fame. He has held appointments in some of the important opera houses in Europe and in America.

It was during Jan Popper's turn as the Chairman in 1964 that I was asked to join the Music Faculty at UCLA as a member of the composition staff. Dr. Popper and I became very good friends. Some years later, when I was back in Persia active as Head of the Music Department at University of Tehran, I organized invitations to Jan Popper to come to Tehran and conduct two operas. The Tehran Opera Company operated under the aegis of Ministry of Culture and Arts and mounted a season of opera production in the Rudaki Hall. I was able to arrange for these invitations through my personal contacts with Mr. Pahlbod, the Minister of Culture and Arts. In 1971, he conducted the *Bartered Bride* of Smetana at the Rudaki Hall to great success. Two years later, he was re-invited to Tehran and he conducted the *Romeo and Juliet* of Charles Gounod. Needless to say, Popper was not very satisfied with the standard of production but he did his part enthusiastically and had excellent results. My friendship with Jan Popper continued after I left Persia and came to Ireland in 1979. He and wife Beta came to Dublin for a visit in 1986, and stayed with me. Sadly, the lecture that he was to give at Trinity College had to be cancelled. He was taken ill quite suddenly and was hospitalized on arriving back in America. He died of pancreatic cancer in 1987. Jan Popper was superb musician and one of the most cheerful and kindly human being I have ever known.

Music Department at University of Tehran

The year before my return to Persia in 1968, a music department had been created within the College of Fine Arts of the University of Tehran. The department was in an embryonic stage. There were only two full time staff members with a curriculum of courses that was no more than a haphazard group of subjects in the theory and history of western music, some piano classes, and instruction in Persian music through performance classes in a few of the native instruments. The nominal person in charge was Dr. Mehdi Barkeshli who was a professor in the Physics Department in the College of Sciences of the University. His supervisory role in the music department was sporadic and directionless. Dr. Barkeshli had studied Persian music in his youth and, as a physicist, had taken interest in the theory of tones and intervals of Persian modes. He had written a number of articles on these subjects some of which had been published in France. He knew nothing about western music.

The two members in the department with regular fulltime university appointment: Dr. Barkeshli's daughter Pari, and Mr. Nurali Borumand. Miss Barkeshli, an assistant professor (*ostadyar*), was a pianist who had studied at the Paris Conservatoire; she had returned from France recently. It was quite apparent that her father was preparing the ground for his young daughter to eventually take over the running of the department. Mr. Borumand was a well-known musician of the traditional school, with no background in academia and no knowledge of any music other than the *radif* (repertory of classical melody models) of urban tradition. At age 60, he had been quite unexpectedly brought to the University and was give a full professorship. Except for instruction in piano and the *radif* of Persian music, all other subjects were taught by part-time lecturers whose attendance was rather sporadic. They were given no office space and students had little contact with them outside class sessions.

In 1969 the president of Tehran University was Alinaqi Ālikhāni. He was a highly intelligent and dynamic man, an economist by profession, but keenly interested in both native music and the classical western

music. He had heard about me through some mutual friends and knew
something of my background. His secretary contacted me one day and
indicated that Dr. Ālikhāni wished to meet me. In our first meeting he
plainly said that the music department that has been established within
the College of Fine Arts was in a shambolic state. He asked if I would
agree to be appointed as the Chairman of the department in order to
restructure the department and put it in proper order. He indicated
very clearly that unless I took charge he would close down the department. This was only a year after I had arrived in Iran and had been
engaged at the National Iranian Radio and Television Organization as
the Chairman of the Music Council. I told Dr. Ālikhāni that I was an
academic and would certainly be interested in the job he was offering
me but it had to be subject to the consent of my present employer.

The director of NIRT, Mr. Rezā Ghotbi, agreed to my move to Tehran
University provided that I continued as the Head of the Music Council
on part-time basis. As of the beginning of the academic year 1969/70, I
became the first appointed Chairman of its Music Department. Within
a year a new curriculum based on the American system was devised.
Three major study areas were created in western musicology, composition and Persian music. With Dr. Ālikhāni's unstinting support and
financial assistance I was able to engage a number of new staff members
some of whom proved to be significant figures in the musical life of
the country. The most important of these was Dr. Mohammad Taqi
Massoudiyeh. He had studied music in France and in Germany, where
he had obtained a doctoral degree from the University of Leipzig. He
was a well-educated all around musician, knowledgeable in western music and also very interested in research on native music. Massoudiyeh
was also a good composer but his interest was increasingly focused on
regional folk music. By the time he died in 1998 – long after I had left
Iran – he had published two very important books on the folk music of
the Baluchestan province of southeast Iran and on the music of Ta'zie
(religious passion plays). He was a hardworking and dedicated teacher;
however, he was not always easy to work with; he was very temperamental and easily aroused.

Another figure of prominence was the composer Ali Rezā Mashāyekhi. He was a difficult man, very proud and disdainful; but he was an active and capable composer who had studied composition in Vienna. Of all composers in Persia at the time, Mashāyekhi's style was decidedly the most radical. I did not particularly like his music but believed it was important to have his contributions available to our students. I managed to have a good working relation with Mr. Mashāyekhi, even though he did not always have a happy relationship with his colleagues and his students.

Another very capable composer was Ahmad Pezhmān. Mr. Pezhmān had also studied in Vienna. On his return to Iran in the mid 1960s he had been employed by the Ministry of Culture and Arts as a resident composer and had written a very successful opera that was produced at the Rudaki Hall. With considerable effort I managed to obtain the consent of Mr. Pahlbod, the Minister of Culture and Arts, to have Pezhmān transferred to Tehran University. He was a good and active composer but an indifferent lecturer; his heart was really not in teaching.

In the area of performance of western instruments, the outstanding figure was Emanuel Melik-Aslanian. He had studied in Germany in the 1930s, was a brilliant pianist and a very competent composer. Mr. Melik-Aslanian was already engaged on a part-time basis, as piano teacher for advanced students, before I took over the Music Department. I wanted to make his appointment full-time but he declined. He had many private piano students and simply did not have the time to avail himself to the University on full-time basis. He was not only an excellent musician but also a cultured man with a wide range of interests. We had an excellent relationship both on academic and friendship levels. I was deeply saddened when I learned of his passing in 2003 at age 88.

Another highly accomplished pianist that I brought to the Music Department was Mrs. Lucette Martirossian. She was the Belgian wife of George Martirossian, an Iranian/Armenian violinist. George also became a part-time member of the Department; he was an excellent violinist and taught advanced violin classes. Mrs. Martirossian was not only a good pianist, she was a well-trained musician and I asked her to take charge of ear-training and solfeggio classes. The aforementioned Miss Pari Barkeshli was an accomplished pianist but with little qualifications to teach any subject in the areas of advanced theory or in music history and analysis.

The Music Department was also involved with Persian music as an area of specialization. The students majoring in Persian music had to sit courses on theory, harmony, counterpoint and history of western music in common with other students. In the third and fourth years, however, they concentrated on subjects pertaining to native music. These were in essence classes in theory and history plus a heavy concentration on the study of the *radif* as played on one of the native instruments. The central figure in native music was Mr. Nurali Borumand who, as mentioned earlier, had been recently installed as the Professor of Persian music. His appointment had been of the sort of arbitrary decision-making that was commonplace in Persia, often on the whim of one person in position of authority. Clearly, he had none of the qualifications required for an academic post. He had no university degrees, had never published anything and was not even a renowned performing musician. He was a gentleman of personal means who, in his youth in 1920s, had begun medical studies in Germany. An accident had led to his loss of sight; he had returned to Persia and, being quite wealthy, had spent his time learning music and being in the company of famous musicians. Mr. Borumand was not a particularly good performer of the two instruments he played: tār and setār, but was reputed to know the entire *radif* by heart. Also, he was known to have memorized a large number of old ballads (*tasnif*).

During the years of my contact with Nurali Borumand I came to know him as an exceedingly shrewd man. He had created an aura of great mastery about himself that was highly deceptive. The *radif* he knew was no more – probably less extensive - than a version of what had been already published by Musā Ma'rufi in 1963. The *tasnif*s he had in his memory were also largely in the common domain. But admittedly there was an air of grandeur and mystery, craftily and effectively cultivated, about this highly polished and dignified blind man.

He came to the University in his big car, driven by a chauffeur; he wore dark glasses, walked assisted by a valet, and always came to my office for a cup of tea before going up to his classroom. Borumand was extremely guarded about what knowledge of the *radif* he was supposed to have. In his lessons he would dwell on one *gushe* (individual melody model) from a *dastgāh* (collections of *gushe*s) for several sessions, the performance duration of which would be no more than a couple of minutes. I had heard from some of his students that he was very nervous about the possibility of his lectures being recorded. Being blind, he always begun his sessions by asking if there was a tape recorder in the room.

In his method of teaching the *radif*, Borumand maintained a procedure that I believe to be the antithesis of the desirable. He would insist that any *gushe* that he taught must be played exactly as he demonstrated; in other words, he forbade any elaboration, variation and improvisation. This procedure, in my view, can only lead to the demise of Persian music. The strength of this music is in its ability to expand and vary in each rendition. To limit this music to a fixed version is to make it intolerably repetitive and tedious. Persian traditional urban music is built on a repertory of melody models that if performed in its entirely will not last more than a few hours. The wealth of this music is in its elusiveness and lack of finality. The fact that those few hours are subjected to the freedom of improvisation and are never repeated the same way twice is the very lifeline of this music.

After years of association with Mr. Borumand, quite frankly, I had come to the conclusion that this was a very clever man who had managed to put across an image of being the fount of knowledge on native music whereas, in fact, he had very little on board. The secret of his success in cultivating this image was the ability to maintain deliberate ambiguity as to what it was that he actually knew. He neither was a good performer nor did he have very much to offer by way of knowledge of the theoretical principles of Persian music, and if he did have something to offer, he was extremely reluctant to do so. What he knew of Persian music — and I am convinced that it was not beyond the routine and the widely available — was to him a personal property that he would part with only at a price. And, I do mean monetary price. Concurrent with his fulltime employment as university professor, Borumand was receiving a handsome salary from the NIRT (National Iranian Radio and Television) as an advisor. In the early 1970s, NIRT asked him if he would perform the *radif* as he knew it, to be recorded for posterity. For this service, he asked for a contract and was paid a huge sum of money, even though he was drawing a large salary. The recording could have been done in ten or twelve sessions. But, to make the project appear much more grand than it actually was, he extended the recording sessions so much that it actually took a couple of years for it to be concluded.

When I took charge of the Music Department I knew that the Persian music program needed additional staff. But it was very difficult to find qualified people who could teach beyond the performance aspects of the music. At that time the musicians who were identified with native music were only performers; there were no genuine scholars among them. I had done years of research on the traditional music and had written a thesis on the *dastgāh* system plus a number of published articles, but my primary area of interest was western music and it was in that area that my teaching services were very much needed. Moreover, I felt certain that with all the famous musicians around surely there must be some who could cover all aspects of native music, both practical and theoretical. On close investigation the reality dawned on me that all the great figures of Persian music were performing musicians; they had very little to offer as lecturers, at university level, on the theory or the history of this music.

The only person who appeared to be a possibility as a lecturer was Dāryush Safvat who had co-authored a book on Persian music, published in France. The book was actually written by the French ethnomusicologist Nellie Caron, but the content was largely based on information provided by Safvat. I knew Mr. Safvat from my secondary school days, we had both attended the same high school in the final three years before graduating in 1947. He had studied *santur* and *setār* with the late Abolhasan Sabā in his youth and was reputed to be a fair performer of these two instruments. I took the issue of the book co-authored and published in France seriously and thought the Music Department could benefit from the services of someone who was evidently both capable as a performer and has also scholarly credentials. By profession Mr. Safvat was an accountant and had been in the employ of the Ministry of Finance for about 25 years. I spoke to him to see if he would be willing to come to the University on full time basis; he was very interested. The process of transferring his employment and pension scheme from the Ministry of Finance to the University of Tehran proved complicated. I asked for the University President, Dr. Ālikhāni's help, which he gave willingly, and with considerable effort and perseverance I had Mr. Safvat moved to Tehran University as Assistant Professor (*ostādyar*). Some years later, he was promoted to Associate Professorship (*dāneshyār*).

I placed Mr. Safvat in charge of course on theory and history of Persian music. Unfortunately, as time went by, it became increasingly evident that my assumptions about his expertise, merely based on his co-authorship of a book published in France, were totally off the mark. Not only had he very little to give to his students, he was grossly derelict in his attendance. Moreover, it was revealed that he was in the full time employ of the National Iranian Radio and Television Organization as the Head of the Centre for Preservation of National Music. Each time the subject of his employment was raised, either by me, or by the Dean of the College of Fine Arts (the Music Department was a unit within that College), and he was told that he could not be a full time employ of two different institutions, he would obligingly agree and give assurance that he would give up the NIRT job. But he would do nothing and hope that the matter would be forgotten. For all I know Dāryush Safvat was still drawing two full time salaries when I left Persia for the last time in the summer of 1979. The full-time members of the Music Department's Persian music section were these two gentlemen, neither of whom really had any place in a respectable academic surrounding.

To teach Persian musical instruments, I engaged, on part-time basis, some excellent musicians. Mr. Asqar Bahāri taught the *kamānche*, which is a spiked fiddle. He was a fine musician, modest and honorable. One of our former students, Mohammad Rezā Lotfi taught the *tār* (long-necked six stringed lute); Mr. Lotfi, some years after my departure from Persia, became one of the country's best-known *tār* players and has enjoyed an international reputation. As the *santur* (dulcimer) instructor, I engaged the country's most celebrated *santur* player, Farāmarz Pāyvar. Mr. Pāyvar was a temperamental and at times difficult person but his technical command of his instrument and his knowledge of the *radif* were unsurpassed.

In 1978, with the revolution in progress, the city of Tehran was in constant turmoil. The campus of the University was one of the major scenes of daily demonstration. The academic year 1978-79 was effectively suspended. I left Persia in July 1979, a few months after the departure of the Royal family and the take over of country by the clerics. The Islamic regime, for a couple of years, closed down all universities. The professed intention was to Islamize all third level teaching. This was such an absurd objective that it could not go much beyond rhetoric. However, music posed a particular problem as Islam has at best an ambivalent, at worst a hostile, attitude towards music. I have learned that the Music Department at the University of Tehran was closed down for a few years. After it was reopened, for a few years, it was named the Department of Sound, as if the name music in itself was sinful. Apparently, a few years later, the word music (*Musiqi*) was rehabilitated and reinstated. Currently, I understand, it continues to function and at least two new members have added weight to its standing. These are my cousin Shāhin Farhat who is a very active and competent composer and Mohammad Rezā Darvishi who is both a composer and an excellent research scholar.

The School of Music at University of Dublin, Trinity College

The University of Dublin was founded in 1592 when Ireland was under British rule and Elizabeth I was the monarch. It was to be modeled on Oxford and Cambridge, the only two universities that existed in England. Like her English sister universities, it was to contain a number of Colleges where students and some of the staff members resided and tutorials were conducted. However, it began with one college called Trinity. As time went by no new colleges were added and, as is the case to this day, Dublin University remained synonymous with Trinity College. For over four centuries it has retained a position of high prestige as one of Europe's distinguished institutions of higher learning.

The Chair of Music at Dublin University was established in 1764, which is quite early as music is not one of primary subjects of concern in the European concept of a university. To have a Chair of Music, and to appoint a Professor to that Chair, did not mean, however, that there was a course of study with regular class sessions, lectures, research programs and examinations. It simply meant that the Professor, a person of musical knowledge and discernment, was in place to be consulted by prospective applicants who, with his guidance, will prepare for examinations that will be administered when the candidate is ready, and upon passing will receive a degree, the Bachelor of Music (BMus). In other words no regular instruction on the university premises was available. The students, usually mature persons of some musical accomplishments, would register for the BMus, prepare for examinations in consultation with the Professor of Music, and on passing those tests will receive the degree. I was told that the first Professor of Music was Lord Mornington, the father of Duke of Wellington; he had not been a professional musician but a man of 'musical erudition'. Since 1764, there were long periods when the Chair of Music was not occupied. Clearly, there were no applicants to sit exams and receive degrees during those periods. Or, if there were any applicants, the university simply did not accept their applications, as there was no Professor of Music in place.

At the University of Dublin, following the old tradition of Oxford and Cambridge, in each discipline there was only one Professor as the holder of the Chair and the Head of the School; other academic members were Junior or Senior Lecturers. In rare cases an individual of exceptional distinction might be granted a personal Chair with the title of Professor of that particular discipline. It is also possible to be pro-moted, for considerable accomplishments, to Associate Professorship.

The formation of the School of Music with fulltime academic mem-bers and a four year course of study, with lectures and regular examina-tions, leading to a B.A. Honors degree, was only established in 1977 by my immediate predecessor, Professor Brian Boydell. I replaced him in 1982 when he took retirement. The School was young, small and had a miniscule budget. In addition to the Professor, there were only three full-time and two part-time lecturers. Of the three full-time members only one had obtained a doctoral degree; the other two only had B.A. in music. They were all quite young and relatively inexperienced; they had no publications of any significance. Only one of them, a few years after my arrival in Dublin, published a book of scholarly standing. By American standards this might have passed as the staff of a music de-partment at a two year college, generally known as a 'Junior College'.

The School of Music was housed in a portion of one of the old build-ings in the 'Front Square' of the College. There were three lecture rooms plus a larger room that could seat up to 60 for recitals. There were no practice rooms and the Music Library was located within the Main (Berkley) Library of the College. The fulltime lecturers had their offices, but the part-time teachers had none. There was a departmental office with secretary, next to The Professor office, which was a large and handsome room.

In 1982, there were only about 40 music students. The curriculum did not include any practical tuition in musical instruments or sing-ing, the emphasis was on theory and analysis. The outcome of students' four years of the B.A. course was determined by examinations at the end of each year. Postgraduate degrees of M.A. and PhD were available on the strength of a thesis prepared under supervision of a staff mem-ber. No taught courses were included in the postgraduate program.

Curiously, the old BMus degree, which only hinged on passing cer-tain examinations, was still in effect. Applicants, who were hardly known to me, or to my colleagues, were to be examined at specified periods and, on passing the tests, they were to receive the BMus degree. This was clearly a leftover from the bygone days when there were no taught courses and no required attendance. I could not countenance the continuation of a degree conferred on persons, who were barely known to the School and who never attended classes, by a mere set of examinations. As my colleagues were in agreement with my position, I set about a gradual phasing out of this degree. There were a number of people who had already registered for the BMus examinations, to be administered at three stages, each normally at one year's interval. They had to be processed. Accordingly, it took four years before this degree was abolished.

In other areas of the School's curriculum I introduced major revisions. The new structure of courses established a uniform program of studies in the first two years; in the next two years, two areas of specialization, in either musicology or composition, were instituted. All students were required to present either a thesis (for musicology majors) or a large composition folio (for composition majors) in their final year. As some of our students were accomplished performers, a recital option was also introduced as partial fulfillment of their degree requirement. As regards students' results at the end of each year, I introduced what I believe the important concept of continuous assessment. I felt that to evaluate the outcome of a student's work solely based on the result of final exams was unjust. Accordingly, 40% of the mark for each course was the result of the student's work done in the coursed of the year. Only 60% of the result was determined by the final exam. In a matter of a few years this approach to assessment of the students' work was adopted by a number of other departments in the University.

I tried to organize periodic concerts in Trinity. In some cases I was able to invite distinguished artists who happened to be visiting Dublin to give concerts or lectures in Trinity. My efforts were not always successful largely due to two problems: apathy on the part of my colleagues who were not supportive, and the absence of a proper venue at the College. University of Dublin, to this day as I write these lines, does not have a hall suitable for concerts or for any kind of stage production. The only place where concerts can be held is the Exam Hall, now also called the Public Theatre, as if the change of name makes the unlikely place into a real theatre. This is an elaborately designed late

18th century hall where students in all disciplines sit for their final examinations. It has an ornate high sealing, but no appropriately elevated stage area that would suit concert of theatrical presentations. It has no lobby or waiting area, no proper dressing room, and no toilet facilities. The hall is acoustically bad and is terribly cold in winter. Trinity, a highly prestigious university with some 15,000 students, does not have a proper hall for public lectures, theatre productions, concerts, commencement ceremonies, or for any number of functions that require a sizable gathering of participants. During my tenure, I tried to press the need for a proper concert hall with different Provosts of the College without success.

Despite inadequate resources and financial constraints, my years at Trinity College were in some ways exceptionally satisfying. Some of the colleagues that I came to know from different departments were highly accomplished academics whose friendship I have greatly enjoyed. Also, I was gratified in assisting in the development of some very talented students. The most outstanding of these was Donnacha Dennehy who began his training in composition with me. His exceptional creative ability was in evidence from the outset. On his graduation, I encouraged him to seek further studies in the U.S. He received a scholarship from University of Illinois for postgraduate studies, returned to Ireland and is now the country's leading young composer. There were a number of other talented young men and women who began their compositional studies with me and are currently major figures in Irish composition.

On the whole, my experience at Trinity College Dublin has been very positive. It is an institution of high standing; some of its departments, and a number of individual academics, are distinguished and have international recognition. The student intake has grown, however, beyond the physical capacity of the College. The campus, located in the very heart of Dublin, is of a size best suited to no more than 5000 students. (Until a century ago it had less than 1000 students.) It has now more than 15000; classroom and lecture hall facilities are entirely inadequate, particularly in the fields of humanities and the arts. While the front areas of the College (Front Square and New Square are of old design and are very handsome, the other parts of the campus are congested with an array of incongruous and disharmonious buildings.

Some traditions that live on from the College's inception seem rather out of place in modern times, but they are tenaciously maintained. A particularly peculiar one, in my view, is the 'scholarship' procedure. Near the end of their second year of a four year bachelors degree, the students can choose to sit Scholarship Examinations in whatever field they have been studying. These exams cover most of the subjects taught in the first two years. If they receive a first class result as an average of their marks, they are awarded 'Scholarship'. Henceforth, they are called 'Scholars of Trinity college' and receive extraordinary privileges. The Scholars do not pay any more fees, they can receive free housing in College, free dinners while the College is in session, and they have automatic access to postgraduate studies, if they so choose, without fees. This is a procedure that was clearly meaningful when there were no more than a few hundred students in the institution and university studies, for the overwhelming number of students, came to an end by the end of the four years. Proven excellence at the midpoint of an undergraduate course, perhaps, could have been taken as a serious scholarly achievement. Now that thousands enroll each year and even the full four years of a BA course in not taken to have great significance, for one who has done very well in two years to be called a 'Scholar' seems rather risible.

Al things considered, the fact that I have had an academic career at various institutions and in different parts of the world has enriched my life. I am grateful for the opportunities I was given and am gratified for being able to contribute to the musical development of many young and promising talents.

❧ 14 ❧

Reflections On Persian Music

In this chapter I shall address various issues related to the urban musical tradition of Persia. I shall begin with an account of how I became interested in this music, followed by a brief historic overview, theoretical foundations of Persian music, socio-religious problems, and its developments in modern (last 120 years) times. In discussing theoretical issues I shall try to avoid getting too 'technical', hoping not to pose difficulties for my non-musician readers in grasping the points that are raised.

My Entry into the World of Persian Music

Before leaving Iran and going to America for my university studies in June of 1949, I had developed very little interest in Persian music. I was aurally familiar with the urban musical tradition, which was practically the only genre of Persian music generally known and practiced in major cities. I had heard this music from recordings we had in our home and also from radio programs. Moreover, my father was a fair player of the tar, a six-stringed plucked instrument. In his youth, he had studied with the famed tar player Darvish Khān. He had two tārs at home and, in my childhood, he did occasionally play which delighted and fascinated me. He did not keep up with his tar practice, however, and by my late teens he rarely touched the instrument.

My earliest musical interests were primarily aroused by western music of the light variety. Initially, I was drawn to dance rhythms of foxtrots, rumbas, waltzes and particularly the Argentine tango; I also loved French chansons such as those sung by the celebrated tenor, Tino Rossi. This awakening to western music had come about after we had bought a radio set. Before the establishment of a local radio station, some well-to-do homes had acquired radio sets. These radios had short wave bands making it possible to tune-in to broadcasts from abroad. There were Persian language news broadcasts from the BBC and from Radio Berlin, each having their own avid listeners, depending on the family's political persuasion. One could also listen to musical programs from various foreign stations. The first local broadcasting station became operative in early1940. From Radio Tehran, as it was called, a daily dose of music entered our home which included programs of Persian traditional urban music, songs and light instrumental pieces composed, in Persian modes, by native musicians, as well as a few scattered hours of western music, both light and classical.

It was through this narrow opening into the world of western classical music, provided by the local radio station, that my abiding commitment to music was born. Radio Tehran had a 45-minute slot, at two in the afternoon, devoted to broadcasts of classical music. Their collection of recordings – 78 rpms, of course – was quite limited. Selected symphonic works by Hayden, Mozart, Beethoven, Schuman, Dvorak, Grieg, Tchaikovsky, Rimsky-Korsakov and a few others were available. There was very little piano solo or chamber music and no operas were ever heard. Baroque and earlier music were apparently not included in their collection, and Debussy was the closest to the contemporary one could ever hear. I became devoted to this afternoon classical music program, although on school days I could not be at home to tune in.

Classical music moved and inspired me beyond any experience I had ever known. I was overwhelmed by the richness, diversity, drama and power of western classical music. By comparison Persian music seemed limited, static and dull. I have recounted in chapter 6 the events leading to my decision to pursue musical studies and how this decision took me to America. What is relevant to this chapter is the fact that, while western music and in particular musical composition, became my all-consuming love, at some point I became also interested in Persian music.

In 1955, when I begun my studies towards a PhD degree at University of California in Los Angles, my attention was turned to Persian music as a possible field of research for my doctoral thesis. I had already obtained a B.A. and a M.A., majoring in composition. At that time, most

American universities did not grant doctoral degrees in composition. Now they do. For the PhD degree I had the option of continuing my studies in composition, but I had to produce a major work of research as my dissertation. The person responsible for drawing my attention to Persian music as the subject of my research was Mantle Hood (he is one of five persons I have written about in Chapter 11: Exceptional People). Dr. Hood was a man of great resourcefulness and resolve. When installed at UCLA, he proceeded to create and expand a whole program of ethnomusicological studies with far reaching applications. In 1955, however, he was at the very beginning of his project and was keenly interested in attracting students who would eventually become a part of, and contributors to, his program.

On a number of occasions, Mantle, whom I had only met recently, asked me about Persian music; he was keen to learn what I knew about it. I had to tell him that I have only aural familiarity and know nothing about its theories and practices. He encouraged me to choose Persian music for my research and produce my thesis on a subject pertaining to it. As I took his advice and as I made a preliminary investigation, I came to realize that no work of any consequence had ever been published on Persian music in western languages. Accordingly, we both concluded that a first hand research on any aspect of this music could be a genuine contribution to the field of musical knowledge. By the following academic year I was convinced that it was fruitless to pursue this research in the United States; the only way to do an effective investigation was to go back to Persia. Early in 1957, I forwarded an application to the Ford Foundation, supported by a strong letter of recommendation by Mantle Hood, for a fellowship grant to finance my return to Iran so that I might spend a year in research. In April of 1957, I was invited to attend an interview, in San Francisco, by a board from the Ford Foundation. A month later I was informed that I had been granted the Fellowship and can travel to Persia as soon as I wished.

In June, exactly eight years after I had left Tehran, I arrived back in my native city. Before the year was up I applied for a year's extension of the Fellowship as I still had more work to do in gathering material for my thesis. This, too, was granted. I remained In Persia for a total of 17 months. On the way back to America, I spent three weeks in Turkey, both in Ankara and in Istanbul. I was able to contact a number of distinguished Turkish musicologists including Kemal Ilerici and Mahmud Gazinihal. I had several interviews with them and received their kind assistance in making comparative studies between Persian and Turkish classical traditions. This was important to my research, as the two traditions have decided historical and theoretical connections.

The research that I conducted during 17 months in Persia was multi-faceted; it included: a) establishing contact with major figures of traditional music, to interview them and learn their views on native music, b) making taped recordings of performances of traditional music by these same reputed authorities, c) obtaining all published material on native music that were available, and d) learning how to play some Persian instruments in order to understand the inner workings of this musical tradition.

Shortly after arriving in Tehran, my first move was to establish contact with well-known Persian musicians. I began by going to the Honarestān-e Musiqi-ye Melli (Conservatory of National Music). The Director of the Conservatory, at that time, was Ruhollāh Khāleqi. Mr. Khāleqi (1906-65) was one of the country's most distinguished musicians whose reputation, quite exceptionally, was based on his scholarship and his compositions. I say exceptionally because nearly every other musician's recognition was essentially as a performer, some of whom also composed occasional pieces. The only other personality who, in addition to being a virtuoso performer of a number of instruments, was also known for his theoretical writings and for his compositions was Khāleqi's teacher and mentor, the highly respected Alinaqi Vaziri who, at that time, was already in semiretirement.

From our first meeting, Mr. Khāleqi seemed to take interest in what I intended to do and offered to help with my research. He was a soft spoken, gentle and dignified man; I remain very much indebted to him and cherish the memory of the times I spent with him. Through Khāleqi's introductions I met a number of other notable musicians. In what follows I give brief accounts of my contacts with major figures of the urban musical tradition, which in many cases evolved into lasting friendship. Two particularly important figures, however, I had only one chance to see and to interview.

One day, with prior arrangement, Khāleqi took me to meet Abolhasan Sabā at his home on Zahirdole Street, which happened to be very close to my childhood home. Sabā (1902-57) was a very well known and highly esteemed musician. His fame was, above all, as a violinist, but he was equally proficient as a performer of *santur* (dulcimer), *setār* (4 stringed plucked instrument) and *tombak* (goblet shaped drum). He was also the composer of a large number of pieces based on Persian modes for the violin. Some of his compositions were available in a series of booklets he published as graded pedagogic methods for both the violin and the *santur*. Saba was also a generous and inspiring teacher; most of the violinists of the younger generation had studied with him and emulated his very individual style of violin playing. My visit with Sabā was largely spent in ceremonial pleasantry so elemental in Persian first meetings. He was very kind, however, and asked that I should pay him repeated visits to discuss any matter that may be of interest to me for my research. Sadly, Mr. Sabā died quite suddenly of a heart attack only a few days after I had visited him; it is a source of much regret that I had no further opportunity to learn from this wonderful musician.

Another important meeting arranged by Mr. Khāleqi was with Alinaqi Vaziri. Mr. Vaziri (1887-1979) enjoyed a rather unique position among Persian musicians. In addition to being a virtuoso player of *tār* and *setār*, in his youth, he had also studied the rudiments of the theory and notation of western music. In his early 30s he had travelled to Europe and had spent four years, between 1918 and 22, in France and Germany, where he had studied violin, piano and composition. Soon after returning to Persia he had founded the first private music school in the country. Within a few years Vaziri had established a reputation as the country's foremost music teacher who was well versed in the native traditions but also was knowledgeable in European music. Among Persian musicians there had been some who had aural familiarity with western music and had some knowledge of the rudiments of western theory, but Vaziri was the only one who had actually studied in Europe. The combination of high credentials in native music and knowledge of western music placed Vaziri in an unassailable position of authority. The fact that he had also a very forceful and charismatic personality added to his stature.

From early 1920s until mid-1930s, Alinaqi Vaziri was unquestionably the dominant musical figure in Persia. His music school, established in 1923, flourished and attracted many students, most of them, in time, became prominent figures in their own right. He published books and articles on music that made a significant impact. Within his music school he established a chamber orchestra composed of both native and western instruments. He wrote compositions to be performed with this orchestra, and encouraged his more advanced students to do the same. His orchestra, made of some twenty players, included native instruments such as *tār*, *setār* and tombak, plus violin, violoncello and piano. Vaziri believed in the 'advancement' of native music through the adoption of harmonic principles of western music; accordingly, he introduced a thin layer of polyphony in some of his compositions. He organized public concerts, and gave lectures on music. Above all, Vaziri made great strides in opening a place of honor for music and musical activity in a society where, due to religious proscription, none existed before.

At the time of our meeting, Vaziri was 71 years old. I found him to be highly intelligent, sharp and focused. He asked me questions about music education in American universities and was very impressed to learn that all institutions of higher learning in the U.S. have music departments. He was very taken by the fact that a third level student in America can pursue further studies in all musical instruments and in composition, in addition to musicology. Our meeting turned out to be more of my telling Mr. Vaziri about what I have been doing in the U.S. rather than my learning from him about his views on Persian music. This was not necessarily disappointing for I had already read his books and was familiar with his theories on Persian music. I did not meet Vaziri again; he left for Europe shortly after our visit, which was in summer of 1958.

Without a doubt, Alinaqi Vaziri has been the most influential musician of early 20th century Persia. Above all, he is responsible for mak-

ing music, at least among the educated middle class, respectable. This, I
believe, is Vaziri's most important contribution to the history of Persian
music in modern times. I have already discussed, earlier in this chapter,
his views on modes, scales and intervals. Here, may it suffice to say that
in his theories he attempts to explain Persian music by way of western
musical concepts which are not relevant to it. As to his compositions,
they are decidedly among the best of the genre of 20th century composed music in Persian modes.

Other musicians I met and interviewed in the course of nearly one
year and half in Iran included Ahmad Ebādi, the country's most celebrated *setār* player. Mr. Ebādi (1906-94) was the son of Mirzā Abdollāh
and a nephew of Āqā Hoseyn Qoli, both great musicians of the late
Qājār period. As a performer, Ebadi had an elegant and very original
style; he had a dramatic and nuanced manner of performance. In his
hands the *setār*, which is basically a rather timid instrument, became
quite powerful. Before him, the *setār* was losing out to more sonorous
instruments (e.g. *tār* and *santur*) that could hold their own in ensembles. But his virtuosity and the rich sonority that he produced went
a long way in popularizing *setār*, both as a solo and as an ensemble
instrument, particularly in the 1960s and 70s. I was fortunate to enjoy
Mr. Ebādi's friendship and, in the course of many visits, made several
hours of recordings of his performances of different *dastgāh*s.

Asqar Bahāri was another important figure; he was a pivotal figure in
reviving another native instrument that was on the verge of extinction.
By the middle of the 20th century, the use of the native bowed instrument *kamānche*, (a spiked fiddle held vertically as in violoncello), in
urban music, was practically abandoned in favor of the western violin.
The violin can easily manage all the varied and fluid intervals of Persian
music; it provides a wider and more colorful tonal range than its native
counterpart, and it is more glamorous. The *kamānche* has a huskier
tone and is technically less versatile. On the other hand it sounds closer
to the human voice and has its own distinctive character. It was most
unfortunate that it was becoming obsolete. Largely through the artistry
of Mr. Bahāri, with his great modesty and mastery of the instrument,
that interest in the *kamānche* was revived; by the late 1970s it had

become quite popular and is widely performed today. I was fortunate to be able to make a number of taped recordings of his performances.

A much younger musician who was soon recognized as the country's leading *santur* player was Farāmarz Pāyvar. He was in his mid-twenties when I met him in 1957. We became good friends and I made several hours of recording of his performances. Pāyvar (1933-2009), who had studied with the great Abolhasan Sabā, was a virtuoso performer, practiced his instrument many hours each day – not a common practice among native musicians - and tended to favor display pieces that showed his dexterity. He sprinkled his improvisations with numerous *chahārmezrāb*s. These are short, fast and rhythmic pieces that demonstrate the performer's technical prowess. In particular, his penchant for introducing rapid scale runs, arpeggios, even chords and parallel thirds into his improvisations seemed totally out of place in Persian music. But his technique was flawless and his knowledge of the *radif* was next to none.

Within a few weeks of my arrival in Tehran, I had met a large number of prominent musicians, too numerous to name here. One of my tasks, in addition to making recordings of their performances, was to interview them and to ask questions about Persian music in order to broaden my understanding of this music. As I was a trained western musician, inevitably my questions related to the theoretic principles, modes, rhythmic element, historic references, etc. Except for the likes of Vaziri, Khāleqi, Sabā and a few others, the responses I received were mostly unsatisfactory. For the most parts, the information I was given was routine and cursory. They all spoke of the seven *dastgāh* and the five *āvāz*; they had little to say about the intervals and scales; except for some vague understanding, and seeming acceptance, of Vaziri's theory of 24 quartertones scale. At times, I even sensed that the answers I received to my questions were rather improvised and misleading.

It did not take long for me to realize that I was dealing with excellent performing musicians who were very good at what they did but did not necessarily have theoretical, scientific and historical knowledge of their own music. In other words, although they were professional urban musicians, they are in essence folk musicians. Like folk musicians in all cultures, they knew how to perform but were not necessarily able to explain theoretical issues. They had learned the music and its repertoire through an aural process, which did not involve learning anything other than how to play the music in keeping with the teacher's instructions. The music they learned had a vaguely fixed core, subject to constant variation in extemporized renditions. Through endless improvised repetitions of the core material they would master both the technique of the instrument and learn the substance of the classical repertoire.

After a few months, as I continued to make new acquaintances, I decided to refrain from asking technical questions; I simply let musicians talk at will about their own background, their likes and dislikes, and about music in the way they wished to discuss it. I became primarily interested in obtaining samples of their performance. Eventually, on returning to the U.S., I made a comparative analysis of these performances and arrived my own conclusions as to any principles that may govern this music.

In my search to find publications on music I found very few books of any significance. The scholarly treatises of the medieval period, for the most part, were in a few libraries, some of them in places like Cairo, Istanbul or the British Library. No treatise on music of originality and significance was written between the 16th and 20th century. Most available recent publications were limited to the books of Vaziri and Khāleqi, which I obtained. There was also a monthly journal, *Majalle-ye Musiqi*, published by the Ministry of Culture and Arts; its content was light but had occasional articles of interest. The most important publication on the urban tradition of Persian music came out a few years after I had finished my research and had returned to America. This book, published by the Ministry of Culture and Arts in 1963, contains the entire *radif* of the 12 collections (*dastgāhs*) written, in western notation, by Musā Ma'rufi, a distinguished musician of the old school. It must be understood however, that this book represents only a notated rendition of the *radif*, as it might have been played at one sitting. The *radif* will not be repeated the same way twice. The book, as a sample of the *radif* in its entirety, is decidedly valuable.

Perhaps the most important part of my research on Persian urban music was to learn how to play two of the native instruments. After all, this is how native musicians learned their own music. They did not go through theory and history classes; any understanding of the traditional repertoire and its governing principles was a byproduct of practical training. To this end, Mr. Khāleqi introduced me to two of the teachers at the *Honarestān*: a distinguished elderly gentleman, a famous *tar* player, Nasrollāh Zarrinpanje, and a young *santur* player called Hoseyn Sabā (no relation to the great violin teacher Abolhassan Sabā). Within a couple of months of my arrival in Tehran I had purchased a *setār* and a *santur* and had begun taking regular lessons from these two excellent musicians. Following Mr. Zarrinpanje's advice I began my lessons on the *setār* instead of the *tār*. The two instruments have identical range and very similar technique. The *tār* is bulkier, has six strings and is played with a plectrum; the *setār* is lighter, has only four strings and is played by the nail of the right index finger. He thought that it would be easier to start with the *setār*.

My *setār* lessons with Mr. Zarrinpanje quickly developed into a close friendship. I went to his house every Friday at 11 in the morning, I played the piece he had asked me to learn with him as he guided and corrected what I played. Initially, I had a few lessons on how to hold the instrument, how to move my plucking finger and how to change the position of the left hand on the long fingerboard. Thereafter we proceeded with learning actual pieces. There were no theoretical introductions, no technical exercises, and no study manual; from the outset I was to work on a simplified version of a *darāmad* to *dastgāh-e shur*. A notated version was given to me but I was not restricted to what was on the paper, I could vary it and elaborate on it. My lessons usually lasted for an hour after which he invariably insisted that I stay for lunch. This became the established pattern for my Fridays: one hour of *setār* lesson with Zarrinpanje followed by lunch with him and his family. Mr. Zarrinpanje never accepted any payment from me.

My *santur* study with Hoseyn Sabā, also, quickly developed into a friendly relationship, which in his case was a friendship of contemporaries since he was closer to my own age. His approach to my *san-*

tur lessons was more westernized; it involved some exercises aimed at building technical dexterity. He had in fact published a book of lessons on the *santur* for the beginners. I followed the book and had weekly lessons with him. On a number of occasions he came to my place of residence and played for me as I made taped recordings of his performances. It was through Saba that I met Farāmarz Pāyvar who, in years to come, emerged as the country's preeminent *santur* virtuoso. Sadly, towards the end of my stay in Persia, in the autumn of 1958, Mr. Sabā, who was suffering periodic severe headaches, was diagnosed as having brain tumor. He died a couple of years later when he was only in his late 30s.

In the course of my nearly one and half years of study and research I collected a vast number of taped recordings of performances of traditional urban music. Analysis of this recorded music, representing diverse renditions of the same repertoire of the *dastgāh* system, contributed to the thesis that I produced when I was back in the U.S. The finalized doctoral thesis was presented in 1965 when the degree was granted. A slightly revised version of his work (*The Dastgāh Concept in Persian Music*), was published by the Cambridge University Press in 1990.

⁕ ⁕

For some eleven years, between 1968 and 1979, I was back in my native country. Both as the Head of the Music Department at Tehran University and the chairman of the Music Council at National Iranian Radio and Television organization, I had much contact with major figures in national music. Also, I conducted periodic research on aspects of Persian music I had not, hitherto, investigated. On one occasion I made recordings of folk music in the mountain villages of the Gilān province on the Caspian Sea. This is a forested region of the country with its own distinct folklore. The trip was sponsored by NIRT and I had a recording team with me. The material collected was deposited in the NIRT's archives.

On another occasion, for a two-week period, in the company of a film and recording crew, I made a trip to Bandar Abbas and the islands of

Qeshm, Hormoz and Lārak in the Persian Gulf. The crew was headed by Naser Taqvāi who later emerged as one of Iran's best film directors. This was an extraordinary visit to some of the least frequented parts of the country. Bandar Abbās is a major port at the mouth of the Gulf, but the islands I visited, at that time, were hardly frequented by anyone from the mainland. The local inhabitants of the islands are a mix of Persians, Arabs and Africans. In their music and rituals the African roots, particularly in ceremonies for the healing of the emotionally disturbed, are clearly in evidence. In these ceremonies, incessant drumbeats together with strumming of a primitive harp, a state of trance is induced. The afflicted person goes through bodily contortions and eventually returns to a peaceful state free of the former mental malaise.

Historic Background

Reliable information on pre-Islamic music in Persia is extremely scanty. We know very little about the musical life in the earliest Iranian empires of the Medes, the Achaemenids and the Parthians. Some information about music at the court of the Sassanids (226-651CAD) can be gleaned from literary sources of the Islamic era. Most of the information comes to us by way of epic poetry as, for example, found in Ferdowsi's *Shāhnāme* or Nezami's *Haft Ganj*. They tend to be fanciful accounts of festive events at the court of Persian kings in which musicians participated. In particular, stories about musical life at the court of Khosro II (ruled from 590 to 628) are featured prominently. The reign of this king, also known as Khosro Parviz (victorious), was a high point of Persian culture and political prominence, and, in its final years, of upheaval and disintegration. It was under his rule that Persians, once again, conquered the Levant and Egypt. Khosro II's court was legendary in its opulence. There were, according to poetic sources, a number of famous musicians attached to the court, including one Bārbod, who was the most celebrated musician of the age. He was, evidently, a virtuoso player of the plucked string instrument called the *barbat*, an instrument that was later disseminated by the Arabs throughout the Islamic world, where it became known by its Arabic name, *al-ud*. It also entered Western Europe, by way of the Iberian peninsula, as the lute (a variant of the name *al-ud*) and became popular in the medieval period and in the Renaissance. In addition to being a great performer, Bārbod is reported to have been also a composer. Names of some of his compositions have survived, but we have no idea as to what the music was like, since, to our knowledge, no system of notation was used. A theory of musical classification is attributed to Bārbod; it is reported that he had devised a system of seven primary and 30 secondary modes plus 360 *dastān* or melodies. The exact nature of the system is not known, and the seeming correspondence of the above numbers to days of the week, the month and the year of the Sassanid calendar remains a matter for conjecture.

We do have some evidence as to the type of musical instruments that were in use at the Sassanid Imperial court. Bas-reliefs from the period clearly show lutes, dulcimers and harps, flutes, shawms and drums; they are shown as employed in ensemble formations.

Numerous treatises on music are extant from the Islamic period, particularly the 10th to 15th centuries. Medieval scholars generally viewed music, in its Pythagorian and Aristotelian connotations, as a legitimate field of scientific investigation. The earliest and the foremost among scholars was Abu Nasr Fārābi who died in 950. His *Ketāb al-Musiqi al-Kabir* is a voluminous and exhaustive work on the physical and mathematical properties of music. It also includes a theory of intervals and modes that were presumably relevant to the learned music of his time in Baghdad, the seat of the Caliphate. Other scientists and musical theoreticians who followed Fārābi, also, have left us with very engaging treatises on what we may call the science of music. Particularly significant are the detailed writings, on the theory of intervals and modes, by Ebn-e Sinā (Avicenna) in the 11th century, and Safieddin Ormavi in the 13th century. Other important contributions on the theory of modes followed, the last of which is by Abdol-Qāder Marāqi in the early 15th century.

None of these treatises, however, gives us a clear sense of how the music of that period sounded. Musical notation was not used and, except for a few pieces that were composed by Abdol-Qāder Marāqi in early

15th century, we have no record of musical compositions. Medieval theories on intervals, and the division of the octave scale, suggest a degree of precision that is virtually unrealizable in actual practice. No musical instrument that was in use at the time – or now, for that matter – and certainly no human voice, can possibly replicate the sort of exactitude of tones and intervals as given by Fārābi, Ebn-e Sinā, Safieddin and the others. To be realistic, one must conclude that the theories, as discussed by these eminent sages, represent idealized versions of the actual music as practiced by performing musicians of their time. In all probability, the scales and intervals discussed in medieval treatises are scientific abstractions rather than true representation of the reality of the music their time.

Given the fact that in eastern societies cultural trends have remained relatively static and all the arts have evolved very slowly over centuries, it would not be unreasonable to assume that Persian traditional music, as known in modern times, is not significantly different from that which might have been practiced centuries ago. If we accept this premise, then it become all the more evident that the medieval scholars may have indulged in the creation of beautiful and neatly argued theoretical systems with only oblique connection with the music of their own time as performed by professional musicians. Their theories certainly cannot be supported by the music that has survived to this day. Persian music, as we know it contemporaneously, is anything but precise. Intervals are unstable and quite irregular; scales concepts have no practical application. It is not without significance that today's musical nomenclature has no word for scale. Contemporary Persian musicians, in their theoretic discussions, which are founded on western musical precepts, use the French word 'gamme'.

Contemporary Tradition: the Radif

It is quite remarkable that the theoretical foundations of Persian music have remained a subject of varying points of view. In a civilization of great depth and antiquity, where written sources in all fields of human knowledge abound, this absence of a firmly established and universally accepted theory for native music is quite exceptional. The problem, in all probability, lies with the proscriptive Islamic position towards music. This prevailing negative religious attitude has cast a shadow over musical activity and scholarship particularly since the 16th century when shiism was established as the national religion and gradually came to dominate the society. I shall discuss the Shiite clerical attitude toward music later in this chapter.

During the golden age of Islamic civilization, from the 9th to 14th centuries, when shiism was only a minor sect, musical scholarship had flourished and significant treatises on the physical and mathematical properties of music were written. But the succeeding centuries, until the modern era, produced little of genuine value other than minor and largely derivative works. By the 19th century musical activity had become an exclusively aural/oral tradition. Theoretical and historical studies, if not altogether absent, were only side issues, a byproduct of the practical training, subject to each teacher's own ideas. This is not to say that each musician had divergent theoretical views, but certainly a clear and universally accepted canon did not prevail. Until well into the second half of the 20th century, Persian musicians were essentially performers, there were no genuine musical scholars.

At this point, it is important to clarify that musical traditions in Persia fall into two distinct categories: the urban or classical and the rural or folk music. The overwhelming majority of Iranians are only familiar with the former, which they know as '*musiqi-ye irāni*', also referred to as '*musiqi-ye asil*' (authentic music), or '*musiqi-ye sonnati*' (traditional music). The far more extensive and diversified regional folk music of Iran is largely unknown outside their own locality, as the country is too vast and contains many distinct cultural units, as well as sub-nations. The urban tradition, as is known and practiced in modern times, can be encapsulated in the concept of the *radif* (row or line-up). The term refers to the entire corpus of melody models, or nuclear themes, on the basis of which a solo musician renders an improvised performance. In the 19th century, these melody models were loosely organized into twelve groups: the seven *dastgāh* (*Shur, Segāh, Chahārgāh, Navā, Homāyun,*

Māhur and *Rāst-Panjgāh*) and the five *āvāz* (*Abuatā, Dashti, Afshāri, Bayāt-e Tork* and *Bayāt-e Esfahān*).

There is no evidence to verify that the *dastgāh* concept and the word *dastgāh* have had any musical application before the 19th century; it does not appear in any of the medieval treatises on music. The temptation to see musical significance in the word *gāh* (place or position), and the conjecture that it has any connection with that word as it appears in *segāh* or *chahārgāh* (titles of two of the 7 *dastgāh*s), can be misleading. *Dastgāh* is a Persian word signifying an assembly of parts into a larger unit, as in, for example, a dwelling with a number of rooms (*dastgāh-e āpārtemān*), or the collective structure of the government (*dastgāh-e dolat*). In musical context, also, a *dastgāh* signifies a large unit that contains smaller parts. The smaller parts, or individual melody models, have their own modal identities and their own names; generically they are called *gushe*. The *gushe*s are not well-defined pieces of music; they are thematic ideas (*māye*) that are not specific but suggestive of patterns or layouts to which I have referred as melody models or nuclear themes. These *māye*s, learned aurally through long experience, are the building blocks for improvisation by the performing musician.

The question arises as to why some of these collections of *gushe*s are known as *dastgāh*, while others go by the name *āvāz*. The common explanation is that the five *āvāz* are not fully independent; four of them (*Abuatā, Dashti, Afshāri* and *Bayāt-e Tork*) are affiliated with *Dastgāh-e Shur*; and the fifth one, *Bayāt-e Esfahān*, is related to *Dastgāh-e Homāyun*. The dependency is demonstrated by similarity of tones or pitch material, which can be arranged as a scale pattern. Early in the 20th century, the eminent musician Alinaqi Vaziri went further by recognizing only five *dastgāh*s; he considered *Dastgāh-e Navā*, also, as a subsidiary of *Shur*, and he identified *Dastgāh-e Rāst Panjgāh* as subordinate to *Māhur*. He also gives the similarity of pitch material, which he constructs into scale formations, as his justification. To Vaziri the scale patterns, within the octave range, are the sole basis for modal identity. Moreover, Vaziri did not favor the word *āvāz*, which also has a different musical application (song); he introduced the term *naqme* for these secondary modal groups. Accordingly, in Vaziri's theories there are 5 *dastgāh*s and 7 *naqme*s (*āvāz*).

In fact, in Persian music pitch material, meaning the tones or the notes, when artificially constructed into scales, are of no significance; what is important is the singularity of melodic patterns (*māye*). Each of the 12 groups (*dastgāh* or *āvāz)*, in its opening section (*darāmad*), and each of the *gushe*s that follow the *darāmad*, has its own *māye*. It is the *māye* that identifies each one of them and not the scales that can be made with the ascending or descending arrangements of notes. Accordingly, it is the melodic individuality of each piece within the *radif* that is important. Each of the 12 collections is melodically identifiable and the question of the dependency of one to the other (*āvāz* as subordinate to *dastgāh*) is rather moot. In my investigations and writings, I have chosen to refer to all 12 as *dastgāh*.

Persian musicians who have expounded views on the theoretic foundations of their music have made a fundamental mistake in equating the concept of mode (*maqām*) with tonality in western music. They have dwelled on construction of octave scales and have identified *maqām*s in terms of pitches and intervals in those scales. Vaziri goes even as far as calling certain pitches, in the scales that he creates for Persian modes, as tonic, dominant and leading-tone, etc. Clearly, he did not understand that these terms relate to the harmonic system of western classical music and have no relevance to a music that is both modal and monophonic. These are ideas borrowed from western theoretical concepts and their application to Persian music is misplaced and misleading.

I am convinced that, in all probability, in the ancient Greek concept of modes, also, the very essence of modal identity was the melodic pattern inherent to each mode and not the mere arrangement of tones and semitones within the octave. Why would Aristotle speak of the heroic quality of some and the degenerative quality of other modes? When Plato in *The Republic* opines that the Mixolydian mode 'would make young men effeminate', or that Ionian mode 'promotes sloth', and that the 'Phrygian is martial and manly', he is surely not talking about the mere succession of pitches into scales that would possess such distinct attributes. The Greek modes of antiquity, also, must have dictated certain melody models from which a sense of character could be discerned.

A performance of the entire *radif*, including all known *gushe*s of the 12 *dastgāh*s, with extensive improvisation, will not yield 12 hours, not even 8 hours, of music. On the face of it, this makes for an extremely small repertoire. The saving grace is that the performance tradition is purely aural and non-specific; it relies heavily on extemporization based on melody models (*māye*) that are the genesis of each *gushe*. Since the very foundation of performance rests on endless variations on these elusive themes, a *dastgāh*, which is an assembly of a group of *gushe*s, is never rendered the same way twice. Improvisation has a paramount role and endows this music, not only with perpetual variations on familiar core contents, but also with a very personal and intimate quality.

It is commonly believed that Persian music, with its many modes (*maqām*s) expresses a wide range of moods and sentiments. Indeed, the feeling conveyed by the *darāmad* of *Dastgāh-e Māhur*, for example, is different from that of *Segāh*, and the mode of *Chahārgāh* has a very different impact from that of *Shur*. Nevertheless, the totality of the *radif* is basically one genre of music. It is monophonic, soloistic, improvisatory, and mostly free of regular rhythmic pulsation. It moves within a range of sound not exceeding two octaves. Moreover, although the initial mode, as given in the *darāmad* section of each *dastgāh*, may convey a variety of emotions, what comes in the *gushe*s that follow frequently blur this distinction by bringing into play associations with other *dastgāh*s. For example some of the *gushe*s in *deastgāh-e Māhur* refer to the mode of *Shur*; some of the *gushe*s in *dastgāh-e Navā* are also modally related to *Shur*; the mode of *Charārgah* can be brought into *Homāyun*; *Dastgāh-e Rāst*, after its *darāmad*, brings into play *gushe*s from a number of other *dastgāh*s. Accordingly, to claim that these *dastgāh*s can convey a wide range of human emotions is a bit of overstatement. They are essentially one type of music and their collective expression is one of sorrow and nostalgia.

Fundamentals of Persian Music

Aside from the medieval theories on tones and scales, in the 20th century, three totally different theories on the tonal structure of Persian music have been advocated. The first of these is the theory of 24 equidistant quartertones that was put forth by Alinaqi Vaziri. Under the influence of western music and intent on introducing the harmonic practice into native music, Mr. Vaziri hypothesized that Persian music is founded on quartertones. He knew well that western style harmony cannot be introduced into a music that has changeable and unstable intervals. He was aware, I presume, that in western music the full flowering of the harmonic practice was only possible after intervals were subjected to the artificial process of equal temperament so that an octave contained 12 equidistant semitones. He knew that in Persian music there are intervals that lie in between semitone and the whole tone. He assumed that these intervals fall exactly halfway between the other two; therefore, he conveniently resolved that they are equal to ¾ tones and he took the ¼ as the basic unit.

Vaziri's theory of the quartertone system, that is the division of the octave into 24 equidistant intervals, was first expounded in his *Dastur-e Tār* (1922), and more extensively in his *Musiqi-ye Nazari* (1934). The fact that the quartertone by itself never occurs in Persian music evidently did not concern him. Thus, the fallacy of building a system on a nonexistent interval was born and received wide acceptance by his disciples. To this day most Persian musicians believe that their music is founded on quartertones. When asked what evidence is there for this quartertone and in which *maqām* do we find it, they point to the tones that are larger than semi but smaller than the whole tone. But if these intervals are larger than the semi-tone, how could they be called quartertone? They figure, I suppose, that since these intervals are about three quarters, then one quarter must also exist! The quartertone, in Persian music, is possible only theoretically, in reality it does not exist. For example, the interval of b flat to b *koron*, or f to f *sori* (*koron* is Vaziri's invented term for half flat and *sori* for half sharp) would make a quartertone, but in no *maqām* do these tones come in succession. This interval, therefore, is a mere theoretic possibility; in fact, it has no application at all in the music itself.

In the 1950's, Mr Vaziri's quartertone theory was challenged by Mehdi Barkeshli. Dr Barkeshli was a physicist who had taken violin lessons in his youth and was fully at home with the traditional music. As a physicist he became interested in the measurement of musical intervals through mechanical means. After a series of examinations of vocal music he published an article in a French magazine in which he identified a totally different scale structure for Persian music. In essence, Barkeshli takes the medieval theories on intervals, particularly Safieddin's 13th century division of the octave into 17 tones, as his point of departure and as reference. He produced a 22-tone scale, which only departs from Safieddin's 17 tone scale by the addition of one more tones in the division of each of the five whole-tones in the octave. Barkeshli's scale is as precise as those given by the medieval theorists. It is equally rapped up in mathematical figurations and is equally unattainable by Persian musical instruments. Its realization by human voice, which is far more unreliable for pitch precision than instruments, is even more problematic.

The third theory of intervals of Persian music was proposed by the present writer in 1965. This was the outcome of the research I conducted in Iran in late 1950s as was articulated in my PhD thesis, *The Dastgāh Concept in Persian Music*, published with minor revisions by Cambridge University Press in 1990.

According to my findings any search for 'the Persian scale' is totally pointless. Octave scale concepts are relevant to many musical cultures including Indian, Javanese, Japanese and certainly the western classical tradition, but not to the Persian. The traditional musician in Persia would never learn scale patterns for the various *maqām*s. In the context of musical studies no such concepts are taught and scales have no place in performance practice.

In Persian music there are five basic tones with which various modes are created. These are the semitone and the whole-tone, which are relatively stable, although not as immovable as they are in the tempered tuning system of western classical music. There are two tones that lie between semitone and whole-tone, one is closer to the former and the other is closer to the later. However, both are quite unstable and, in different modal contexts, can be slightly larger or smaller. If, for the sake of argument, we would take the semitone of the tempered tuning system to be represented by the number 100 and the whole-tone by 200, one of the tones that lie in between these two would be around 135 and the other around 165. There is also an interval larger than the whole-tone that has application in only a few *maqām*s. It is not as large as the augmented tone of western music (6th to 7th degree in harmonic minor scale). This tone is also very unstable.

We need not go, I believe, beyond the recognition of these five basic intervals, and the acceptance of their relative fluidity. All theories must be justified if they are derived from the reality of a musical practice. The music, as is practiced, must be considered first, any theorizing must follow, not the other way around. There is no law that would necessitate a musical practice to be neat, orderly and mathematically perfect. Persian music does not yield exact and unchanging intervals. That does not make it inferior. There is no need to impose on it idealized and rigid systems that are not borne out by evidence in its performance practices. As to the theories of medieval scholars, in which intervals and scales are described with great precision, as stated earlier, we have no way of knowing if they were supported by actual musical practices of the time. In all probability they were not. If in our own era theories can be proposed that misrepresent existing musical practices, perhaps the learned scholars of the past also expostulated neat and scientifically precise theories that were, at best, idealized representations of the music as practiced by performing musicians.

No music needs to be loved, honored or justified only if it yields neat and precise intervals and scale structures. The fact that Persian music has unstable intervals and does not adhere to an orderly system takes nothing away from its beauty. It simply does not need the kind precision that western art music has come to possess. The highly regulated and systematized art music of the west is the by-product of the polyphony that gradually emerged in the late Medieval and Renaissance periods. The artificial equal temperament, necessitated by the harmonic system that evolved in the Baroque period, came much later. Persian music has not developed the kind of exactitude of intervals essential to the harmonic system; the need did not arise because the music is monophonic. Moreover, it is not performed on musical instruments with built in fixed pitches such as the organ, piano, or the metalophones and xylophones of Java and Bali, or the gongs and stone chimes of China. It can be even argued that the pliability of tones in Persian music is to be cherished, as it is an integral part of its eminently personal and heartfelt intimacy.

Music in Islamic Society

Before the advent of recorded music and the coming of radio, the average Iranian city dweller had very limited opportunities to hear music of any kind. There were no concerts and, contrary to the practice in the Christian church service, there is no music in Moslem religious rituals. Ceremonial lamentation for Shiite saints that are peculiar to Persia, such as *rozekhni*, *nohekhāni*, *sinezani*, and *ta'zie*, involves some singing and chanting. However, these are not musical presentations per se; they are aspects of commemorative ceremonies in the religious calendar; they are not considered to be, nor are they experienced, as musical events. Moreover, these rituals that involve chanting occur in a few specified days in the lunar calendar; they are not daily or even weekly events.

The only genre of religious ceremony that involves music, beyond mere repetitive chants, is the *ta'zie* or *shabih-khāni*. I have referred to *Ta'zie* in Chapter 9, in connection to the Shiraz Festival. To remind the reader, this is a form of drama based on different episodes related to the martyrdom of Imam Hoseyn, the grandson of the prophet Mohammad, in the year 680 CE. In these dramas, enacted on a stage, the protagonists sing while the antagonists deliver their lines in a declamatory fashion. There is some instrumental participation, mostly for creating atmosphere and as a kind of intermezzo between events that take place on the stage. Instruments used are of wind and percussion varieties. *Ta'zie*s may have had pre-Islamic roots; as they are known in modern times, however, they originate from the Safavid era (1501-1722). This is the period when shiism was promoted and became the state religion of the Empire. The high point of ta'zie's development was reached in the second half of the 19th century, during the reign of Nāsereddin Shah (1848-96). *Ta'zie* performances took place during the lunar month of Moharram when the tragedy of Hoseyn's martyrdom had occurred. Even if many of the citizenry attended these shows it cannot be said that it amounted to a significant musical experience.

Music of a festive nature might have been heard at weddings, as performed by bands of three or four professional musicians known as *motreb*s (merry-makers). A *tār* and a *tombak*, plus a singer were fixed components of these bands, while the addition of a violin became increasingly fashionable. The pieces played by these bands were standard dance tunes and bawdy songs connected to the lighter side of urban traditional music. (It is a sad fact that the society at large generally regards *motreb*s with derision.) It would not be far off the mark to say that an ordinary city dweller's life provided for no other opportunity to hear music of any kind. The aristocratic families, on the other hand, had a wider field of contact with music. It was not uncommon for some members in such families to have gained the mastery of an instrument. This was also true of some female members of noble houses. Nevertheless, even among the wealthier class, who were but a small fraction of the population, occasions for contact with music were extremely limited.

All things considered, before modern times, social conditions had been generally inhospitable to a flourishing musical life in Persia. A civilization that has produced a staggering poetic heritage, a magnificent school of miniature painting, a splendid architectural style and the most graceful handcraft of all kinds, has but a small, static and monochrome urban musical tradition. The absence of any musical orientation, let alone training, in the education of the young has perpetuated this regrettable situation. Even among the social elite music is not likely to be regarded as a serious endeavor; it is seen merely as an aspect of entertainment. To the average Persian of all stations, a musician is someone who plays an instrument; there is virtually no comprehension as to what composition, musical theory or musicology are all about.

The problem is undoubtedly rooted in Islamic, and particularly Shiite, hostility towards music. The control that Islam has maintained over every society, where it has been the dominant religious persuasion, has tended to stifle musical growth and flourish. It is true that music, as a branch of natural sciences, was a subject of study by medieval Moslem scientists. Indeed, as stated earlier, there are important books and treatises extant from the medieval period that were written by scholars whose interest was primarily centered on theoretical issues, or the mathematical properties of music as a science, a continuation of classical Greek scholarship. What is important, in the present argument, is that there is no historic evidence to indicate what part, if any, did music play in the life of the average citizen. Significantly, no system of musical notation, as a practical tool for communicating music from one person to another, was ever developed. The need did not arise because music making was only a private, and, probably, a furtive affair.

A system of musical notation is developed when there is a need to disseminate pieces of music, to pass them on to others, and that has to do with its presentation to a public. In Persia, until about a century ago, music did not have a public forum. Music making was a rarified and private endeavor, and its performance had remained mostly soloistic and improvisatory. Any creative impulse was subordinated to the art of performance. Compositions were mere individualized elaborations on known themes, which would come into play in the course of improvisation. Accordingly, there was no need to write any of it down; in the next extemporized performance, the same themes would receive a slightly different elaboration.

The invention of notation in western music was necessitated by: a) the need to perform set pieces on specific texts every day in the service of the church, b) the development of polyphony which requires the coordination of simultaneous sounds of different pitches in a fixed and orderly fashion, and c) group singing and group instrumental participation. All three factors required a means for performance of music that is fixed and repeatable in every detail. That could only be done through the invention of written symbols that we call notation. None of these factors presented themselves in an Islamic society; hence the need to develop a system of notation as a practical tool for performance did not arise.

Some of the more sophisticated musical cultures in the Far East have also developed their own methods of musical notation. Court, religious and ceremonial music in both China and Japan has relied on systems of notation for centuries. Again, this was necessitated by musical traditions that involve performance through group participation, both vocal and instrumental. Theirs is also a richly textured music that has to be performed in a stable and repeatable fashion. In these cultures, also, there exists a repertoire of composed music from the past centuries that have been written in various methods of notation.

There is no history of musical composition in pre-20th century Iran, and there is no extant repertoire of composed pieces by past masters. I am fully informed as to the existence of a few compositions, written in a personally devised manner of notation, by Abdol-Qāder Marāqi, from the early 15th century. But the survival of a few pieces of music by one individual, written some 600 years ago, can hardly testify to the presence of a tradition of composed music. Also, the efforts by Persian musicians in recent times who, influenced by western music and employing western musical notation, have produced a genre of light music in Persian modes (*tasnif, tarāne, pishdarāmad, reng*, etc.), is not part of this argument. The emergence of this type of composed music, written in western notation, only points to the reform trends and westernization that have influenced all aspects of modern life of the country in the course of the last 150 years.

Also, I am aware that the royal courts, particularly that of the Safavid shahs, supported bands of musicians, and that musical performance must have had a place at courtly ceremonies. There are miniature paintings in manuscripts, showing musical instruments from that period, and there are some mural paintings that show bands of musicians. None of these, however, gives any indication as to the role, if any, of music in the life of the average citizen. Where and how did a city dweller hear any music? It is difficult to avoid the conclusion that

Islamic hegemony over the society at large has consistently stifled the development of a flourishing musical culture.

What is about music that gives rise to religious hostility? According to those who know the Quran, there is no mention of music in the holy book. This in itself can be a source of the problem, as it leaves the question of how to regard music to the individual points of view of the *olamā* (religious scholars). Music is made of sounds that are abstract without any clear meaning. That such meaningless sounds affect and move the listener is inherently enigmatic. Since the cause of the sensation aroused by music cannot be explained, the tendency is to view it with suspicion. Suspicion can in turn lead to condemnation and prohibition. There is always safety in abstinence.

The problem is essentially related to instrumental music, since purely vocal music is not really considered as anything but a stylized manner of delivering a text. It is viewed as an extension of declamation. Any sensation that may be experienced by the listener in hearing vocal music is attributed to the meaning of the words, and if the text is in no way objectionable then the question of impropriety does not arise. The singing of the *azān* or call to prayer, or the preacher's chanting on the pulpit, is not objectionable; they are viewed as stylized delivery of an approved text. It is not without significance that, in the Persian language, the same word (*khāndan*) – clearly of the same root as the Italian *cantare* and the French *chanter* - means both to read and to sing. It is instrumental music, with its indefinable meaning, and the impact it has on the listener, that is inexplicable and therefore objectionable. This, I believe is the very essence of the problem that Abrahamic religions have had with music. In Jewish orthodoxy also musical instruments have no place in the synagogue. And, while chanting was part of the service in the Christian churches from the outset, it took many centuries before musical instruments, even the organ, were admitted to the church.

An ordinary Moslem cleric's proscriptive view on music, however, is based on something altogether different. The above argument is fundamentally foreign to him. His objection, to put it bluntly, stems from sheer ignorance. He knows of only one type of music, the music that accompanies gaiety, dancing, clapping and merriment. To him, this music is the tool of the devil for, he believes, it leads to frivolity, licentiousness and debauchery. He knows of no other kind of music. At best, he may also have read about a type of music used in ancient warfare, or what may be called martial music. He knows nothing about music as an expression of the loftiest human sentiments; he knows nothing about music as a serious and highly artful creative endeavor; he knows nothing about music drama, devotional music, symphonic, choral, and myriads of other musical genres that are among mankind's greatest artistic creations.

An anecdote from my own personal experience may illustrate the point I am raising about the Moslem cleric's limited range of musical understanding. In the spring of 1976 I was travelling to Paris by Iranair. Seated next to me in the airplane was a well-attired *mollā* (shiite cleric). After a short while into the flight he commenced conversation with me. He was clearly a high-ranking cleric, a *mojtahed*. He gave his name as Abdol-Jalil Jalili and indicated that he was the *Emam Jom'e* (Leader of Friday communal prayer) of Kermānshāh, a provincial capital in western Iran. He was flying to Paris for some health-related reason. I also introduced myself and told him that I was a university professor and was the Head of the Music Department at the University of Tehran. Since he was clearly a cleric of eminent standing, at some point during our conversation, I asked him whether he could clarify for me Islam's position in regards to music, and to explain if there was any prohibition of music in Islamic scriptures. After struggling with the question for a while he said that after a few days in Paris, on his way back to Persia, he intended to make a stop in Iraq to visit the holy shrines in Karbala and Najaf, and that he would have an interview with the Grand Āyatollāh Khoie. Khoie (1898-1992) was the highest Shiite authority and the most respected source of emulation (*marja'*), and, at that time, Najaf was the seat of the highest Shia authority. He suggested that I could write down my question and that he would request the Grand Āyatollāh to respond to it. Although I could not place much faith in the outcome of this manner of inquiry, I asked the plane attendant for a piece of paper. On a sheet of paper, with Iranair emblem on top, I wrote down my question as to the position of Islam in regards to music.

Before long, I forgot all about my encounter with Kermanshah's *Emam Jom'e*. About three months had passed and I was back at my job in the University of Tehran when among the letters placed on my desk I notice one from Kermanshah. The envelope contained a brief note of greetings from the *Emam Jom'e*, His Eminence Mr. Jalili, plus the sheet of Iranair stationary, on which I had written my question about Islam and Music. On the bottom of the sheet, which is still in my possession, Grand Āyatollāh Khoie had written his response. It states: There are different commands as concerns music. Festive music, which is for merriment and frivolity, is forbidden and must not be heard. Music for warfare and appertaining ceremonies is not forbidden. The statement is signed and the Āyatollāh's seal is pressed under his signature.

This was the scope of the knowledge of the highest Shiite authority about music.

In October of 1979, the distinguished Italian journalist, Oriana Fallaci, conducted an interview with Āyatollāh Ruhollāh Khomeini in Tehran. The interview is well documented and can be viewed on You Tube. This was a few months after the triumph of the Revolution of 1978-79 that brought Khomeini to power as the supreme leader of the Islamic Republic he had created. One of the questions she put to the Āyatollāh was about music. After he had denounced music for 'it tarnishes the mind', and that 'it carries with it the same pleasure and ecstasy as drugs do', she asked if he had any objections to the music of great masters such as Bach, Beethoven and Verdi. His response was that he does not know these men and their music but that music is basically a corruptive force to be avoided. He only gave approval for some 'marches and hymns'. One can easily see that Āyatollāh Khomeini's position on music was in line with that of Āyatollāh Khoie, as expressed in his response to my letter in 1975.

Is it any wonder then that, under conditions regulated for centuries by such narrow and ignorant views, the musical life in Islamic societies, until modern times, remained confined and inert? For all we know, from the time that Islam became the dominant religion in Persia, and particularly since the beginnings of the 16th century with the increasing sway of shiism, a state of semi-prohibition has been imposed on music in a society where the clerics have been vociferous and powerful. The prevailing stifling conditions have been responsible for the fact that urban music is essentially soloistic, which points to the private, almost furtive, nature of music making. Ensemble playing was largely developed in the 20th century, due to western influences together with the diminishing power of the clerics during the Constitutional Movement and particularly in the Pahlavi era.

Only during the rule of the two Pahlavi monarchs (1925-79) was clerical domination curtailed and hence musical activity received real impetus. Particularly significant was the Rezā Shah period (1925-41), when he set out to virtually destroy the power of the clergy. Indeed, much that the country has achieved in the advancement of the cause of music begun under Rezā Shah. This included new movements towards creativity within the bounds of traditional music, the promotion of western music both serious and light, and the establishment of conservatories, orchestras, and public concerts. It is quite remarkable that Rezā Shah had even ordered the construction of an Opera House in Tehran. The building was not completed when the Shah was forced to abdicate; the crumbling unfinished building was torn down some years later.

Further reform and greater development of the musical life of the country were achieved under Mohammad Rezā Shah. By mid the 1970s Tehran boasted an opera company, a ballet company, a large symphony orchestra, and a chamber orchestra, plus a number of Persian music ensembles that provided daily music programs for radio and television. Masters of traditional music were honored public figures who performed regularly on Radio and TV. Importantly, not only were there two large conservatories in Tehran (one mainly concerned with national music and the other with a curriculum entirely devoted to western art music), there was a thriving Music Department at the University of Tehran and the beginnings of one at the newly founded Fārābi University.

Almost immediately after the take-over the country by the clerics in February of 1979, all musical establishments were disbanded or suspended. The Tehran Symphony Orchestra, the Opera Company, the Ballet Company, and the Folkdance Ensemble were all dismissed. All music broadcasts from radio stations, and musical programs on television were brought to a halt. After a couple of years the ban on music from radio and television was partially lifted. This change of heart was due to the realization that without some relief through musical programs nobody would listen to the radio, or watch the TV, and that their incessant lectures on Islam and their self-promoting propaganda were being wasted on a disinterested public. There was such trepidation about music that when the universities were reopened, the Music Department at the Tehran University was renamed Department of Sound, as if the very word 'music' was sinful. (I understand that a few tears later the word music was rehabilitated.)

Into the second decade of the 21st century, as I am writing these lines, the Islamic regime in Iran remains uneasy about music. The fact that a great deal of musical activity takes place is entirely due to citizens' initiatives, without any state support. The regime has effectively admitted defeat in its attempt to stamp out music from public life. However, musical presentation faces the constant hazard of state intervention and prohibition. A woman's singing voice cannot be heard in public, and close-up of musical instruments cannot be shown on TV, even though it is permissible to hear them. Public presentation of dance music of any kind with participation by dancers is totally banned.

In a recent interview with the current Leader of the Islamic Republic, Āyatollāh Ali Khāmenei, he states with incredulity that he has learned that music is taught at some universities. He then goes on to say that this is wrong and it must be stopped. (This interview can be seen on You Tube.) Fortunately not much attention is paid to Mr. Khāmenei's pronouncements on music and, I am told, no one has heeded his recommendation against music teaching.

Further Observations

Since childhood, I had heard many times from my father, among others, that: 'the sounds of any kind of music, from what ever part of the world, can be found in Persian music'. Not only that, I had also heard the amazing claim that even birds sing in Persian *maqām*s. This is, of course, all nonsense. Not only is music of other cultures fundamentally different, even those with a common theoretical background, such as Arabian and Turkish music, have evolved along separate paths. It only takes a few seconds before one can identify Arabic or Turkish music as distinct from Persian. As to other eastern musical systems some common ground may exist with north Indian music. This can be supported by the fact that the Moghul dynasty that ruled for some 300 years in northern parts of India was heavily Persian in its culture. However, not a second of Indian music can be mistaken for Persian. The music in the Far Eastern cultures of China, Korea, Japan, Java, Bali, Thailand and the rest is totally different; their musical systems are mostly based on pentatonic scales and are largely orchestral.

There is a particular eagerness, on the part of Persian musicians, to prove common ground with the music of the west. Perhaps, subconsciously they believe all things western to be superior and therefore any connection with the west is a proof of equality. Ali Naqi Vaziri and his disciples claimed that the major and minor tonalities are duplicated in the modes of *Māhur* and *Bayāt-e Esfahān*, respectively. They equate the 'scale' of the first with major and 'scale' of the second with harmonic minor, as if this were something to be proud of! This is a spurious claim; I have already made clear that the notion of a scale pattern, an ascending line-up of notes within the range of an octave, has no relevance to Persian music. Moreover, of the hundreds of thousands of compositions, by western composers, in the major mode, not one can be said to be in *māhur*. Why? Because the *māhur* melody model (*māye*), as given in the *darāmad*, is not suggested by these pieces. The same goes for the myriad of western compositions in the minor tonality; none of them is in *Bayāt-e Esfahān*, because the *māye* of *Bayāt-e Esfahān* is not in them.

Misinformation, combined with nationalistic pride, has led to fundamental misconceptions about Persian music among both the general public and professional musicians. A case in point was a televised program, in 1974, about Persian music in which I was invited to participate. Other participants were Mr. Morteza Hannāne and Mr. Homāyun Khorram, both reputable musicians with wide experience in both native and western music. The discussion had turned to the question of the comparative evaluation of different musical traditions. Mr. Khorram, who is a respected violinist of the Persian style, in attempting to show the richness of Persian music as compared with the music of the western world, stated that the Europeans have only the major and the minor modes, where as we have seven modes (presumably referring to the 7 *dastgāh*s). I had to inform him and the viewing audience that if we include the ecclesiastic modes, on the basis of which the magnificent legacy of musical composition from late medieval and renaissance eras rests, then western tradition has used, in addition to the major and minor, eight more modes. (These are the both the authentic and the plagal versions of Dorian, Phrygian, Lydian and Mixolydian modes, in both authentic and plagal versions). More importantly, I also suggested that in Persian music, not seven but nearly sixty modes have actual application.

This statement caused some bewilderment around the table and required clarification. I went on to explain that the seven, or in my count the 12 *dastgāh*s, are in reality 12 collections of modes (*maqām*s). Each *dastgāh* embodies a group of *gushe*s most of which possess their own modal identity distinct from that of the opening mode. The initial mode is that of the *darāmad* of the *dastgāh*, most of the *gushe*s that follow have distinct modes of their own. If we consider all these different modes that are classified under the heading of the 12 *dastgāh*s, we end up with nearly 60 different modes. However, the number of modes in any musical tradition, in itself, is of little significance. Modes are no more than tools, or the raw material, for musical creativity. The western musical tradition, even with only the major and minor tonalities, has created thousands of musical masterpieces in a great variety of genres, forms and styles. In the west musical notation was developed and, as a consequence, eight centuries of music written by thousands of composers is available to us. With only major and minor tonalities they developed chamber, vocal, choral, dramatic, and religious music, in countless varieties of styles with different compositional techniques. What we have achieved with our wealth of modal possibilities is the *radif* that provides us with a few hours of improvised monophonic music of a single genre.

In the days that followed the showing of this televised program, I received a number of hostile letters, including one that was life threatening. There appeared a number of letters in newspapers accusing me of not knowing anything about Persian music, of lacking national pride, and of being a servant of foreigners. One of the letters published in the daily *Ettelāʾāt*, had very harsh words about me; its author was Mr. Assadollāh Malek, another violinist of the Persian school. He went on to state that the only thing in which Persian music fall short is orchestration, if his own compositions were to be orchestrated, they will be just as great as those of Beethoven.

The day after the program was shown, when I entered the university building where Music Department was located, I met one of the staff members who did not return my greetings and thereafter never spoke to me. He was a man who, with much time and effort, I had managed to transfer from the Ministry of Finance to the University of Tehran in order to teach some of the courses in the national music section of our curriculum. Although he had no formal musical education, he played *santur* and *setār* and was reputed to be knowledgeable in Persian music. Unfortunately, as a teacher, he had proved to be totally incompetent.

How can Persian Music be 'advanced'?

Countless times in discussions with my compatriots, as well as in formal interviews, I have been asked: How can we advance our music? How can we make our music more 'scientific'? The answer of course is that we cannot advance what is already there. The classical tradition is the heritage of the past and must be preserved; those who are interested in it should continue to learn it and perform it as true to its authentic norms as possible. At the same time, we must accept that in today's society music has a far greater application than it ever had before. The *dastgāh* system is only one genre of music and cannot possibly respond to present day needs. Today's world lives with music, music of all kinds, and so does the society in the Islamic Republic, whether the *mollā*s like it or not. There is nothing wrong with importing music. Western classical music in its ever-evolving stylistic manifestations, is the only music that is international. It is incomparably varied and vast; it is the highest musical art there is. All advanced nonwestern nations have accepted it and have made it their own without misplaced national pride and without abandoning their own music. It is embraced not as a replacement of their own heritage, but as an addition to it. Iran needs to follow – and in fact is following whether the *mollā*s approve or not - the same rout as other eastern cultures like Turkey, Japan, Korea and China have done. In addition, it needs to produce more composers, composers who are both gifted and well trained. Their work will be the future of the country's music. What they compose is up to them; whether or not their compositions are informed and inspired by native music is for them to decide.

The history of musical composition in Iran is barely a century old. In this one hundred years, two types of music have been created by native composers: pieces that are essentially committed to the *dastgāh* system, and those that are rooted in the western technique of classical composition. The first of these are largely of vocal chanson type, mostly monophonic with simple instrumental participation. It is a limited genre of basically light music comparable to popular songs of early 20th century (*chanson* type) in the west. The second category is more serious and also much more varied; it includes symphonic and operatic and chamber music, which may or may not involve aspects of native music. They are based on western techniques of composition and demonstrate much stylistic diversity. Works in the first category have popular appeal, of which the present Islamic regime seems to disapprove. The second genre is serious and therefore not within easy grasp of many, including the regime itself, which seems willing to tolerate it. This is the future hope of our music. It may not be strictly 'Persian music', but will be music by Persian composers. It will be part of the musical culture of the country, in the same way that works of Kodaly and Bartok are not Hungarian music but are music of Hungary, and the works of Sibelius are not Finnish music but are music of Finland.

The history of serious compositions by Persian composers began in early 20th century with Aminollāh Hossein and Parviz Mahmoud. It has continued with Emanuel Melik Aslanian, Samin Bāghchebān, the present writer, Loris Tjeknavorian, Ahmad Pezhmān, Alirezā Mashāyekhi and Shāhin Farhat. These composers have been followed by many more, the generation of composers who were born after the Second World War, some of whom are active in Europe and America. It has been a beginning but a great deal more needs to be done before Iran has a genuine reservoir of composed music of serious quality. I believe we must not be chained to Persian music that we already have. The heritage of the past, the *radif*, is fine and noble and must be preserved and perpetuated. The future of our music, however, is in the hands of composers. In time, the superior and the inferior of their work will be determined; the weak will be forgotten and the strong will remain. There is nothing else that can be done; we surely cannot recreate the past of Persian music, we can only place hope in its future, which rests with creative artists now and henceforward.

I am well aware that some of the views expressed in this chapter will displease some of my compatriots. Persian music, which to most Iranians means the *dastgah* system, is a national heritage and many have feelings of love and protection for it, as indeed I do. What I have written about it is, I believe, realistic and certainly detached from sentimentality, which I hope the reader will accept and appreciate.

❧ 15 ❧

Reflections on Western Classical Music

In the course of the past seven centuries, Western civilization has produced a staggering artistic heritage. In literature, poetry, music, architecture, painting, sculpture, theatre, cinema and handcrafts of all sorts, the combined creative output of western societies is quite overwhelming. It is not within this writer's competence to comment, or to evaluate, the merits of western artistic output in literature, theatre and the plastic arts, nor is it within the remit of this chapter to do so. Equally, it is not for me to make comparisons between what the western civilization has produced in the said areas with that of other civilizations. But, I believe that I have the sort of professional background to proffer a conviction that western civilization's accomplishments in music stand, not only at the pinnacle of her artistic achievements, but also that they are without equal in other cultures. There is no doubt that the great civilizations of Asia and the Middle East have also produced magnificent literature, architecture, sculpture and painting, although perhaps with more limited scope and variety, as compared with the creative output of the west. In music, however, no culture can remotely come close to what the western civilization has accomplished. I say this from the position of some knowledge of non-western musical traditions. For several years, in the course of my postgraduate studies, I was a student of ethnomusicology; I have familiarity with the music of many cultures including those of China, Japan, Korea, Thailand, Indonesia, India, Persia, Turkey and the Arab World.

In no way do I mean to degrade the importance of music from these named civilizations. They all have their own noble cultures; they all have musical traditions possessing beauty and refinement. However, the unique attribute of the art music of the west is polyphony, which, in my view, sets it apart from anything that other cultures have produced. Polyphony has led to a diversity of styles and genres beyond the reach of all other traditions that are essentially monophonic. The development of systematic polyphony, that is the deliberate and structured use of simultaneous layers of sounds, is the supreme achievement of western music; it has no parallel in any other culture. Polyphony is the most singular attribute of western music that invests it with limitless stylistic diversity leading to a vast range of expressive possibilities. It is through the systematized polyphony of the Renaissance and its evolution in the disciplined harmonic practice of the Baroque and Classical periods that a boundless treasury of great music has been created. Through the richness of the polyphonic texture every conceivable emotion: grandeur, drama, joy, pathos, ardor and excitement, has been brought within reach of the creative minds of composers. No other musical system has been able to achieve a comparable diversity and expressive power. It is through this line of musical development that the splendor of the symphonic sounds of Strauss and Mahler, the richness of the keyboard music of Bach, Chopin, and Debussy, and the enchanting dramas of Monteverdi, Mozart, Verdi and Wagner, have been made possible. It is through the wealth of polyphonic possibilities that such diversity of genres as symphonic music, chamber music, keyboard music, choral music, opera and ballet have been developed. It is with the tools of polyphony that different technical approaches to composition have been made possible, resulting in the distinct styles of the High Renaissance, Baroque, Classical, Rococo, Romantic, Impressionistic, Expressionistic, Serial, etc. Without a systematized polyphonic and harmonic practice none of these could have been created in the way that we know them. No monophonic musical system can possibly lead to such a vast range of styles and wealth of expressive possibilities.

All musical cultures have professional musicians who are performers of various instruments or are singers. In some cases these performing artists have also composed pieces of music that were primarily part of their own performing repertoire. There are instances when a piece of music, composed by one person, has circulated and was learned and performed by other musicians. In such cases the dissemination has been usually done aurally. On rare occasions, a method of notation was developed so that music, as composed by one person, could be learned by others. Examples of notated music can be found in the Carnatic music of south India, also in Javanese, Japanese and Chinese ensemble and ceremonial music. But reliance on a highly precise system of notation for all composed music was necessitated by the development of polyphony and is unique to western culture.

The very emergence of the composer as a singular figure, above all other professional musicians, is a western phenomenon. The concept of the creative artist in music, the composer who makes music that is entirely his own and is written down for others to perform, is also exclusively western. Of course the composer can also be a performer and very often they were. But, his recognition as an exalted figure, a creative genius, equal to the poet or the painter, is exclusively western. In other cultures only after the arrival of western music, and the impact it has had on native musicians, have composers appeared on the musical scene. A notable example is the emergence of composed music and composers at the court of Ottoman sultans from the 17th century. By that time Turkey was very much a European power, and the Empire had more Christian subjects than Moslem. Gradually, the influence of Christian Europe, in both secular and sacred music, led to the founding of a whole school of musical composition, in which modal features of Turkish music were blended with western techniques of composition. Similar influences, at a much later date, paved the way for the rise of composers in Japan, Persia, Egypt and elsewhere. These were for the most part musicians who were trained in western music and worked in accordance with western ideals and techniques of musical composition.

An additional attribute of western music, leading to its incomparable richness, is the quest for change and variety that since the Renaissance has been a dominant feature of western civilization. Styles and techniques of musical composition have constantly evolved, as the central objectives have been innovation and novelty. The course of musical development in the west demonstrates the creative artist's attempt at self-assertion, and the pressing urge to do something different from what has been done by others. This is a uniquely western characteristic in artistic creativity, as has been the quest for exploration, discovery and innovation in scientific fields.

It may be argued that polyphony is not exclusive to western art music and that certain types of polyphony is practiced in some non-western musical cultures. I am well aware that a comparatively meager application of polyphony can be found in the music of certain Far Eastern cultures. For example, the Gamelan music of Java and Bali is not strictly monophonic. But the polyphonic sound emanating from a gamelan is the outcome of instrumental stratification rather than polyphony for its own sake. As instruments with differing sound registers, some with only a few low pitches and others with many at higher register, are to perform simultaneously, the outcome is a kind of inevitable polyphony. The same sort of polyphony, necessitated by the simultaneous participation of instruments of unequal range and capability, can be also heard in ensemble music of China and Japan. Even in Indian music the use of a drone instrument, such as the *tampura*, as a fixed sound background to an ensemble, I suppose, can be taken as deviation from purely monophony. Or, one can point to the bi-phony as heard in the vocal folk songs of the Serbs and the Bulgarians. But none of these can come remotely close to the richly textured, highly diversified and systematized use of multiple sound layers of western classical music from the late Middle Ages to the present. Systematized and deliberate simultaneous combination of different pitches is fundamental to the art of western musical composition; that is its crowning achievement. In that, it stands without rival. Everything that distinguishes western classical music: keyboard music, chamber music, symphonic music, choral music, opera and ballet - even jazz and Blues - they all issue from that achievement. And, for that reason, I believe in the realm of the arts, 'classical music' is the most singular glory of western civilization.

The grand sweep of the development of western classical music began in the late Middle Ages. Its gradual growth, leading to the emergence of professional composers, can be traced from the 14th century to its high point of refinement, in sonority and richness of texture, in the choral works of 16th century masters such as Josquin, Tallis, Lassus and Gesualdo. In the 17th century the course of musical development was more directed towards dramatic (opera) music by Monteverdi, Cavalli and many others. Also, instrumental music began to receive greater attention by composers such as Frescobaldi and Corelli, among others. In the 18th century, it was further advanced in every musical domain by supreme geniuses such as Bach, Handel, Gluck, Hayden and Mozart. The grand gestures of symphonic, operatic, chamber and keyboard music reached their apogee in writing of the 19th century: masters such as Beethoven, Berlioz, Liszt, Chopin, Wagner and Verdi, to name but a few.

The 19th century ushered in a high point in musical development that, by the end of the century, resulted in a kind of impasse. Some composers, already in the late 1800s, and certainly many in the 20th century attempted innovations of a revolutionary nature. Some of them even considered the established formats for composition, such as sonata, symphony, concerto, suite, and the rest as having been worked to death and no longer valid. The concept of tonality itself was seen, by some, as having outlived its usefulness. They embarked on new paths leading to what has been generally identified as 'modern' music.

What is modern in music? Is it the music composed in a style that differs from the established norms? If a style that was deemed modern at one time becomes the norm, should we still call it modern? Should we continue to label deviations from the norm as 'modern' even after it has been, in turn, superseded by other stylistic novelties? These questions have always been relevant to the course of musical developments, but they are pressingly central to stylistic changes in composition during the past one hundred years. No comparable period in the history of composed music – which has about seven centuries of history – has seen such wide range of stylistic diversity. Arguably not even the combined three centuries prior to the 20th century have produced such variety of musical styles.

Marked departures from stylistic norms were already in evidence, at the close of 19th century, in the works of composers such as Claude Debussy, Alexander Skryabin and Charles Ives, for example. Their music was referred to, at the time, as modern, but not any more. Bartok, Stravinsky and Hindemith, who were contemporaries, were certainly modern composers, but do we still call them by that label? And, what about the Viennese School of Schoenberg, Berg and Webern? They were very modern ninety years ago, but the professional musician of today knows them as the classics of the 20th century.

It is, perhaps, unnecessary to quibble about the appropriate application of the word 'modern', what is important is that to most music-loving people – if not to professional musicians – much of the music of the past one hundred years of the classical tradition in known as modern. Equally important is the fact that the public who support classical music, go to concerts and buy recordings, mostly dislikes this music. This is particularly true of musical types that are, or were, identified as 'avant-garde'.

The creators of this type of 'modern' music resent the public's rejection. They draw comfort, however, from the support of a small coterie of non-musician adherents to the cause of the avant-garde modernity. The supporters of radical trends in composition often see a kind of elitism in their support. A notion seems to prevail to the effect that if a musical composition is incomprehensible to the general public it must necessarily possess intellectual values that are over their heads. Needless to say, I fully agree that serious music, that is a musical creation with intricate construction and multi-layered content, cannot be readily accessible to all. There is no question that a genuine appreciation of all great music of all periods, from the renaissance to the present, requires intimate familiarity, if not in-depth study. However, I do believe that often the question of comprehension is taken too far, which only serves to justify any sort of noise making that has crowded the world of serious music, but fails to win the favor of the music-loving public.

A spurious argument, that I suppose has given comfort to some composers, is the often repeated claim that great musical innovations were never appreciated at the time they were made. Also, one often hears the proposition that great composers were not recognized for their greatness until after their demise. These claims are categorically false. No music that is recognized and revered today for possessing originality, inventiveness and freshness of ideas, has been rejected by the collective community of musically informed listeners at the time it was presented, or soon thereafter. There have been cases when a fine piece of music was faulted, even ridiculed at first by some; but such criticisms were always balanced with praise of others. This is only natural; after all, musical creativity is not rooted in empirical science that would possess irrefutable rights and wrongs. There are always differing opinions, even on proven masterpieces. A radically contradictory view has, at times, been rendered by the most qualified to render judgment. Even the works of Beethoven, possibly the most universally esteemed of all composers, have not escaped serious criticism. Stravinsky consistently claimed to dislike the music of the great German master. Tchaikovsky considered Brahms a second rate composer, and Shostakovich could not stand the operas of Puccini. There are countless other examples demonstrating that even the most revered of compositions do not necessarily receive unqualified approval, whether at the time they were written or thereafter. Setting aside individual proclivities, however, the worth of a good piece of music has always been recognized by consensus and by the informed public. It is the consensus view, over a long period of time, that cannot be ignored and must be taken as the ultimate judgment on the value of a work of art, not individual likes or dislikes.

As to composers and how they were regarded while living, I cannot think of even one major composer who was not recognized for his greatness in his own lifetime. There have been composers whose work, with passage of time, has been even more appreciated. Bach is a case in point. In his own lifetime he was admired and revered; but he was mainly in the service of the church, did not travel beyond Germany and, most importantly, did not write operas. (Opera composers invariably enjoyed greater fame because operas usually were given repeated performances, at different opera houses, attended by large audiences made of the lay public.) Accordingly, his music did not circulate much and his fame did not reach far. Yet, there is no question that his works were known and were highly regarded. Bach's collection of 48 preludes and fugues in the *Well-Tempered Clavier* was studied by most composers of instrumental music who came after him. Beethoven, in particular, was significantly influenced by Bach's contrapuntal writing. Chopin was an avid student of Bach's keyboard music. All this was before the celebrated revival of interest in Bach's music instigated by Mendelssohn's performance of the St Mathew Passion in Berlin in 1829.

If any great composer was to go unappreciated in his own lifetime it should have been Schubert. He hardly ever moved beyond the city of Vienna, was not a virtuoso performer (very often composers' fame was associated with their ability as a performer), and died when only 31 years old. Yet, he was widely known in Vienna, and, most importantly, many of his compositions were published while he lived. What better recognition can there be for a composer than to have his music published, sold and therefore circulated and performed? The most revolutionary of all composers was Richard Wagner. He turned the world of music upside down. His innovations included a highly advanced harmonic technique to the extent of obscuring tonality; he extended the orchestral participation in his operas beyond the established norms, even incorporating instruments of his own specifications; he gave orchestral participation equal importance to the development of the drama, as the text itself. He revamped the traditional operatic format of dividing the plot into small sections, by creating a continuous musico-dramatic flow epitomized by his opera, *Tristan and Isolde*. Yet, well before his death in 1883, Wagner was revered almost as a prophet. Not only after his death, but while he lived, his music influenced more composers than anyone else in the history of music.

Much is made of the raucous premier, in Paris, of Stravinsky's *Rite of Spring* in 1913, as evidence of how a work is rejected when it breaks the bounds of tradition. The event did cause a riot partly due to the suggestively risqué dancing and Vaslav Nijinsky's provocative choreography. The music also sounded harsh and savage; but in the riotous premier strong supportive voices were also part of the clamor. Moreover, it did not take long after its initial presentation for the work to be hailed as a break-through masterpiece, a position it holds to this day. Arnold Schoenberg had received noisy rejection on the first performance of the *Five Pieces for Orchestra*, but only a year later was given tumultuous applause on the first performance of the much more attention demanding *Gurrelieder*.

It can be said emphatically that there are no cases of a work that was a universal failure when first presented but was recognized as a great work of art much later. These arguments: the genius who was scorned and the masterpiece that was derided, are romantic myths and do not stand proper scrutiny. They are self-serving and specious propositions that are cited to elevate works of little merit at the expense of the listener who is often made to feel like a fool. It seems to me that if someone, be it a musician or a non-musician, who loves music, understands and appreciates the works of Josquin des Pres, Lassus, Monteverdi, Bach, Mozart, Beethoven, Chopin, Verdi, Wagner, Tchaikovsky, Debussy, Strauss, Stravinsky, Poulenc, Britten, Schnitke, Lutoslawski, and Philip Glass but he/she cannot really come to appreciate the music of X, Y and Z, then the problem lies with X, Y, and Z.

The 'modern', or more to the point the 'avant-garde', in music has somehow fostered the notion that if a piece of music has no discernable ties to past traditions, and if it draws on absolutely virgin ideas, and if it is very convoluted in its structure, then it possesses intellectual values that may be inaccessible to ordinary mortals. There is a fundamental fallacy in such a premise. Music is a sound phenomenon, abstract and unnatural. Detached from a given title or explanatory literature, it cannot convey ideas and therefore the question of intellectual communication does not arise. Intellect, or more accurately artistic skill, can play a part in the way a work has been structured, but to the listener it is the emotional impact that really matters. Even that emotional impact cannot be predetermined as it is never uniform to all listeners.

Undeniably, on getting to know a piece of music, whether by studying it or by repeated listening, one can come to admire its structural design, if it is well crafted. But that hardly attests to an intellectual achievement, either by the composer who has made it, or by the admirer who has come to appreciate it. The composer has employed the craft of musical composition and the listener has used his ears. Intellectual achievement has to do with the formulation of ideas that convey meanings, meanings that bear significance towards the advancement of human condition. Music simply cannot be a tool for such advancements; it cannot convey specific ideas of any kind. Regrettably, it has become almost a matter of embarrassment to speak of music as evocative of emotions. But, in fact that is the only thing it can do. As such, it rides above the mundane, above ideas; it soars to the heights of sensations and feelings that are personal and non-specific. The power of music is in its ability to exalt; it cannot enlighten.

It is ironic that when composers come up with very complicated structural designs: inversions, retrograde movements, superimposed motivic ideas, and all sorts of what are supposedly intellectual devices, then they have to write lengthy explanatory notes to tell the listener in words all about the clever things they have done. The sad fact is that often the music by itself cannot reveal its structural design if it is overly complicated; the composer has to resort to language in order to inform and impress the listener. Moreover, the complexity that is supposed to prove the intellectual merits of the work is, in fact, always very simple to explain and requires no great mental exercise. On the intellectual level, they are child's play. Yet, sadly, they have to be explained in words, as music cannot do it on its own.

The case of vocal music is different; where a text is involved, as in a song, a choral piece, or in operatic music, the words convey ideas to the listener and the musical expression is necessarily derived from the meanings of those words. The only problem in vocal music is the difficulty of hearing the words as they are sung, not read or recited. Inevitably, a text when sung as a moving line with highs and lows of pitch, sudden leaps, and long held or rapid movement of notes, becomes audibly hard to follow. This problem is accentuated in choral music when different voices do not necessarily deliver the same words at the same time.

There are also musical genres that stimulate bodily movements; dance forms and marches are examples of this type of music to which a more uniform response can be expected. Also, a piece of music, such a national anthem, can be assigned a certain application. These types represent music that is functional and is meant to serve an extra-musical purpose. There is also the type of music that, by virtue of its title, is expected to direct the mind of the listener to a certain imagery: The 'Four Seasons', 'Harold in Italy', 'Hamlet' (Symphonic Poem), 'Ein Heldenleben', Claire de Lune, 'The Planets', 'The Lark Ascending', etc. But, take away the title and the music invariably will fail to evoke the intended imagery.

As a sound phenomenon, music may be able to replicate some non-musical sounds such as the wind, thunder, bird songs, and possibly a few other things. Such imitations of natural sounds by musical means are invariably rather naïve and less than satisfactory. It is important to understand and accept that music deals essentially with sounds that do not exist in nature. Musical sounds are artificially produced; they are unnatural, and there rests the power and the beauty of music. Music does not deal with worldly matters, and there lies its specialness. As such, it differs from the other creative arts such as painting, sculpture and poetry. They deal with the common experiences; music does not. They suggest the tangible; music does not. They aim at a collective response; the music does not.

Much of the music composed in the past one hundred years has been created with the overriding aim of being interesting or different. These are commendable objectives provided that the outcome is also beautiful. To say that beauty is in the eye - the ear in this case - of the beholder is really a copout. Of course the perception of beauty can vary from person to person. But, again, there is such a thing as consensus. The composers whose work we admire and that history upholds as great creative artists wrote music that is regarded as beautiful by consensus. The limitless treasury of compositions of the past eight hundred years is cherished because, by consensus, they are known to be beautiful. They may have other attributes, structural ingenuity, richness of harmonic texture, colorful instrumentation, etc. But all these combine to make a work of beauty. By hearing them the listener is touched, is emotionally moved, and importantly they are memorable.

The merits of a musical composition, and its durability, rest with the emotional impact that it can engender. In the context of western classical music, this has been best achieved through coherent and memorable melodic content, discernible rhythmic structure and harmonic richness. I accept that folk music, both in the western world and elsewhere, is mostly monophonic and is, therefore, devoid of structured harmonic properties. Also, some African music is purely rhythmic. But the argument here is concerned with western art music where all three elements combine. It is in the context of this musical tradition that to concoct musical sounds that have no recognizable melodic content, project no regulated rhythmic structure, and have no harmonic cohesion would simply deny that which centuries of musical development has upheld. A music that is supposed to be interesting by virtue of its novelty alone will not remain interesting on repeated hearing; novelty does not wear well and can soon become hackneyed. What shocks at first usually will turn out to be mightily boring once the shock has worn off.

All musical traditions, from all cultures, seem to have one common ingredient, a discernible melodic feature. The Grove Dictionary of Music states: "Melody is a universal human phenomenon traceable to prehistoric times." How do we define a melody? Such definitions as given by Webster's Dictionary: "a sweet and agreeable arrangement of sounds", or "a rhythmic succession of single tones organized as an aesthetic whole" are not really very helpful. What is 'sweet' or 'agreeable'; what is 'aesthetic whole'; and, does the succession of tones need be organized rhythmically?

I believe that a key point in describing a melody, overlooked in the above definitions, is the singability of the 'arrangement of sounds' or the 'succession of single tones'. By raising the issue of singability I am drawing attention to the fact that the earliest and the most basic instrument for music making has always been the human voice. All research into the origins of music in all societies points to the human voice as the earliest means of music making. It is the first and foremost musical instrument because it requires no means of production beyond the individual who is making the music; it is as elemental as speech itself. It is not unreasonable to conclude, therefore, that a melody must be an arrangement of sounds, or tones, that can be sung by an ordinary, untrained, human voice.

The above argument is admittedly overly simplistic. It would be quite reasonable to argue that a definition of melody need not rest on its most primitive foundations. It can be said that music making has evolved, it has become more complex, and it need not project melodies that can be sung by untrained voices. I agree, but I also believe that music ought to possess melodic or motivic ideas that are, if not singable, at least memorable, that they make an impact on the listener and can be retained in his or her memory.

It may be argued that melody as such is not essential to music. In fact, it has been fashionable, at least since the mid 20th century, to say that music is merely 'organized sound'. (Not to complicate matters further, I am leaving out other propositions such as chance or aleatory music, or John Cage's 'random sound' music, where no attempt at organization is admissible.) These arguments may satisfy the professionals who make and perform the avant-garde, but they don't seem to placate the average music loving public. If the professionals can be happy with the endorsement of their own ilk and forsake the public at large, then there is no problem. But, can they afford to do that? The music loving public will go on listening to Bach, Mozart, Schumann, Puccini, Ravel, Rachmaninoff, Shostakovich, Villa-Lobos, Part and hundreds more, and will ignore the avant-garde. There is so much proven great music that no one can in ten lifetimes get to the bottom of it. All that the 'moderns' can do is to insult the public by calling them 'conservative', 'ignorant', 'out of touch', etc. Would it matter? The fact remains that no one can possibly claim that by not appreciating some bizarre sound concoction, anyone is missing on anything that is at all important, or that they are rejecting that which improves or elevates human mind or human existence.

Composers must come to realize that, unless they are commissioned to write something, or that they write music as a job assignment (e.g. motion picture scores), they are not needed. To satisfy the ardent music lover, the greats of the past are very much alive. In fact, with recorded music, Haydn, Schubert, Tchaikovsky, Bartok and hundreds of others are musically far more alive today that when they were living. This is not to say that there is no more room for new compositions. Of course there is, as there is room for more books of literature, more poetry, more plays, more painting and sculpture. But, as is the case with books, plays and paintings, it has to be a work that uplifts, exalts and is enjoyed, not something that is at best curious and bizarre on first hearing and boring or irritating thereafter. It is a grievous mistake for composers, given the availability of the unlimited treasury of great music in recordings, to think that by shocking the listener, or by insulting him or her, they can find a place for themselves, to be loved and honored.

It is also important to appreciate that music is the only art form that has a pre -determined experience duration. No other art form imposes its own time limit. One can look, examine and ponder over a tableau of painting, or a sculpture, or an architectural structure, for minutes, hours or days. One can read Dostoyevsky's *Crime and Punishment* slowly or rapidly, or reread passages for better understanding of the content, take hours, days or weeks; it will not harm the work itself, and it will not defy the intentions of the author. The book a do noes trquire a time frame for it to be read. As a listener one cannot do that with music. A piece of music lasts just so long, no less and no more. You cannot cut it short if you want to hear it all, and you cannot lengthen its duration without distorting it.

The life of a piece of music is very short. Even the longest single compositions live only for a few minutes. (I am not referring to operas that are made of many sections and collectively may last for hours.) Take the slow movements of most Bruckner symphonies, or the last movement of Beethoven's 9th symphony. These are among the longest continuous compositions of importance ever written, but still they last less than 30 minutes. That is less than the time needed to read thirty pages of any book of fiction; and the book may have ten or twenty times as many pages. Yet greater effort, skill and artistry has gone into the creation of the 25 minutes of the Bruckner or the Beethoven piece than most works of literature, even those written by reputable authors. And, in fact, by far most individual pieces of music are much shorter than 25 or even 15 minutes.

We see therefore that a musical experience is necessarily very short lived. What has the composer given the listener beyond the few min-utes of sounds with no meaning? Is it anything more than the sensa-tions aroused in those few minutes? Yes, it can be! It can be, if some-thing from the experience of those few minutes remains with the listener. It can be if something from those few minutes affects us in such a way that we want to relive the experience over and over again, dozens perhaps hundreds of times. That something is not going to be the bewildering sound effects, but it can be melodic ideas that move the listener and have been even retained in the memory. Memorable melodic ideas make for lasting impressions; that is what we remember from the experience of hearing a great piece of music; that is what becomes ours to keep; we can take home with us, live with it and love it.

Another issue that I wish to address is the question of progress in music. I find a fundamental problem with the notion of progress when applied to creative arts. If by progress we mean moving forward, then an objective or a goal must exist for us to move towards. It would not make much sense to aim at the unknown. What is the objective in the creation of a work of art other than the work itself? If, on the other hand, by progress we mean moving from one manner of expression to another, then the correct definition is change and not progress. Still further, if by progress a move to something better or more satisfying is implied, then it becomes questionable if such an objective is applicable to artistic creations that are self-expressive and non-utilitarian.

Western civilization, since the Renaissance, can be characterized as dynamic and consistently evolving. Movement and change have been a central force. In matters pertaining to the betterment of the human condition, as in scientific investigations, this movement has been largely the conveyer of improvement in that condition. When there is a goal and innovation has brought us closer to the attainment of that goal then progress has taken place. In creative arts the question of progress arises if the work of art is to serve a utilitarian purpose, not if it is fundamentally self-absorbed, or is creation for its own sake.

Lets us clarify the proposition by some examples. If we are considering the development of polyphony we can establish that Bach's *B minor Mass* represents a progress – an actual improvement – as compared with the *'L'Homme arme'* Mass of Guillaume Dufay. It is richer in texture, its polyphonic structure is more diversified, and greater variety of sound combination is employed. So, as to the question of the development of polyphony and richness of harmonic texture, the Mass of Bach shows a definite progress, but it cannot be argued that it is therefore a better work of art; it can only be said that it is a different work of art. Within compositional norms of its time Dufay's mass is as accomplished a work of art as is that of Bach. If the issue of diversity of sound combination or orchestral enrichment is in mind, then we can say that the symphonies of Sibelius show progress as compared with those of Haydn, but they are not better. The same goes, needless to say, for the other arts. Paintings of Cezanne are no better than those of Titian, but they are different. The poems of Ted Hughes are not improvements over those of William Wordsworth, but they are different. So, let us have no illusions about modern music representing any kind of progress in the sense of improvement in the expressive aims of music.

It is also important to appreciate that styles and mannerisms change; all that is modern and novel, in time, becomes old. Does anyone care today that Bach was writing music that was, at the time, quite old-fashioned? Beethoven is revered because he wrote powerful music that is highly charged with human emotion, not because he was trampling on the established norms of his time. Brahms was considered quite conservative in his style; does it matter? Rachmaninoff was writing deeply romantic music when emotionally expressive music was out of fashion, when the likes of Varese, Schoenberg and Antheil were causing modernistic revolutions. Today Rachmaninoff is loved and listened to more than ever; nearly everything that he composed is consistently performed and recorded; one certainly cannot say the same for some of his contemporaries who were causing sensation with their revolutionary movements. Schostakovich, Britten and Lutoslawski are widely performed; but how many people listen today to the sensation makers of forty years ago, the likes of Xenakis, Stockhausen and Kagel?

I am aware that some of the views expressed here may have created a false impression about where I stand. I do not have a negative view of all 'modern' music. As a composer, I belong to the modern school. Every piece of music that I have written can be readily recognized as having been composed in the age that I have lived; that certainly includes a major portion of my compositions that are in the atonal dodecaphonic style.

I believe that the last one hundred years have given birth to a great diversity of styles and the term modern is not indicative of any specific type. There have been many good composers and a great deal of excellent music has been written. The 20th century has produced the likes of Bartok, Schoenberg, Stravinsky, Prokofiev, Szymanowski, Berg, Copland, Carter, Poulenc, Schostakovich, Barber, Walton, Britten, Lutoslawski, Schnitke, Penderecki, Part, Tavener, Dutilleux, William Schuman, Glass, Corigliano and many others, whose music I enjoy and admire. They adhered to very different styles but they all have created music that is memorable. The music loving public may not love them all, but on the whole, these are the composers who do have a public.

Interestingly, in the last century some nationalities that were not particularly prominent in the past have produced outstanding composers. American, British and Polish composers have been among the foremost figures, whereas countries that usually led the way in the past, such as France, Germany, Austria and Italy, have not maintained their former high standing. As some nations of the east, such as Japan, China and Korea are more and more entering the arena of western musical composition, the future may witness great musical contributions from that unlikely region. In fact, already Japanese composers, the likes of Toru Takemitsu and Akira Miyoshi are recognized among the major figures of the 20th century. Could it be that even my native country Persia might produce composers of international stature in this as yet new 21st century?

Epilogue

By a curious twist of fate I have lived in Ireland longer than anywhere else. For nearly 36 years, amounting to more than half of my adult life, I have been a resident of this beautiful island at the extreme northwest of Europe. Forty years ago, Ireland might have seemed as improbable a place to spend my remaining days as New Zealand. But it has been all for the good and I am grateful. Contrary to what some who do not know this country, and are influenced by news of sectarian conflicts that plagued Northern Ireland may think, this is an exceptionally peaceful country. The freedom enjoyed by citizens and residents of the Republic of Ireland is unsurpassed by any other nation that I know of. The Irish are for the most part friendly, warm and gregarious; they have the 'gift of gab', which is very engaging, although I find myself consistently disadvantaged for not being equally gifted.

The climate in Ireland, a source of endless discontent for the natives, I find very agreeable. Irish summers are particularly pleasant, as I do not favor hot weather. The days are long and the temperature does not exceed the mid 20s, which is about ideal for me. Winters are long and can be gloomy, but it never gets really cold; seldom does the thermometer descend to zero or a few degrees below. Irish winters are usually milder than any place in the rest of Europe except the costal margins of the Mediterranean Sea. Springs and autumns are about perfect; even the Irish may be willing to admit that. As to the perennial complaint about the rain, in fact, rainfall in Ireland is quite moderate. I believe there is a fundamental misunderstanding about rain in this country. It does not rain as much as most think, but the sky is cloudy much of the time. The threat of rain is more real than the actual rain itself. Of five cloudy days only one may produce actual rainfall. I do share some unhappiness with my Irish friends about the lack of enough sunshine, particularly in the fall and winter. But on the whole I have no complaints about the natural conditions in Ireland. Here, we have no tornadoes, no hurricanes, no typhoons, no ruinous floods, no heat-waves, no blizzards and no earthquakes. I think we are quite blessed and we should be grateful.

Dublin is a city with charm and gaiety. It is not a big city nor is it too small. Except for the central square mile, it is a collection of neighborhoods – originally outlying villages – that are now incorporated into the city. These districts largely maintain their separate characters. Places like Sandy Mount, Ranelagh, Rathmines, Terenure, Drumcondra, Ballyfermot, Clonskeagh and many others are self-contained with their own commercial zones. Dublin is also a most confounding city. Except for a few avenues in the central sector, there are hardly any roads in Dublin that are laid in a straight line for any distance. There are no geometric patterns to the layout of streets. In many areas there are no regular intersections. There are hardly any main thoroughfares that go in an east/west direction. The few major avenues that do exist run north/south, but never in a straight line or maintaining a consistent width. Dublin is a port city, it lies next to the Irish Sea. But it is very difficult to get to the seashore; the sea is to the east of the city and there are no through roads that go east. To reach the coast one has to maneuver through a series of narrow residential streets, or drive a few miles south to Black Rock or many miles north to Sutton. The traffic congestion, particularly in morning and afternoon rush hours, is very troublesome. This not because there are too many cars, it is due to the inadequacy of the driving surface. There are not enough roads and what there is, is narrow, winding and confused. Nevertheless, once you get used to it, Dublin is a lovable city and in parts quite attractive.

I came to the Republic of Ireland on being appointed to the Chair of Music at Trinity College. The Chair was founded in 1764. I have learned that first holder of the Chair was Lord Mornington, the father of Duke of Wellington, Napoleon's main adversary at the battle of Waterloo. I understand that he was not a professional musician but a gentleman of musical erudition and an occasional composer. The Chair was occupied sporadically by various individuals of note, a few of whom were actually distinguished musicians, for two centuries. My immediate predecessor was Brian Boydell who was very active as a composer and lecturer. The honors degree of Bachelor of Arts in Music, with a taught curriculum, was established during his tenure. Before mid 1970s, only a BMus degree, based on a series of examinations was on offer. I succeeded him in 1982.

After thirteen years of teaching and managing the affairs of the School of Music, I became of retirement age in 1995. Since retirement, as a Fellow Emeritus of the College, I have had the privilege of being given an office space in the College premises. This is quite an exceptional bonus; to my knowledge no university anywhere – perhaps with the exception of Oxford and Cambridge – offers such facilities to their retired Fellows, no matter how distinguished their services might have been. I greatly value this privilege. It is enormously important that I can maintain a lifetime habit of rising early, dressing up and 'going to work'. What I do in my office in College can, no doubt, be done at home. But I think it important, when old and lawfully – not out of incapacity – retired, to have a place to go outside one's home and to maintain the work habit of the past.

My years in Ireland, particularly since retirement, have passed peacefully. This has been a source of much satisfaction, as I have not had an easy life. But that is all now in the past. I enjoy my end years with my philosopher wife Maria Baghramian, who is in the whirlwind of an active academic career, and with our son Robert Kambiz, an accomplished pianist and a good all around musician. He was born in Ireland, does not easily relate to his parental heritage, and feels very Irish. Maria has been my prime motivator for my taking on the task of writing this book; I have benefited greatly from her advice on restructuring of some of the chapters. We are fortunate to have many good friends, all well educated, urbane and always helpful. On learning of my endeavors to produce this work of selected reminiscence and essays, they have all shown interest and have given encouragement. I like to thank, in particular, my learned friend Ian Cornelius for accepting to read the preceding chapters and for his valuable suggestions.